T0093389

Hacker Culture A to Z

A Fun Guide to the People, Ideas, and Gadgets That Made the Tech World

Kim Crawley

Beijing · Boston · Farnham · Sebastopol · Tokyo

Hacker Culture A to Z

by Kim Crawley

Copyright © 2024 Kim Crawley. All rights reserved.

Published by O'Reilly Media, Inc., 1005 Gravenstein Highway North, Sebastopol, CA 95472.

O'Reilly books may be purchased for educational, business, or sales promotional use. Online editions are also available for most titles (*http://oreilly.com*). For more information, contact our corporate/institutional sales department: 800-998-9938 or *corporate@oreilly.com*.

Acquisitions Editor: Simina Calin	**Proofreader:** Tove Innis
Development Editor: Sarah Grey	**Interior Designer:** Monica Kamsvaag
Production Editor: Ashley Stussy	**Cover Designer:** Susan Thompson
Copyeditor: nSight, Inc.	**Illustrators:** Jose Marzan and Kate Dullea

November 2023:   First Edition

Revision History for the First Edition

2023-11-06:   First Release

See *http://oreilly.com/catalog/errata.csp?isbn=9781098145675* for release details.

The O'Reilly logo is a registered trademark of O'Reilly Media, Inc. *Hacker Culture A to Z*, the cover image, and related trade dress are trademarks of O'Reilly Media, Inc.

978-1-098-14567-5

[LSI]

This book is dedicated to all of the people who have been consistently wearing high-quality respirators in public and continue to do so, despite all opposition. The future of humanity is in our hands.

Contents

Preface

Hello! I'm Kim Crawley. I've worked in the cybersecurity field as a writer for over a decade, and I've met many brilliant hackers over the years. Ordinary people think hackers are cybercriminals, as I wrote in an article for *2600 Magazine*.[1] But hackers are people who find new and inventive uses of technology. And we owe most of the cool stuff about computer technology to hackers. Hackers have also created the culture of computing—hacker culture.

These days, computers are for everyone, and computer technology is integrated into nearly every facet of our everyday lives. Laypeople sometimes call a PC a computer and call their iPhone their phone, but their iPhone is also a computer. Most of us are on the internet several hours per day, and that's just a huge collection of networked computers.

In my apartment building, you can't use the elevators without interacting with a touchscreen. Guess what? That's a computer too. There are embedded computers in so many places in our retail stores, hospitals, factories, office buildings, and government institutions. If you drive a car, there's probably an embedded computer in that too.

So, inevitably, a lot of everyday computer usage is done by people who don't think they're very technologically skilled. But we wouldn't have a computer-technology-driven world without hackers. Hackers aren't cybercriminals; they're clever people who explore innovative new uses of computer technology. We wouldn't have what we have today without their curiosity. Yet mainstream news reporters have the nerve to call people who attack medical clinics with ransomware "hackers." That seems rather disrespectful to me. Instead, we should honor their legacy and their culture. My book is one of the ways that I'm doing that.

---

1 Kim Crawley, "What Do Ordinary People Think a Hacker Is? (*https://oreil.ly/I-Vw_*)" *2600 Magazine: The Hacker Quarterly* 31, no. 4 (Winter 2014–2015).

This is a multipurpose book. You can use it as a desk reference and, when a computer or hacker-related topic comes up in your work or studies, look up the terms in this book. It's all conveniently presented in alphabetical order! You can also read the book from cover to cover. It's up to you! If you're reading the ebook version, you will find hyperlinks in the text to web content and to related terminology and entries in this book. You can explore how concepts are connected to each other, like in James Burke's *Connections* (*https://oreil.ly/B31p1*). (Google it!)

I hope you have as much fun reading this as I have had writing it.

Conventions Used in This Book

The following typographical conventions are used in this book:

Italic

Indicates new terms, URLs, email addresses, filenames, and file extensions.

`Constant width`

Used for program listings, as well as within paragraphs to refer to program elements such as variable or function names, databases, data types, environment variables, statements, and keywords.

O'Reilly Online Learning

 For more than 40 years, *O'Reilly Media* has provided technology and business training, knowledge, and insight to help companies succeed.

Our unique network of experts and innovators share their knowledge and expertise through books, articles, and our online learning platform. O'Reilly's online learning platform gives you on-demand access to live training courses, in-depth learning paths, interactive coding environments, and a vast collection of text and video from O'Reilly and 200+ other publishers. For more information, visit *https://oreilly.com*.

How to Contact Us

Please address comments and questions concerning this book to the publisher:

O'Reilly Media, Inc.

1005 Gravenstein Highway North

Sebastopol, CA 95472

800-889-8969 (in the United States or Canada)

707-829-7019 (international or local)

707-829-0104 (fax)

support@oreilly.com

https://www.oreilly.com/about/contact.html

We have a web page for this book, where we list errata, examples, and any additional information. You can access this page at *https://oreil.ly/hacker-culture-a-to-z-1e.*

For news and information about our books and courses, visit *https://oreilly.com.*

Find us on LinkedIn: *https://linkedin.com/company/oreilly-media*

Follow us on Twitter: *https://twitter.com/oreillymedia*

Watch us on YouTube: *https://youtube.com/oreillymedia*

Acknowledgments

I'd like to thank my romantic partner, Jason Smith, for loving me and enthusiastically supporting my career.

To the Smith family, my father-in-law Joe Smith and my stepmother-in-law Laurie Collins-Smith, you both have been really enthusiastically supportive of me as well! Thank you for welcoming an eccentric and nearly middle-aged orphan into your family.

To my late father, novelist and creative writing tutor Michael Crawley, I hope you're looking up at me from down there with pride. You've always encouraged my interest in computers since I was a little girl. You lent me your PC and let me fix it for you. And you showed me at a very impressionable age that writing is a career. I followed your footsteps, in my own way.

To Ossington the bear, you've made damn sure that I sleep well every night. I cannot work well without proper rest! To Amelia Bearhart for supporting me as another woman in STEM. I'm sorry the industry doesn't provide professional opportunities to teddy bears. Indie, Insfjull the polar bear, Luci, Annie Aurora, Bao Bao, Leonard the lion, Bronto the dinosaur, Paddington, Abyss, Baphie, Algonquin, Dormé, Hiver, Ickles the thing, Nocturne the bat, and all the rest of my stuffed animal family, thank you for your softness.

I must thank the O'Reilly Media team, because this book was a group effort. Thank you Development Editor Sarah Grey for your patience with my ego and lack of brevity, Acquisitions Editor Simina Calin for taking a chance on my big idea, Production Editor Ashley Stussy, and Interior Designer Monica Kamsvaag for your crucial work behind the scenes. Karen Montgomery, for your innovative eye-catching cover art that's as quirky as the author, and José Marzan and Kate Dullea for your beautiful illustrations that bring my ideas to life.

If a book is published but no one's ever heard of it, would it really sell? To my team at PR by the Book, Marika Flatt, Melissa Teutsch, and Rebekah Epstein, thank you for bringing my book to the masses.

Thank you, Hoyt Kesterson, Marc Loy, Daniel Kurnath, Matt Jackson, Johnny Justice, Bill Jacqmein, Stacey Champagne, and Mekki MacAulay, for your technical feedback, assuring this book's accuracy.

Thank you, Jennifer Sunshine Steffens, Chris Chon, and John Sheehy at IOActive, for your professional support of me. I hope that I honored Barnaby Jack's ATM jackpotting cyberattack research well. May he rest in peace. Thank you, Tanya Janca, for keeping me connected with the cybersecurity community, because the pandemic has made me a hermit. Thank you, CloudDefense CEO Anshu Bansal, for your professional support of me.

Thanks to Larry Ewing and The GIMP for the use of the image in the Linux listing.

Hack the planet!

A

Abacus

The abacus is perhaps the earliest mathematical device, if you don't count making marks in the sand or cave paintings. It's the ancient equivalent of a pocket calculator. The "hackers" of the Bronze Age definitely used abacuses.

The full story of the invention of the abacus is unknown. Historical records of its use date back as far as 2700 BC in Mesopotamia (approximately where Iraq and parts of Iran, Kuwait, Syria, and Turkey exist today), as well as ancient Egypt, Greece, Rome, China, India, Persia (the precursor to modern-day Iran), Japan, Russia, and Korea. The revolutionary abacus traveled the world centuries before motor engines and the printing press! But the device might be even older.

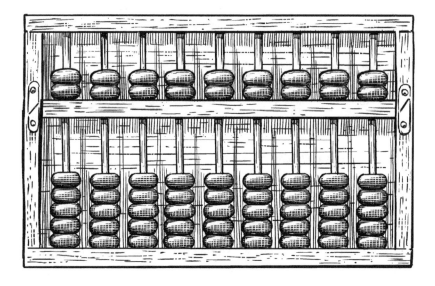

Abacuses are still manufactured, and they are frequently seen in young children's classrooms. Some modern abacuses are also designed for blind people, such as the Cranmer Abacus (*https://oreil.ly/WOYqm*), invented by Terence Cranmer of the Kentucky Division of Rehabilitation Services for the Blind in 1962.

Abacus designs vary, but their defining feature is a set of bars in rows or columns, usually in some sort of frame, with beads or similar objects as counters that can slide across each bar to change position horizontally (on a row) or vertically (on a column).

Here's how an abacus works. Each bar can represent a position in a numeral system, and then the placement of the counters on a bar indicates the position's integer. For example, an abacus that would work well with the base 10 or decimal numeral system we're most familiar with in the modern world would have 10 bars and 10 counters on each bar. On the bar farthest to the right, I could slide three counters up. On the bar to its left, I could slide two counters up. And on the bar left of that, I could slide seven counters up. That value represents 327. If I wanted to perform a very basic arithmetic operation and add or subtract, I could reposition the counters accordingly. If I wanted to add 21, I could slide two more counters to the two that have already been placed in the tens position, and one more in the ones position. So I could see that 327 plus 21 equals 348.

There are a lot of other arithmetic and algebraic methodologies that can be applied to an abacus, as well as different numeral systems. If you're an imaginative math whiz, you could even create some of your own. Now you're thinking like a hacker!

See also "Binary" on page 35, "Hexadecimal numbering" on page 133

Abandonware

See "Shareware/freeware/abandonware" on page 223

Activision

Activision is one of the biggest names in video games. Its founders, David Crane, Larry Kaplan, Alan Miller, and Bob Whitehead, were definitely hackers. In the earliest era of console game development, they had to invent the craft almost from scratch. They started their careers making games for the Atari 2600, the most commercially successful second-generation video game console, which debuted in 1977. (The first generation consisted of the Magnavox Odyssey and a variety of home Pong clones released throughout the 1970s. The third generation was defined by Nintendo.)

After a couple of years, Crane, Kaplan, Miller, and Whitehead realized that the games they developed accounted for 60% of all Atari 2600 game sales. Their games made Atari about $20 million, whereas their salaries were about $20,000 a year. "The Gang of Four" felt significantly underpaid and wanted to be credited, so gamers would know who crafted their games. They left Atari in 1979 to form Activision, the very first third-party console game developer.

In 1983, however, the video game market crashed in North America—partly triggered by a plethora of low-quality Atari 2600 games. The crash forced Activision to diversify if it wanted to survive. It started to produce games for home computers. In the late 1980s the company rebranded as Mediagenic and expanded to games for Nintendo Entertainment System (NES), Commodore, and Sega systems, as well as text-adventure games (as Infocom) and business software (as Ten Point O).

Mediagenic struggled to make a profit as the video game console and home PC markets evolved. In 1991, Bobby Kotick and a team of investors bought Mediagenic for about $500,000 and restored the company's original name and its focus on video games. Activision rapidly grew and became profitable throughout the 1990s and 2000s. Notable titles from that era include *Quake*, the *MechWarrior* series, the *Tony Hawk* series, the *Wolfenstein* series, *Spyro the Dragon*, and the *Call of Duty* series.

In 2008, Activision merged with Vivendi Games to form Activision Blizzard, which Microsoft acquired in 2002. Kotick still leads Activision Blizzard and is one of the wealthiest people in the industry.

See also "Atari" on page 22, "Commodore" on page 53, "Microsoft" on page 174, "Nintendo" on page 185, "Sega" on page 221

Adleman, Leonard

Adleman (*https://oreil.ly/IkpLs*) was born in San Francisco in 1945. According to his bio on the University of Southern California Viterbi School of Engineering's website (*https://oreil.ly/sj3IR*), a very young Leonard Adleman was inspired to study chemistry and medicine by the children's science show *Mr. Wizard* (*https://oreil.ly/KweB9*). Adleman would actually become known for his innovations in computer science, but his destiny would cross into medicine later on in a peculiar way.

Adleman acquired his first degree (*https://oreil.ly/Ho1P_*), a bachelor in mathematics, from the University of California, Berkeley, in 1968. Back then, mathematics degrees often led to computer programming jobs, and after graduation Adleman got a job as a computer programmer at the Federal Reserve Bank in San Francisco. He did return to Berkeley soon after and got his PhD in computer science in 1976.

With his doctorate in hand, Adleman went right to MIT to teach mathematics. There he began collaborating with his colleagues Ron Rivest and Adi Shamir, who shared his enthusiasm for public-key cryptography and the Diffie-Hellman key exchange. The three developed RSA (Rivest-Shamir-Adleman) cryptography in 1977. RSA's big innovation was the ability to encrypt and decrypt messages without a shared private key. This made public-facing cryptography, like we use on the internet, a lot more feasible.

In 1980, Adleman moved to Los Angeles and became a pioneer of DNA computing, likely inspired by his childhood memories of *Mr. Wizard*. The Viterbi School (*https://oreil.ly/X5iL_*) says, "He is the father of the field of DNA computation. DNA can store information and proteins can modify that information. These two features assure us that DNA can be used to compute all things that are computable by silicon based computers."

In 2002, Rivest, Shamir, and Adleman received a Turing Award (*https://oreil.ly/CTyel*), the highest honor in computer science, for their work. Mr. Wizard would indeed be proud. All three of the inventors of RSA encryption have entries in this book: Ron Rivest, Adi Shamir, and Leonard Adleman.

See also "Berkeley, University of California" on page 32, "Cryptography" on page 63, "Rivest-Shamir-Adleman (RSA) cryptography" on page 215, "Rivest, Ron" on page 214, "Shamir, Adi" on page 223

Advanced persistent threat (APT)

APT stands for advanced persistent threat, a cool-sounding name for teams of malicious cyberattackers with advanced technological skills and knowledge. Most are nation-state-sponsored cyberwarfare units or sophisticated organized-crime entities. APTs create their own malware, find their own exploits, and do technologically complex reconnaissance work—that's the "advanced" part.

Different cybersecurity vendors and organizations (*https://oreil.ly/jjuAC*) have different ways (*https://oreil.ly/WlEKp*) to describe the phases of an APT attack. But it all boils down to infiltrating a targeted network, establishing persistence, and spreading the attack to more parts of the targeted network. Here's the National Institute of Standards and Technology's definition:

> An adversary that possesses sophisticated levels of expertise and sig-
> nificant resources that allow it to create opportunities to achieve its
> objectives by using multiple attack vectors including, for example, cyber,
> physical, and deception. These objectives typically include establishing
> and extending footholds within the IT infrastructure of the targeted organ-
> izations for purposes of exfiltrating information, undermining or impeding
> critical aspects of a mission, program, or organization.... The advanced
> persistent threat pursues its objectives repeatedly over an extended
> period; adapts to defenders' efforts to resist it; and is determined to
> maintain the level of interaction needed to execute its objectives.[1]

Among cybersecurity people, "script kiddie" is a term for a generally low-skilled threat actor: someone who conducts attacks by running malicious scripts or applications developed by other people. APTs are the polar opposite of that!

APTs are "persistent" in that they don't strike and run, like a computerized drive-by shooting. They can maintain an unauthorized presence in a computer network for a few weeks (*https://oreil.ly/an9OQ*) or even years.

APTs are the kind of "threats" that have malicious intentions. They're capable of doing great harm. They rarely bother with ordinary computer users: APTs are behind attacks on industrial facilities, like the 2010 Stuxnet attack (*https://oreil.ly/pVoH_*) on a uranium enrichment plant in Iran and thefts of terabytes' worth of sensitive data from financial institutions.

See also "Cybersecurity" on page 68, "Stuxnet" on page 232

Agile methodology

See "DevOps" on page 82

Airgapping

No computer is 100% secure. The closest we can get is by *airgapping*: that is, restricting access to a computer's data as much as possible by not having any connections to any networks whatsoever. Not to the internet, not to any internal

---

1 National Institute of Standards and Technology (NIST), Special Publication 800-160 (Developing Cyber-Resilient Systems).

networks, not even to any printer devices or network-attached storage. That's the most literal network-security (*https://oreil.ly/dTcL7*) definition, at any rate.

If you want to do a really proper job, you should physically remove any network interface cards and disable any USB ports and optical drives that aren't absolutely necessary for the computer's authorized use. Those aren't computers, but they *are* potential *cyberattack surfaces*: places where a threat actor could send malicious data. Ideally, an airgapped computer should also be in a room protected by excellent physical security, including locked physical doors that require the user to authenticate.

As you might have gathered by now, airgapping a computer makes it very inconvenient to use. For that reason, they're typically only used for highly sensitive data in situations with extremely strict security standards, like military and national security agencies or industrial control systems in power plants. They also have applications in digital forensics and incident response (DFIR), when digital forensics specialists need to assure a court of law that their evidence hasn't been tampered with through networks or other means of data transmission.

As with all cybersecurity techniques, there's a constant battle between security professionals and those who seek to outwit them. Mordechai Guri, director of the Cybersecurity Research Center (*https://oreil.ly/KufYF*) at Ben-Gurion University, is well known for coming up with exploit ideas in hopes of staying several steps ahead of attackers. If you're curious about his ideas, I wrote about Guri for the Tripwire blog back in 2017 (*https://oreil.ly/qoYef*), and *Discover* magazine (*https://oreil.ly/fpLXj*) reported on another one of Guri's scenarios in 2022.

See also "Cybersecurity" on page 68

Akihabara, Tokyo

Akihabara, a neighborhood of Tokyo, Japan, is just as relevant to hacker culture as Silicon Valley is.

Some hackers are total *weeaboos* (*https://oreil.ly/BxVQW*) (Westerners who are fans of Japanese popular culture), as I am. And in Japan, an *otaku* (*https://oreil.ly/jAmcL*) is pretty much any sort of obsessive nerd, including those with technological fixations. Akihabara is a hub for Japanese hackers and otaku culture.

During the Meiji period (*https://oreil.ly/DBvZb*) in 1869, a massive fire destroyed large parts of Tokyo, including what is now Akihabara. Railways were part of the city's reconstruction, and in 1890 when Akihabara train station was built, the surrounding neighborhood was named after the station, still a major fixture of the area.

When World War II ended in 1945, an unregulated "black market" for radio components appeared in Akihabara, earning it the nickname "Radio Town." Until 1955, when Sony launched the TR-55 radio, hobbyists in Japan typically built their own radios (*https://oreil.ly/X-rsj*). If you wanted to find the postwar equivalent to hackers, they'd be in Akihabara, feeding their passion. Akihabara was also close to Tokyo Denki University, and bright young minds from the technical school poured into the neighborhood's radio component shops.

Radio broadcasting boomed in 1950s Japan, becoming an important source of news and entertainment, and the growing demand for radio equipment fed Akihabara's economy. The US General Headquarters (*https://oreil.ly/89Idc*), which had a governing role throughout the mid-20th century, directed electronics shops to move to Akihabara. This expanded the variety of nerdy goods sold in the neighborhood, which soon became known as "Electric Town."

This was also the period in which anime and manga culture started to thrive. The seeds of that phenomenon were sown through the genius of Osamu Tezuka (*https://oreil.ly/66dlh*), known as the God of Manga. Tezuka pioneered manga and anime, and many other Japanese artists followed his lead. His 1950s *Astro Boy* and *Princess Knight* manga series kicked off the widespread popularity of Japanese comics. In the 1960s, TV shows based on his work, such as *Astro Boy* and *Kimba the White Lion*, made anime a commercially profitable medium.

From the 1970s until roughly 1995, Akihabara was still known as Electric Town. The built environment went from a series of rustic electronics flea markets to impressive multistory retail buildings covered in neon signs. Then, in 1995, the launch of Windows 95 brought thousands of computer hackers to the neighborhood, eager for their own copy of Microsoft's operating system. More electronics shops opened, selling more PC and computer networking equipment, as well as video game consoles.

Video games also began to incorporate anime and manga art and culture, most notably in Japanese role playing games (JRPGs) and visual novels. For instance, Akira Toriyama (*https://oreil.ly/Q_tZo*) created the *Dragon Ball* manga series and illustrated the *Dragon Quest* series, Japan's most popular JRPG franchise. Once shops in Akihabara started selling video games, anime and manga products of all kinds followed.

In the 2020s, Akihabara remains a hacker paradise where you can pick up PC hardware, electronics components, PS5 games, and even a ¥30,000 *Melancholy of Haruhi Suzumiya* figure for good measure.

See also "Atlus" on page 24, "Nintendo" on page 185, "Sega" on page 221, "Tokyo Denki University" on page 245

Alderson, Elliot

See "Mr. Robot (TV show)" on page 181

Alphabet Inc.

Alphabet Inc. is the holding company that owns Google and thus has a massive amount of control over the internet. Google founders Larry Page and Sergey Brin founded Alphabet in 2015 to enable a variety of projects, including:

Calico (https://oreil.ly/sJKC2)
A project to improve human health and longevity via technology

CapitalG (https://oreil.ly/8i11A)
A venture-capital endeavor

Waymo (https://oreil.ly/Ck9cn)
Formerly known as the "Google Self-Driving Car Project"

Google Fiber (https://oreil.ly/lVcp2)
An internet service provider and telecommunications company

DeepMind (https://oreil.ly/5nZqU)
For artificial intelligence research

See also "Google" on page 114

Amazon Web Services (AWS)

Amazon Web Services (AWS) is a major provider of cloud computing infrastructure and services for businesses. In the early 2000s, Amazon built on its success as one of the earliest successful online retailers by offering datacenter services to other major US retailers, such as Target. Many of these big retailers had started as brick-and-mortar stores and needed Amazon's help to scale their online offerings.

Scaling, in this context, means expanding to meet demand. If a company needs 1x storage and bandwidth one month, 8x storage and bandwidth the next, and 3x storage and bandwidth the following month, the degree to which that infrastructure adjusts accordingly is called its *scalability*. Big retailers need a datacenter backend that is huge, scalable, and flexible, and creating that was a real challenge. As John Furrier writes in *Forbes* (*https://oreil.ly/Yo3n8*), "The idea grew organically out of [Amazon's] frustration with its ability to launch new projects and support customers."

In 2006, Simple Storage Service (S3), the first major AWS component, went online (*https://oreil.ly/o4PyA*). AWS features have been expanding ever since. In the wake of the success of AWS (*https://oreil.ly/kDFo_*), other major tech companies launched cloud platforms and services. Its two biggest competitors, Google Cloud Platform (*https://oreil.ly/HJKMg*) and Microsoft Azure (*https://oreil.ly/PmiFK*), both launched in 2008.

See also "Cloud" on page 51

AMD (Advanced Micro Devices)

Advanced Micro Devices (*https://oreil.ly/SzG98*) (AMD) was founded in 1969 in Sunnyvale, California, in the heart of what is now Silicon Valley (*https://oreil.ly/JFOh2*). AMD makes billions from graphics processors (GPUs), chipsets, and motherboard components, but its competition with Intel is what made AMD the huge tech company it is today.

The x86 CPU architecture debuted with Intel's groundbreaking Intel 8086 (*https://oreil.ly/KBBha*) processor in 1978, and it has been predominant in PCs ever since. In desktops and laptops, the two main CPU competitors are Intel and AMD.

In 1982, IBM wanted at least two different suppliers (*https://oreil.ly/dZlY3*) of CPUs, to have redundancy in their supply chain in case something happened with either supplier that would slow down production. Intel couldn't afford to lose IBM as a customer, so it made an agreement with AMD for both companies to produce processors based on 8086 and 8088 technology. But by 1984, the agreement had fallen apart; Intel stopped sharing its research and development with AMD. In 1987, AMD sued Intel for developing the 386 without cooperating with them. After a long battle through the courts, the Supreme Court of California (*https://oreil.ly/EBtDI*) ruled in AMD's favor in 1994.

Intel released its first 486 CPU (*https://oreil.ly/7DFL2*) in April 1989. AMD's equivalent, Am486 (*https://oreil.ly/WYKS1*), came out in 1993, but Acer and Compaq, PC manufacturing giants at the time, used it frequently in their products. In 2006, AMD bought ATI for a whopping $5.4 billion and became a major competitor with NVIDIA.

AMD's Ryzen CPU series, launched in 2017, has been AMD's most commercially successful foray into the gaming CPU market. It features x86-64 architecture and Zen microarchitecture, for you CPU nerds out there.

See also "CPU (Central processing unit)" on page 57, "IBM" on page 139, "Intel" on page 144

Amiga

The Commodore 64, first released in 1982, was the world's top-selling PC by 1984. It was technologically impressive for its time and had a large third-party software library that included business and programming utilities and a huge variety of games. But Commodore knew it needed to produce PCs with more advanced and innovative technology to compete with Atari, IBM, and Apple.

Activision cofounder Larry Kaplan approached Atari hardware designer Jay Miner about starting a new company to produce a new video game hardware platform with its own proprietary operating system. That produced Amiga in 1982, with Miner leading its research and development team in creating a Motorola-68000-based prototype, code-named "Lorraine." Trouble was brewing in Commodore's C-suite, however, despite the massive success of the Commodore 64. Founder Jack Tramiel fought with primary shareholder Irving Gould and was dismissed from the company in 1984. Tramiel moved to Atari, and many top Commodore engineers followed him.

January 1984 was probably the most important month in the history of hacker culture. Tramiel left Commodore, *2600 Magazine* published its debut issue, the historic Apple Super Bowl commercial (*https://oreil.ly/9O8Pw*) launched the Macintosh, the author of this book was born, and the Amiga team presented their working prototype at the Consumer Electronics Show. Attendees were mesmerized by the Boing Ball, a red-and-white checkerboard-patterned 3D graphic that showcased the Amiga's astonishing graphical capabilities.

PC World (*https://oreil.ly/wVEwv*) called the Amiga 1000 "the world's first multimedia, multitasking personal computer." It featured the fully graphical and mouse-navigable AmigaOS 1.0, cutting-edge graphics, a Motorola 68000 CPU, and built-in audio. It had a variety of audio and video outputs—great for gaming, but also a great computer for digital video editing. There had never been such a graphically advanced PC before, and the Amiga's Video Toaster software became the professional standard for digital video editing. Commodore couldn't produce enough Amiga 1000s to meet demand. But by 1993, it was losing market share to multimedia "IBM-compatible" PCs (and, to a lesser extent, the Apple Macintosh line). In a dramatic move, Commodore reconfigured its Amiga PC hardware into the Amiga CD32, which (probably deliberately) looked a bit like the Sega Genesis. It wasn't enough; in 1994, Commodore went into voluntary bankruptcy liquidation. What a sad end! But hackers look back on the Amiga fondly.

See also "Activision" on page 2, "Atari" on page 22, "Commodore" on page 53, "Consumer Electronics Show (CES)" on page 57

Android operating system

(For androids as in humanoid robots, see "Robotics" on page 216.)

There is only one mobile operating system that gives Apple's iOS any real competition: Android. If iOS is the Coca-Cola of the mobile OS world, Android is its Pepsi.

The world's first mobile OS was the short-lived PenPoint, introduced for PDAs in 1991.[2] It was followed in 1993 by Apple's Newton OS (*https://oreil.ly/F6TwA*) and then Symbian, a joint venture between several mobile phone manufacturers that claimed 67% of the smartphone market share in 2006 (*https://oreil.ly/9ed98*). But Apple introduced the iPhone in 2007, and iOS became the first mobile platform to sell devices in the hundreds of millions (and then billions). Apple operating systems like iOS and macOS are only supposed to run on Apple hardware, although hackers have been installing them on non-Apple hardware for years.

Android Inc. was founded in 2003 (*https://oreil.ly/vXAYF*) by Rich Miner, Nick Sears, Chris White, and Andy Rubin, who originally conceived of it as an operating system for digital cameras. Google bought the company in 2005. In 2007, hoping to compete with the iPhone, Google founded the Open Handset Alliance (*https://oreil.ly/9ImW3*) in November 2007 with HTC, LG, Sony, Motorola, and Samsung.

Android first launched in 2008, running on the slider smartphone HTC Dream (*https://oreil.ly/xSONj*), which had a physical keyboard rather than a touchscreen. Like Symbian, it was designed to run on devices made by multiple manufacturers. It is based on a Linux kernel. Android entered the market at the right time and replicated some of what Apple was doing right.

---

2 Personal digital assistants (PDAs), such as the BlackBerry and PalmPilot, were handheld mini-tablet devices for notes and calendars.

The 2009 Android 1.5 Cupcake was the first Android version to have a touchscreen keyboard, and 2010's Android 2.3 Gingerbread (*https://oreil.ly/YswD1*) really established Android's "visual language," as a UI designer might say. The 2019 Android 10 introduced the ability for users to decide which permissions to grant which apps—for instance, you can deny apps camera access—a big step forward for privacy.

See also "Google" on page 114, "Linux" on page 161

Anonymous

Anonymous (*https://oreil.ly/Iir8E*) is the most notorious hacktivist group ever. Laypeople may not have heard of LulzSec or the Cult of the Dead Cow. But if they read "We are Anonymous. We are Legion. We do not forgive. We do not forget," and see Guy Fawkes masks, their imaginations run wild.

The origin of Anonymous can be traced back to the infamous 4chan forum in 2003 (*https://oreil.ly/bILmV*). In 4chan culture, it's very poor form to enter a username when you post. To be able to generate posts for the "lulz" without the inconvenience of accountability, you'd better leave the name field blank. So whoever you are and wherever you are in the world, your name is posted as "Anonymous." And all the l33t posters on 4chan are "Anonymous."

One of the earliest Anonymous "ops" to get public attention (*https://oreil.ly/WVYtF*) was 2008's Operation Chanology. Operation Chanology was a massive online and offline protest campaign against the Church of Scientology. That's how I first got involved. Offline protests took place in various US, Canadian, Australian, British, and Dutch cities between February and May of that year.

Some other campaigns that have been attributed to Anonymous include 2010's Operation Payback, against the Recording Industry Association of America (RIAA) and the Motion Picture Association of America (MPAA); 2011's Operation Tunisia, in support of the Arab Spring; 2014's Operation Ferguson, in response to the racism-motivated police murder of Michael Brown in Ferguson, Missouri; and 2020's vandalism of the United Nations' website to post a web page supporting Taiwan.

Let me let you in on a little secret that's actually not a secret at all: Anonymous doesn't have strictly verifiable membership, like a motorcycle gang, a law enforcement agency, or the Girl Scouts would. Anyone can engage in hacktivism online or protest offline in the name of Anonymous. Anyone who posts on 4chan is "Anonymous," and that extends to the hacktivist group. Do not forgive and do not forget, 'kay?

See also "Hacktivism" on page 125

Apache/Apache License

The world's first web server was launched by Tim Berners-Lee in December 1990. The second was httpd in 1993 (*https://oreil.ly/l8RoL*), developed by the National Center for Supercomputing Applications (NCSA). However, as the Apache HTTP Server Project website (*https://oreil.ly/GsHSH*) explains, "development of that httpd had stalled after [developer] Rob [McCool] left NCSA in mid-1994, and many webmasters had developed their own extensions and bug fixes that were in need of a common distribution. A small group...gathered together for the purpose of coordinating their changes (in the form of 'patches')." Eight of those core contributors (known as the Apache Group) went on to launch Apache HTTP Server (*https://oreil.ly/lnTsS*) in 1995, replacing NCSA httpd.

Microsoft launched its proprietary IIS (*https://oreil.ly/kN7_Q*) (Internet Information Services) software the same year, and the two have dominated web-server market share ever since. IIS is optimized to run on Windows Server, whereas Apache was originally only for Linux distributions, but now there are versions of Apache for Windows Server and UNIX-based servers as well. Apache is open source under its own Apache License (*https://oreil.ly/7zwox*). Anyone who develops their own open source software may use the Apache License if they choose.

See also "Berners-Lee, Tim" on page 33, "Open source" on page 189

Apple

Apple, a little tech company you might have heard of, became the world's first $3 trillion company in 2022 (*https://oreil.ly/l7d9X*). It has more money than many nations now, but when Steve Jobs and Steve Wozniak founded it on April 1, 1976 (*https://oreil.ly/r3q2h*), Apple was indeed little (and it was no April Fool's joke, either). Not long before Jobs and Wozniak founded Apple, they were phone phreaking and attending meetings of the Homebrew Computer Club. As Jobs said in an interview: "If it hadn't been for the Blue Boxes, there would have been no Apple. I'm 100% sure of that. Woz and I learned how to work together, and we gained the confidence that we could solve technical problems and actually put something into production."

Wozniak designed the first Apple product, the Apple I (*https://oreil.ly/2jupp*), as a kit. Users could buy the motherboard but had to add their own case, peripherals, and even monitor. Homebrew, indeed.

In 1977, Woz and Jobs debuted the Apple II (*https://oreil.ly/z9202*) at the first West Coast Computer Faire in San Francisco. The Apple II was more user friendly, with a case, a keyboard, and floppy-disk peripherals. But the really exciting feature that set it apart from the Commodore PET (which also debuted at the Faire) was its color graphics. When color television was introduced in the 1960s, NBC designed its peacock logo to show off the network's color broadcasting; similarly, the original rainbow Apple logo was designed to show off the Apple II's colors. Apple II was the first Apple product to become widely successful. It inspired many early game developers.

In 1983, Jobs chose former Pepsi president John Sculley to be CEO of Apple. According to biographer Walter Isaacson,[3] Jobs asked Sculley, "Do you want to spend the rest of your life selling sugared water, or do you want a chance to change the world?"

The first product Apple introduced during Sculley's tenure, the Lisa (1983), was the first Apple product to have an operating system with a graphical user interface (GUI). It was ambitious but a commercial failure. It was priced at US$9,995 (a whopping US$27,000 today) and marketed to businesses, but only sold about 10,000 units.

The following year, Apple launched the Macintosh (known today as the Macintosh 128K) with a George Orwell-themed Super Bowl commercial (*https://oreil.ly/z2obt*) that only aired once. The ad declared, "On January 24th, Apple Computer will introduce Macintosh. And you'll see why 1984 won't be like *1984*."

At US$2,495, or about US$6,500 today, the Macintosh was still expensive, but Apple was targeting hobbyists with some disposable income. It featured a Motorola 68000 CPU, 128K RAM, a built-in display with a floppy drive, and the first version of (Classic) Mac OS, then called System 1 (*https://oreil.ly/cwNA2*) or Macintosh System Software. It even came with a mouse and keyboard. The Macintosh sold very well in its first few months, but then sales tapered off.

In 1985 (*https://oreil.ly/a569c*), Wozniak stopped working for Apple in a regular capacity, though he never stopped (*https://oreil.ly/smQ1M*) being an Apple employee. Steve Jobs also left (*https://oreil.ly/sOKIq*) that year, citing his and Sculley's conflicting visions for the company. Sculley was replaced as CEO by Michael Spindler in 1993 (*https://oreil.ly/-1V6f*), followed by Gil Amelio (formerly of Bell Labs) in 1996. Amelio laid off a lot of Apple's workforce (*https://oreil.ly/wwuAX*) and engaged in aggressive cost cutting. I'm not a fan of the reputation

---

3 Walter Isaacson, *Steve Jobs* (Simon & Schuster, 2015), pp. 386–87.

Steve Jobs has (*https://oreil.ly/_SeJc*) for mistreating employees, but it seems like Amelio was an even more destructive leader.

Many different Macintosh models were released before Jobs rejoined Apple in 1997. The Macintosh II came out in March 1987, featuring a Motorola 68020 CPU, a whopping 1 MB of RAM, and System 4.1. It showed how much PC hardware had improved since 1984's Macintosh, full colors and all. Yes, the Apple II also had colors, but not the Macintosh II's computing power!

The 1980s and 1990s brought the Macintosh Portable (1989), Apple's first proper laptop computer, followed by the Macintosh PowerBook (*https://oreil.ly/dtOB5*) series (1991–97) and, for businesses, the Macintosh Quadra (*https://oreil.ly/-YUJF*) (1991–95) and Power Macintosh (*https://oreil.ly/Zo-6P*) (1994–98) lines.

Apple also produced some experimental yet commercially released mobile devices, such as the Apple Newton line of personal digital assistants (1993–98). Although 1997's eMate 300 (*https://oreil.ly/wY-vg*) had a physical keyboard, most Newton devices (*https://oreil.ly/Ws_-T*) used touchscreen input with a stylus. However, Newton OS's handwriting recognition feature didn't work well (*https://oreil.ly/gFUGB*). Such mistakes definitely informed Apple's later development of iPods, iPhones, and iPads.

In 1997, Apple convinced Jobs to merge his new company, NeXT, with Apple (*https://oreil.ly/BuxJP*) and become its CEO in 1997. One of his first moves was to get rid of 70% of Apple's product line.

The iMac (*https://oreil.ly/sZM-c*) (1998) ushered in the new vision Jobs had for Apple products, featuring striking designs by Jony Ive (*https://oreil.ly/V_xN9*). Its monitor and motherboard resided in one unit, available in a variety of candy colors at a time when most PCs were some shade of beige. Ive also designed Apple Park, the corporate campus, in Cupertino, California.

A new operating system, Mac OS X (*https://oreil.ly/W7K9k*), debuted in 2001—and so did the iPod (*https://oreil.ly/UanhG*). For the first time, Apple began selling mobile devices in the billions of units, as well as entering digital-music sales. From the late 1990s to the mid-2000s, iMacs and iPods made Apple an extremely profitable company. The first MacBook (*https://oreil.ly/K-nxP*) line launched in May 2006 and is still Apple's top-selling Mac line as of today.

The first iPhone (*https://oreil.ly/d8uLT*) launched in 2007 with its own OS, iPhone OS 1.0. Some were skeptical that consumers would want a smartphone without a physical keyboard, but Apple had the last laugh, since now we all carry phones that are just one solid touchscreen interface with a motherboard and lithium-ion battery behind it. The iPhone line continues to sell like hotcakes. Meanwhile, the first iPad (*https://oreil.ly/61yse*) debuted in April 2010, and by the time this book is published, will be on its eleventh generation.

In 2003, Jobs was diagnosed (*https://oreil.ly/-K1MN*) with pancreatic cancer. As his health worsened, Jobs became Apple's chairman and made Tim Cook CEO. Jobs died in 2011; Cook is still CEO as of this writing, and billions more iPhones, iPads, and MacBooks have been sold.

See also "Captain Crunch (John Draper)" on page 41, "Commodore" on page 53, "Graphical user interface (GUI)" on page 117, "Homebrew Computer Club" on page 136, "Jobs, Steve" on page 150, "Personal computers" on page 196, "Silicon Valley" on page 224, "Wozniak, Steve" on page 269

ARM (Advanced RISC Machines)

ARM (Advanced RISC Machines) is a family of CPU architectures used predominantly in mobile devices and embedded computers. (RISC stands for "reduced instruction set computer.") The vast majority of non-Apple PCs these days use x86 CPUs, which are now only produced by two companies: Intel and AMD. (Apple has been putting its own ARM architecture CPUs in its MacBooks these days.) But ARM licenses its architectures to lots of semiconductor brands—kind of like how Android phones are produced by a wide range of companies. Small single-board computers designed for hobbyist hackers, such as the Raspberry Pi series, also use CPUs (*https://oreil.ly/XTrFa*) with ARM architecture.

ARM's design facilitates advanced computing while consuming a lot less electricity and producing a lot less heat than x86 CPUs. It's why we've got computers in our pockets that are more powerful than PCs from 10 years ago, but they don't need fans, nor external vents for thermal regulation.

Acorn Computers (*https://oreil.ly/y4XI5*) (1978–2015), a mighty British tech company people seldom talk about anymore, is the reason this great ARM technology drives our very small computers. Its first major product was the 1981 BBC Micro (*https://oreil.ly/3maPD*) line of PCs, made for the British Broadcasting Corporation's Computer Literacy Project. Acorn developed the world's first RISC CPU in 1985. In the late 1980s, Acorn worked to develop a CPU for Apple's Newton line of touchscreen mobile devices (a precursor to iPhones).

See also "AMD (Advanced Micro Devices)" on page 9, "CPU (Central processing unit)" on page 57, "Intel" on page 144, "Raspberry Pi" on page 211

ARPAnet

The Advanced Research Projects Agency Network (*https://oreil.ly/BKqim*) (ARPAnet) was the precursor to the modern internet, developed in 1969 under what is now the US Defense Advanced Research Projects Agency (*https://oreil.ly/Td47V*) (DARPA).

One of ARPAnet's earliest tests (*https://oreil.ly/evGp7*) came when Charley Kline sent the first packet-switched message between two computers at University of California at Los Angeles (UCLA), under the supervision of professor Leonard Kleinrock. The system crashed before Kline could type the "G" in "LOGIN"! They eventually worked out the bugs and proved that ARPAnet could send short messages. ARPAnet gradually came to connect US military facilities, academic computer science departments, and technological development facilities in the private sector. At its apex in 1976, ARPAnet had 63 connected hosts.

One of the main differences between ARPAnet and the modern internet is that the latter is built on TCP/IP, the standard internet protocol suite that makes it possible for devices and applications from any makers to communicate. ARPAnet was a technological mess (*https://oreil.ly/4LDBp*) in its earliest years, because there was little technological standardization between the hosts that were trying to send each other packets.

In 1973, Vinton Cerf and Bob Kahn (*https://oreil.ly/C8vJ3*) started work on the development of TCP/IP to solve that problem. In 1982, the US Department of Defense declared TCP/IP to be the protocol standard (*https://oreil.ly/oM9k2*) for all military computer networking. ARPAnet was completely migrated to TCP/IP (*https://oreil.ly/2jQnr*) on January 1, 1983, the date many computer historians consider the birthdate of the internet. (ARPAnet was a Scorpio, but the modern internet is a Capricorn.) The ARPAnet project (*https://oreil.ly/POqfH*) was decommissioned in 1990. But from 1983 to 1990, as Tim Berners-Lee started development on the World Wide Web, ARPAnet and the internet overlapped.

See also "DARPA (Defense Advanced Research Projects Agency)" on page 72, "Internet" on page 145, "TCP/IP (Transmission Control Protocol/Internet Protocol)" on page 239, "World Wide Web" on page 268

Artificial intelligence (AI)

Artificial intelligence (*https://oreil.ly/zMWqt*) (AI) is all about making computers think. There was a lot of buzz around OpenAI's ChatGPT project in the early 2020s, but AI development and research began in the 1950s (*https://oreil.ly/M5Csd*). Improvements in computer technology over the decades have just made

AI more versatile and sophisticated. Most people encounter AI in a wide variety of areas, from Google search suggestions to computer-controlled bad guys in video games.

In 1963, DARPA began funding AI research at MIT. The 1968 film *2001: A Space Odyssey* predicted that machines would match or exceed human intelligence by 2001. A major milestone in AI development was when IBM's Deep Blue computer beat world chess champion Garry Kasparov in a 1997 game.

A foundational concept in AI is the Turing test (*https://oreil.ly/nj-1k*), based on Alan Turing's 1950 paper "Computing Machinery and Intelligence" (*https://oreil.ly/KxhUY*). His proposal was about answering the question "Can machines think?" Today the term "Turing test" commonly refers to whether or not a computer program can fool someone into thinking that it's human. (This includes via mediums like text; an AI doesn't have to have a human-like body to pass the Turing test.) Advanced AI chatbots like ChatGPT do usually pass the Turing test—unless you ask if they're human. ChatGPT's reply to that was, "No, I'm not a human. I'm an artificial intelligence language model created by OpenAI called ChatGPT. My purpose is to understand natural language and provide helpful responses to people's queries."

See also "ChatGPT" on page 47, "DARPA (Defense Advanced Research Projects Agency)" on page 72, "IBM" on page 139, "Massachusetts Institute of Technology (MIT)" on page 170, "Turing, Alan" on page 248

Assange, Julian

Julian Assange (*https://oreil.ly/mMGYe*) (1971–) is most notable for founding WikiLeaks, a controversial online platform for journalists and sources to expose classified information to the masses. Born in Townsville, Queensland, Australia, Assange has spent his life exposing dark truths hidden by many of the most powerful people, militaries, and intelligence agencies in the world.

Assange's childhood featured a lot of homeschooling and correspondence courses as his family traveled around Australia. He had an unusual talent for computers and, in the late 1980s, joined International Subversives (*https://oreil.ly/15OtK*), an early hacktivist group. Under the handle "Mendax," Assange hacked (*https://oreil.ly/49mJY*) into some impressively prominent networks, including those of NASA and the Pentagon.

This got the Australian authorities' attention, and in 1991, Assange was charged with 31 counts of cybercrime and sentenced to a small fine. (In 1991, people who weren't computer professionals likely would not have understood computer networks very well, so perhaps the judge didn't comprehend the serious implications of hacking into the Pentagon!)

Assange launched WikiLeaks in 2006 and began publishing sensitive data that December. The site became world-famous in 2010 when former US soldier Chelsea Manning, a hacker herself, published nearly half a million classified documents that exposed horrific US Army activities in Iraq and Afghanistan. For doing so, Manning was imprisoned from 2010 to 2017, much of that time in profoundly psychologically traumatizing solitary confinement. She was subpoenaed to testify against Assange in February 2019 (*https://oreil.ly/4lPgR*), but, with much integrity and conviction, refused. A judge found her in contempt of court and Manning spent two more months in prison.

Courts in the Five Eyes (*https://oreil.ly/1Q8g7*) realms of Australia, the United Kingdom, and the United States became harsher to Assange in the wake of the Iraq and Afghanistan leaks. In 2010, Sweden issued an international warrant (*https://oreil.ly/EPXbm*) for Assange's arrest on rape allegations.[4] Assange was arrested, held for a few weeks, and then granted bail. In May 2012, however, a British court ruled (*https://oreil.ly/enVLJ*) that Assange should be extradited to Sweden to face questioning over the rape allegations. Instead, he sought refuge in the Ecuadorean embassy in London. Ecuador granted him asylum, and Assange lived in the building for years! London Metropolitan Police entered the embassy and arrested him in 2019 for "failing to surrender to the court." He has been incarcerated (*https://oreil.ly/rNOkK*) at HM Prison Belmarsh in London ever since, and has been infected with COVID (*https://oreil.ly/Tz5ky*) at least once.

The US Department of Justice has been working (*https://oreil.ly/AoEWb*) since 2019 to extradite Assange to the United States, where he could be harshly punished for the Iraq and Afghanistan leaks. Social justice activists and his lawyers have been fighting his extradition, and even Australian Prime Minister Anthony Albanese has suggested (*https://oreil.ly/16KUK*) that Assange has suffered enough and implied that it might not be right to extradite him to the United States.

See also "Manning, Chelsea" on page 168, "WikiLeaks" on page 266

Assembly

The vast majority of computers that came after ENIAC (the early digital computer, from 1945) have some sort of CPU: game consoles, smartphones, PCs, internet servers, and even the embedded computers in your Internet of Things car and in the elevators in my apartment building. ENIAC didn't really have a CPU per se; 1949's BINAC (*https://oreil.ly/DN-MQ*) (Binary Automatic Computer) introduced vacuum-tube-based CPUs. When microprocessors emerged in the 1970s, CPUs began to take the form we're familiar with today.

Computer programming languages can be classified according to how much abstraction they have from a CPU's instruction set. The most abstracted high-level programming languages (*https://oreil.ly/l-fWL*) are the most human readable and intuitive, such as Perl and Python. Low-level programming languages, by contrast, speak the most directly to the CPU. Most are *assembly languages*, the most esoteric of programming languages. Assembly languages

---

4 Is Assange really a rapist, or were the allegations made up to arrest him for the Iraq and Afghanistan leaks? I honestly don't know, and I can only speculate, but I definitely think that people should be believed when they say they were raped. Rape victims are usually treated horribly and seldom receive justice in the courts, as the advocacy group Rape Abuse and Incest National Network (RAINN) has documented (*https://oreil.ly/bAscH*).

are human-readable mnemonics representing individual machine instructions. There are different assembly languages for different types of CPUs.

Hello World code examples illustrate how different high-level programming languages are to assembly code. Here's a Hello World program by René Nyffenegger in Microsoft's Macro Assembler (MASM, commonly used on Windows PCs before booting the operating system), with the comments removed:

```
EXTRN __imp_ExitProcess:PROC
EXTRN __imp_MessageBoxA:PROC

_DATA SEGMENT

  $HELLO DB 'Hello...', 00H

  ORG $+7

  $WORLD DB '...world', 00H

_DATA ENDS

_TEXT SEGMENT

start PROC

    sub rsp, 40        ; 00000028H

    xor ecx   , ecx

    lea rdx   , OFFSET $WORLD

    lea r8    , OFFSET $HELLO

    xor r9d   , r9d

  call  QWORD PTR __imp_MessageBoxA

  xor ecx, ecx
  call  QWORD PTR __imp_ExitProcess
  add rsp, 40
  ret 0

start ENDP

_TEXT ENDS

END
```

Compare that to how simple it is to create a Hello World program in Python 3:

```
print('Hello, world!')
```

The technologically sophisticated software we use these days would be nearly impossible to create without high-level programming languages. But there's probably some assembly-language code on your phone and on your PC, where it's most often used to develop hardware drivers (which let your devices talk to their operating systems) and bootloaders (which boot up your machine and check its hardware).

Some older personal computers and video game consoles, like the Commodore 64 and Nintendo Entertainment System, don't support high-level programming languages, so even their fun games were developed with assembly languages. Those early game developers must have been very patient people.

See also "ENIAC (Electronic Numerical Integrator and Computer)" on page 98, "Hello World" on page 130, "Programming" on page 204, "Syntax" on page 236, "Turing, Alan" on page 248

Atari

The Atari company, founded in 1972 by Nolan Bushnell and Ted Dabney, was integral to the creation of today's video game industry. Atari led the direction of tropes, mechanics, and standards in arcade-game machines and, later on, video game consoles. Today, it's a mere shell (or shell-company-owned shell) of its former self, with the value of the Atari brand completely anchored to nostalgia. But early Atari was saturated with hacker culture and the hacker spirit.

Most historians point to *Spacewar!* (*https://oreil.ly/3Eqvv*) as the very first video game. In the game, players control a dot spaceship shooting at other dot spaceships. *Spacewar!* was developed in the 1960s by electronic engineering and computer science specialists using MIT's groundbreaking, massive TX-0 (*https://oreil.ly/4dELV*) and DEC PDP-1 (*https://oreil.ly/MVpEo*) computers, both of which played revolutionary roles in the development of computer science. Its display was a CRT-based scope using output technology developed for military aircraft. It was made by hackers, for hackers.

Bushnell and Dabney formed Syzygy Engineering to produce the game *Computer Space* (*https://oreil.ly/qQTnv*), their own version of *Spacewar!*, in late 1971, and formed Atari Inc. in June 1972. Bushell's background working with electronic engineering and at amusement parks helped him see the commercial potential of video games. At the time, the hardware and overall technology were so expensive that home consoles would have been impractical, so the business revolved around gathering game machines in spaces where players could gather—arcades.

The pioneering research and development work of Ralph Baer (*https://oreil.ly/OZ_yI*) in the 1960s was also instrumental in Atari's early arcade games and consoles. Baer conceptualized a simple table-tennis video game in November 1967, five years before Atari released *Pong*. Baer also created a "Brown Box" prototype in 1969, which formed the basis of the Magnavox Odyssey (*https://oreil.ly/vcgE_*), the very first home video game console.

Through the 1970s, Atari's arcade released *Space Race, Gotcha, Rebound, Tank!, PinPong, Gran Trak 10* (*https://oreil.ly/DfyJY*), and *Breakout*, which Steve Wozniak helped to design (*https://oreil.ly/d3naO*) in the months before he co-founded Apple with Steve Jobs. Bushnell sold Atari to Warner Communications (*https://oreil.ly/HGO5S*) in 1976.

Likely inspired by the Magnavox Odyssey's commercial success, Atari released its first home game console in 1977. It was first known as the Video Computer System (VCS) (*https://oreil.ly/hZZle*), then renamed the Atari 2600.

Atari's in-house game development team (*https://oreil.ly/z8Kao*) mainly consisted of David Crane, Larry Kaplan, Alan Miller, and Bob Whitehead. Unhappy with their pay and treatment at Atari, in 1979 the four went on to found Activision, the very first third-party video game developer and publisher, where they continued to make games for the Atari 2600.

Atari released its 400 and 800 home computers (*https://oreil.ly/SrYcv*) in November 1979, but the competition was stiff as the early 1980s brought the Commodore 64 and the Apple Macintosh. (Commodore founder Jack Tramiel would eventually buy Atari.) Home consoles and, later, handheld consoles from Nintendo and Sega dominated the market into the early 1990s. Atari's glory days pretty much ended there.

See also "Activision" on page 2, "Baer, Ralph" on page 29, "Commodore" on page 53, "Nintendo" on page 185, "Sega" on page 221, "Wozniak, Steve" on page 269

Atlus

Atlus, founded in 1986, was one of the top Japanese video game development and publishing companies before it was acquired by Sega (*https://oreil.ly/hg-tK*) in 2013. While US-based companies like Activision and Electronic Arts developed out of Silicon Valley's hacker community, Japan has a hacker culture of its own, based in the Akihabara area of Tokyo (*https://oreil.ly/TZUod*).

Atlus's first original game was 1987's *Digital Devil Story: Megami Tensei* (*https://oreil.ly/bCaD5*). Its plot was based on a novel by Aya Nishitani (*https://oreil.ly/lusqB*) in which the protagonist summons demons from a computer, unleashing horrors on the world. Players must negotiate with the demons as well as fight them. *Megami Tensei/Shin Megami Tensei* became a massive game series (I'm a huge fan, personally). Its most recent entry as of this writing is 2021's *Shin Megami Tensei V*. Because only the more recent games have been officially localized into English, hackers created unofficial fan subs and ROM hacks to play the older games in English.

The *Persona* series, a spin-off from the *Shin Megami Tensei* games started in 1996, features a dark, psychological story set in a high school. It has surpassed the original series in worldwide sales and popularity.

See also "Akihabara, Tokyo" on page 6, "Nintendo" on page 185, "Sega" on page 221

Augmented and virtual reality

Augmented reality (AR) is often compared and contrasted with *virtual reality* (VR). When you put on a VR headset, everything you perceive in your environment is generated by a computer: you're inside the video game. In AR (*https://oreil.ly/iDFso*), you see the real world around you, but it's *augmented* with digital elements.

AR caught on in the public consciousness in 2016, with the release of the mobile game *Pokémon GO* (*https://oreil.ly/Z9zuy*). The game uses the phone's rear camera to show the world behind it. For example, if you were playing *Pokémon GO* and standing in front of a rosebush, you'd see the rosebush exactly as you'd see it in your phone's camera when taking video—but, if you were lucky, an AR-generated Charmander might appear, and you could throw an AR-generated Pokéball to catch it. That summer, it seemed like everyone and their uncle was wandering around towns and cities, desperate to catch an Eevee or a Squirtle. Some people still play *Pokémon GO* today, but 2016 marked the height of the game's popularity.

In 1968, Ivan Sutherland (*https://oreil.ly/OupvL*) created the "Sword of Damocles" (*https://oreil.ly/s1-fg*), a head-mounted device that looked like a contraption you might find in an optometrist's clinic. It could display cubes and other very simple graphical objects within the user's field of vision.

VR and AR overlapped in a 1974 experiment by the University of Connecticut's Myron Krueger. A 1985 demonstration video (*https://oreil.ly/8Ya3Q*) of his Videoplace "artificial reality" lab shows a silhouette of a real person, moving in front of the viewer in real time, while interacting within a completely computer-generated world.

Boeing's Tom Caudell coined the term *augmented reality* in 1990. The US Air Force's Armstrong Research Lab sponsored AR research, hoping to improve piloting tools and training. There, in 1992, Louis Rosenberg developed his Virtual Fixtures system, which involved a lot of custom hardware peripherals for the user's head, arms, and hands. AR's utility in aviation extended to space exploration as well: NASA created a hybrid synthetic-vision system for its X-38 spacecraft that could generate a heads-up display in front of the pilot's view. Hirokazu Kato's open source ARToolKit (*https://oreil.ly/9RlmG*) launched in 2000, opening the way for more AR video games and software utilities in the years to follow.

Google Glass, launched in 2014, was Google's first venture into AR, but was commercially unsuccessful. Google Glass looks very much like vision-correcting glasses, but with a tiny display and camera in front of one lens. Google Glass resembles augmented reality glasses prototypes made by Steve Mann (*https:// oreil.ly/5_3Uq*). Mann has been called "the father of wearable computing" and "the father of wearable augmented reality."

With Google Glass, users could see graphical user interfaces (GUIs) for applications in their field of vision. The release of Google Glass provoked some public backlash when it emerged that users could take photos and film video without alerting anyone around them. Its $1,500 price tag (*https://oreil.ly/nggw1*) probably didn't help sales, either. Google is continuing to develop AR glasses and peripherals (*https://oreil.ly/gAPkZ*), perhaps with lessons learned from Google Glass.

See also "Google" on page 114

Autistic

It's believed that many hackers are autistic, and that there may be an association between hacking skills and autistic traits (*https://oreil.ly/5KoT6*). I speculate that many hackers are autistic, including some of the people I mention in this book.

Being autistic (*https://oreil.ly/wxloF*) means having a distinct sort of neurology that makes people more interested in creative, intellectual, and sensory pursuits than pointless small talk and group conformity. Autistic people often have intense sensory sensitivities, loving or avoiding certain sensations or foods (it's different for everyone). Some autistics need direct support with their daily activities; some are nonspeaking or situationally nonspeaking. Nonautistics often fail to recognize the intelligence of nonspeaking autistics (*https://oreil.ly/DMbuz*) because nonspeaking autistics don't share their ideas in societally accepted ways. Each and every autistic person is unique, and autism presents uniquely in each of us (*https://oreil.ly/IhN64*).

I'm autistic, and I'm fully verbal. I live and work alone, communicating with colleagues via emails and Zoom chats. In public, conscious of being watched, I use body language and posture that are generally perceived as "normal." In private, I stim with broken earbud cords while pounding away at my laptop keyboard,[5] engrossed in my work. I learn quickly from computers and books, and can focus on my interests with greater depth than nonautistics. While that's led me into a successful career as a cybersecurity researcher and writer, autistic people shouldn't be judged according to whether or not we have marketable talents.

Modern medicine has pathologized autism (*https://oreil.ly/akA4B*), treating it as a disease. It has been defined, studied, and treated almost exclusively by nonautistic so-called experts. We are not treated as the experts on ourselves, and it's no coincidence that almost all autism treatments, both mainstream and fringe, have been tremendously harmful.

The harm caused by such "treatments" is the reason why I and many other autistic people reject being called terms like "person with autism" and "high functioning/low functioning,"[6] as well as Lorna Wing's "spectrum" model (*https://oreil.ly/V7TpI*). There's no such thing as being "more autistic" or "less autistic." Either you're autistic or you're not.

As an autistic critic of capitalism and ableism, I have two coinciding ideas. The first is that, although not all autistic people are technically inclined, eliminating us and our traits would significantly slow down technological progress. Each and every autistic life has value, and each and every autistic should be accepted as they are. Our value as a people should not be determined by how useful we are to capitalism or whether our talents can be monetized. Defining our value in these absurd ways has had tragic results (*https://oreil.ly/Xc1pf*), including many autistic suicides (*https://oreil.ly/IJ1TK*).

I believe that official diagnosis by nonautistic "experts" will one day be considered as absurd as treating homosexuality as a psychiatric disorder (*https://oreil.ly/cbvKD*). I hope that in future generations, people will discover that they're autistic the same way LGBTQ+ people today discover their sexual orientations: through self-discovery and a community of their peers.

AWS

See "Amazon Web Services (AWS)" on page 8

---

5 Many autistic people do self-stimulation movements that aid us in focusing. When nonautistic people do this, it's often called "fidgeting." In autistic culture, we call it "stimming."

6 Another term best avoided is *Asperger syndrome*, named for Hans Asperger (*https://oreil.ly/b8fr3*), who conducted his autism research under the auspices of Nazi Germany. Unfortunately, even current research (*https://oreil.ly/pMO5y*) often falls into the pseudoscience of eugenics.

Azure

Microsoft Azure, launched in 2008, is Microsoft's cloud platform and a major competitor to Amazon's AWS.

Azure originates from Microsoft's acquisition of Groove Networks in 2005. It appears that Microsoft hoped originally to spin Groove into something that would look like a combination of today's Office 365 software as a service (SaaS) and Microsoft Teams. Instead, Microsoft used the infrastructure and technology from Groove as the foundation of Azure. (Groove cofounder Ray Ozzie (*https://oreil.ly/_7sOO*) also created Lotus Notes.)

Azure was launched as Windows Azure (*https://oreil.ly/4kaPm*). Microsoft originally marketed it toward developers with niche web deployment needs, as an alternative to Amazon EC2 (an AWS service that provides virtual machines) and Google App Engine. Instead of infrastructure as a service (IaaS), which simply provides server machines and networking hardware, Azure introduced platform as a service (PaaS), which deploys infrastructure with a computing platform layer.

Between 2009 and 2014, Windows Azure gradually launched features and services for content delivery networks (CDNs), Java, PHP, SQL databases, its own proprietary .NET Framework, a Python SDK (software development kit), and Windows and Linux virtual machines.

Possibly because its features went well beyond what people think of in the Windows desktop and Windows Server realms, it rebranded in 2014 as Microsoft Azure. By 2018, Azure had datacenters on all major continents (Antarctica doesn't count!), beating AWS and Google Cloud Platform to become the first major cloud platform with a physical presence in Africa (*https://oreil.ly/IKEal*), launching datacenters in Cape Town and Johannesburg, South Africa.

See also "Cloud" on page 51, "Microsoft" on page 174

2

B

Babbage, Charles

See "Lovelace, Ada" on page 164

Baer, Ralph

Ralph Baer (1922–2014) is considered the "Father of Video Games," even more than Nintendo's Shigeru Miyamoto, Atari's Nolan Bushnell, or even Fairchild's Jerry Lawson. I survey my home with its multiple video game consoles and gaming PC, and I thank the late Mr. Baer for making it all possible.

Baer (*https://oreil.ly/81DKS*) was born Jewish in Pirmasens, Germany, in 1922. He fled Nazi Germany as a teenager, making his way to the United States via the Netherlands. In 1940, he graduated from the National Radio Institute with a radio service technician diploma. Between 1943 and 1946, he served in the US Army, spending most of his deployment in France working in military intelligence.

After the war, Baer enrolled in Chicago's American Television Institute of Technology and earned his bachelor's degree in television engineering in 1949, at a time when most Americans didn't know what TV was (*https://oreil.ly/65wh5*). Early televisions existed by World War II (*https://oreil.ly/GeL2C*), where they were expensive toys for the very rich; radio broadcasters CBS and NBC had just begun television broadcasting around 1947.

Throughout the 1960s, Baer worked as an engineer (*https://oreil.ly/oVyYk*) for military contractors. During that time, he got the idea to use electronics technology to use televisions for interactive gaming. He made several prototypes from 1966 to 1968 that are now considered the very first video game consoles (at least conceptually) and are displayed at the National Museum of American History (*https://oreil.ly/9u5PS*).

Many of us who got into gaming in the 1980s fondly remember *Duck Hunt*, which came with the Nintendo Entertainment System Action Set (*https://oreil.ly/UxdqE*) and was played with a Zapper light gun. Well, one of Baer's prototypes was a lightgun (*https://oreil.ly/wHg2a*) for his "Brown Box" console concept, his most advanced prototype yet. The National Museum of American History notes that it "had basic features that most video games consoles still have today: two controls and a multigame program system" and "could be programmed to play a variety of games by flipping the switches along the front of the unit...[including] ping-pong, checkers, four different sports games, target shooting with the use of a lightgun and a golf putting game, which required the use of a special attachment."

Sanders Associates licensed Baer's "Brown Box" and patents to Magnavox, and that was the foundation of the very first commercially available video game console, 1972's Magnavox Odyssey. That same year, *Pong* (*https://oreil.ly/MlOVg*) became available as an arcade machine.

While Atari and Nintendo were responsible for making home video game consoles common, Baer's "Brown Box" and the Magnavox Odyssey predate all of that. Every video game console in existence has some features of the "Brown Box." Baer is no longer with us, but his website (*https://oreil.ly/1_Txk*) features a quote from Apple cofounder Steve Wozniak: "I can never thank Ralph enough for what he gave to me and everyone else."

See also "Miyamoto, Shigeru" on page 178, "Nintendo" on page 185

bash

The earliest computer operating systems were all orchestrated with input commands and output responses through text only. Command line interfaces (*https://oreil.ly/EHcwW*) (CLI) replicate this sort of environment in all kinds of operating systems, including current operating systems with graphical user interfaces (GUIs), enabling users and computer administrators to run commands on their computers in text from a command line.

There are a variety of CLI tools available. For example, the default CLI in Windows is CMD.exe, which shows up in my GUI as the "Command Prompt" app.

Most casual computer users don't interact much (if at all) with a CLI these days. But hackers and programmers certainly do. If you know the commands to perform the actions you want to do, like copy a bunch of files to a different folder, you may find the command line more efficient and more powerful than using your mouse and the File Manager.

The Bourne shell (*https://oreil.ly/Sxsl7*) was first developed for Version 7 UNIX by Steve Bourne for Bell Labs (*https://oreil.ly/oZOrE*) in the late 1970s. While it was a great tool, it ran on closed, proprietary code owned by a corporation. This bothered free and open source activist hackers like Richard Stallman, who argued that computer users should be able to see and control all the code their machines use. This was especially true for CLIs, the primary application for administering one's computer. In the 1980s, activist hackers, including Stallman, thus worked to create an all open source, freely shared CLI program. That program, bash (which stands for "Bourne Again Shell"—get it?), was first released in 1989. Today it is the default CLI in most Linux- and UNIX-based operating systems. To learn more about CLIs, see Launch School's free online book, *Introduction to the Command Line* (*https://oreil.ly/OXTCo*).

See also "Bell Labs" on page 31, "Graphical user interface (GUI)" on page 117, "Linux" on page 161, "Stallman, Richard" on page 229, "UNIX" on page 253

BASIC

See "Gates, Bill" on page 109, "Microsoft" on page 174, "Programming" on page 204

BBS

See "Bulletin board systems (BBSes)" on page 37

Bell Labs

Bell Labs (*https://oreil.ly/tUkK_*) has gone through a number of iterations and names in its nearly century-long history—Bell Telephone Laboratories, AT&T Bell Laboratories, Bell Labs Innovations, and now Nokia Bell Labs. Bell Labs is where many of the technologies that are central to the world of hacker culture were invented. It holds an overwhelming number of patents, a plethora of Nobel Prizes and Turing Awards...and multiple Emmys, Grammys, and Oscars. (No Tony Awards so far, though.)

Bell Labs traces its origins to Alexander Graham Bell, inventor of the telephone, and the American Telephone & Telegraph Company (AT&T). Bell Telephone Laboratories, Inc., was formally established out of several AT&T engineering departments in 1925.

A comprehensive history of Bell Labs would take up at least an entire book, but its website (*https://oreil.ly/cPA42*) is a great starting point. Instead, I'll give you a quick timeline of some of Bell Labs' most important inventions and innovations.

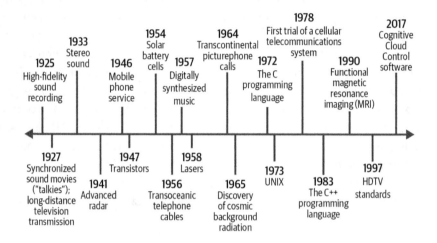

Nokia Bell Labs, as it's known today, continues to employ many of the world's most innovative hackers, who conduct research and development in computing, telecommunications, medical imaging, and physics.

See also "Turing, Alan" on page 248, "UNIX" on page 253

Berkeley, University of California

University of California, Berkeley, is the founding campus of the University of California. Berkeley is in the San Francisco Bay Area, but not quite in the geographic region known as Silicon Valley. Nonetheless, Berkeley has had a major impact on Silicon Valley and hacker culture. Its College of Engineering (*https://oreil.ly/tS_M1*) alumni include Eric Schmidt, Marc Tarpenning (cofounder of Tesla), Douglas Engelbart (inventor of the computer mouse), Andrew Ng (chief scientist of Baidu, a massive Chinese tech company on the level of Google), Leonard Adleman (of RSA cryptography fame), and Steve Wozniak, famous for returning to Berkeley as a student after his massive success co-founding Apple.

The Computing Sciences at Berkeley Lab (*https://oreil.ly/v-H23*) is a major hub of hacker activity. Berkeley Lab is notable (*https://oreil.ly/vnlOv*) for having the first supercomputer connected to ARPAnet back in 1974.

See also "Adleman, Leonard" on page 3, "ARPAnet" on page 17, "Pirates of Silicon Valley (1999 film)" on page 202, "Silicon Valley" on page 224, "Wozniak, Steve" on page 269

Berners-Lee, Tim

Sir Timothy John Berners-Lee (1955–) was born in London to computer-scientist parents. He studied physics at Oxford in the 1970s and was knighted by Queen Elizabeth II in 2004. His notable invention is the World Wide Web, a massive network of hyperlinked pages that mainly contain text (but can also contain embedded media and applets), perhaps the single greatest factor in popularizing the internet worldwide.

The birthdate of the internet is debated, but the most accepted date is January 1, 1983. That's when ARPAnet, the precursor to the modern internet, officially changed to the TCP/IP (*https://oreil.ly/I18OC*) computer networking standard. But nothing like the web existed yet.

His work at the European Organization for Nuclear Research (CERN by its French initials) inspired Berners-Lee to invent the web. He was frustrated by how difficult it could be for researchers to collaborate and by how much research work was lost when people left the organization. In March 1989 he wrote "Information Management: A Proposal" (*https://oreil.ly/CxeVY*) to describe the problem and his idea.

He saw the web as a means for academic researchers to share their knowledge freely and in a way that can be referenced long even after a researcher left the organization, and that is much more dynamic and collaborative than books. Researchers could cite someone else's work or provide further information sources using hyperlinks, which readers could click to go to a different web page on the same web server or a different one. The concept was revolutionary.

Berners-Lee called this enormously popular internet service the World Wide Web, or WWW for short. That's why "www" is still often used as a subdomain for web pages. The web of the 1990s and early 2000s is sometimes known retrospectively as Web 1.0.

In 1990, Berners-Lee published a proposal for the foundational technologies that would underlie the web: the HTTP internet protocol, the HTML markup language, the first web server, and the very first web browser, WorldWideWeb (*https://oreil.ly/EQzVC*). A problem he noted at CERN was the high turnover of people. When two years is a typical length of stay, information is constantly being lost. The introduction of the new people demands a fair amount of their time and that of others before they have any idea of what goes on. The technical details of past projects are sometimes lost forever, or only recovered after a detective investigation in an emergency. Often, the information has been recorded, but cannot be found.

From 1989 to 1991 (*https://oreil.ly/tixtG*), Berners-Lee worked on inventing what he had proposed. To do so, he used a NeXT Computer, an advanced workstation whose hardware and operating system were both created by the same vendor, similar to Apple computers. Indeed, NeXT was founded by Apple cofounder Steve Jobs during his 11-year period away from Apple.

In 1991, Berners-Lee published a summary of his World Wide Web project on the Usenet group alt.hypertext, seeking collaborators. Through the early 1990s, the web gradually grew in usage, particularly among academic institutions. Foreseeing a need to maintain technological standards, Berners-Lee founded the World Wide Web Consortium (W3C) in 1994.

Berners-Lee continues to work as a computer scientist and still frequently gives talks at events and institutions around the world. Some of his policy positions are well received within the hacker community, such as his advocacy for net neutrality. Others cause friction with the ideals of hacker culture, such as his approval of encrypted media extensions for digital rights management (DRM).

See also "DRM (Digital Rights Management)" on page 89, "Usenet" on page 255, "World Wide Web" on page 268, "World Wide Web Consortium (W3C)" on page 268

Binary

Binary data existed long before the invention of the first electronic computer, ENIAC, in the 1940s. Base-2 (binary) numeral systems date back as early 2400 BC in ancient Egypt. The Western Arabic numeral system we most commonly use in everyday life today is base-10 (decimal): numerals 1, 2, 3, 4, 5, 6, 7, 8, 9, and 0, with each digit positioned to the power of 10. The first two-digit number is 10 × 1, 100 is 10 × 10, and so on.

In binary numeral systems, there are only two numerals, 0 and 1. In the 17th and early 18th centuries, German mathematician Gottfried Wilhelm Leibniz was inspired by the *I Ching*, a Chinese text from the 9th century BCE that used its own binary number system. In 1703 in his *Explication de l'arithmétique binaire*, Leibniz devised a binary numeral system similar to the one we use today.

The mechanical (pre-electronic) computers of the 1930s, such as Bell Labs' "Model K" and Konrad Zuse's Z1, calculated based on binary data. Every electronic computer in production use, from ENIAC to the 2021 model AMD Ryzen 9 5900HX-based Windows 11 gaming laptop I'm using now, is based on binary data.

Here's an example of converting decimal to binary:

0 = 0

1 = 1

2 = 10

3 = 11

27 = 11011

256 = 100000000

So each digit multiplies by 2. That's why numbers like 8, 16, 32, 64, 256, 512, and so on are so commonly found in computing when it comes to data capacity and data bus size.

Binary data is measured in *bits*. A *byte* is a unit of eight bits and is typically used to encode a single character, such as an ASCII character. In modern computing, we often measure data quantity and capacity in bigger units, such as you'll See in Table 2-1.

Table 2-1. Units of measurement for binary data

Byte	B	1 B
Kilobyte	KB	1,024 B
Megabyte	MB	1,024 KB
Gigabyte	GB	1,024 MB
Terabyte	TB	1,024 GB
Petabyte	PB	1,024 TB
Exabyte	EB	1,024 PB
Zettabyte	ZB	1,024 EB

You may see petabytes (1,024 TB) and exabytes (1,024 PB) in enterprise computing, supercomputers, and massive data lakes. A zettabyte (1,024 EB) was the total volume of global internet traffic in 2016.

Not all computers are binary. Quantum computing has been in research and development for the past few decades, but has never been properly used in production as of this writing. Quantum computers are based on *qubits*, which can be 0, 1, or both 0 and 1 simultaneously! When quantum computers properly enter the market, they'll mark the first phase in post-binary computing.

See also "ENIAC (Electronic Numerical Integrator and Computer)" on page 98, "Quantum computing" on page 207

BitTorrent

See "Peer-to-peer (P2P) networks" on page 195, "Piracy" on page 200

Blockchain

See "Cryptocurrency" on page 61

Botnet

See "Cybersecurity" on page 68, "Robotics" on page 216

Bug

A bug is an error (*https://oreil.ly/pEPoK*) in a computer program. If I write a Hello World script, but "Hello World" doesn't print because I spelled print "pirnt" (I was probably typing too fast), that typo is a bug. Computers don't interpret information subjectively; they take your instructions literally. If a program doesn't run or execute the way the programmer expected because they made a mistake, that's a bug. Not using the correct syntax in a script creates a "syntax error" bug. (*Syntax* is how a programming language uses punctuation, spaces, and the structure of instructions. It's equivalent to how spelling, grammar, and punctuation operate in natural languages like English.)

While malware is deliberately malicious software, a bug is an innocent mistake. Bugs can be cybersecurity problems, though, if they make it possible for a threat actor to attack something. This kind of bug is called a *software vulnerability*.

Ever wonder why your PC, MacBook, and phone are always having you install updates? Part of the reason is to fix, or *patch*, such vulnerabilities as cybersecurity practitioners track them down and rework (or *debug*) their code. Bug hunting and bug reporting are huge areas in software development.

It's usually possible to completely debug a very simple script (say, 100 lines of code). But as computer software gets more and more complicated, with hundreds of files and potentially millions of lines of code, a totally bug-free complex application is pretty much impossible. The computer I'm currently using has bugs, as does yours. It's inevitable. The important thing is to patch and mitigate security vulnerabilities, and patch bugs that negatively impact your experience of using the software.[1]

See also "Common Vulnerabilities and Exposures (CVE)" on page 56, "Cybersecurity" on page 68, "Hello World" on page 130, "Programming" on page 204, "Syntax" on page 236

Bulletin board systems (BBSes)

Before the modern web, *bulletin board systems* (BBSes) were a popular way for computers to share information through the telephone system, primarily using dial-up or Telnet connections. The first BBS was created by Ward Christensen and Randy Suess in 1978.

---

[1] For a fascinating etymology of the term *bug* that involves Grace Hopper, Thomas Edison, and actual bugs, see Christopher McFadden, "The Origin of the Term 'Computer Bug,'" (*https://oreil.ly/G27d-*) *Interesting Engineering*, 2020.

Connecting to a BBS loads a text interface with a menu and usually some beautiful *ASCII art* (the craft of using ASCII characters you can input from your keyboard to make pictures). The "bulletin board" aspect is a sort of comment thread on which users can leave messages. Some BBS servers also have file transfer capabilities.

Anyone with a computer, the right software, and the right sort of modem and telephone connection can create their own BBS, and back in the 1980s and 1990s (*https://oreil.ly/Pdz3r*), there were hundreds of them all over North America. In the early 1990s, BBSes were especially popular for distributing shareware and pirated software.

Some of the first online communities came about via BBS. As Scott Gilbertson reports in *WIRED* (*https://oreil.ly/epiav*), "BBS took its basic premise from the community bulletin boards that once adorned the entrance of public places like libraries, schools and supermarkets," with "the notion of digital meeting place in mind."

The rise of the World Wide Web in the 1990s killed their popularity, but some BBSes still exist, and you can find them through the Telnet BBS Guide website (*https://oreil.ly/N4vB-*). Exploring some of them would be a great way to learn about hacker culture.

Jason Scott maintains a huge BBS content archive on his site *textfiles.com* (*https://oreil.ly/floyo*), and he also made a documentary (*https://oreil.ly/YDKC8*) on the BBS phenomenon that is worth a watch.

See also "IRC (Internet Relay Chat)" on page 147, "Piracy" on page 200, "Usenet" on page 255, "World Wide Web" on page 268

Byte magazine

Byte (1975–1998) was an influential computer magazine founded by Wayne Green (*https://oreil.ly/5qH49*). During its run, it spawned many of the best ideas in hacker culture and counted the best and brightest hackers among its readership. Some even wrote letters, such as groundbreaking computer scientist Werner Buchholz, who wrote a letter to explain how he coined the word byte (a very meta occurrence indeed). *Byte* was also part of the inspiration for *2600* magazine. You can read the Byte archives for free through the Internet Archive (*https://oreil.ly/Xyz_w*).

See also "2600 (Twenty-Six Hundred): The Hacker Quarterly (magazine)" on page 250

3

C

Calce, Michael "MafiaBoy"

Michael "MafiaBoy" Calce (1984–), of Montreal, Canada, made his name as a malicious hacker, conducting a series of distributed denial-of-service (DDoS) attacks against corporate websites in the year 2000 (*https://oreil.ly/wKwo-*). A *DDoS attack* is when multiple computers overwhelm an entity on a computer network with more packets or datagrams than it can handle, forcing the entity to shut down. Web servers are the most common targets.

In an interview with NPR (*https://oreil.ly/5s21l*), Calce says he was motivated by competition with other cyberattackers: "The overall purpose was to intimidate other hacker groups. The whole of the hacking community was all about notoriety and exploration, whereas you look at hackers today and it's all about monetization."

Calce fell in love with computers (*https://oreil.ly/PMAun*) when his dad got him his first PC at age six, around 1990. He learned how to hack past AOL's 30-day free-trial limit, then learned about DoS attacks through AOL chat rooms.

His first DDoS attack briefly took down Yahoo! in February 2000, when Yahoo! was as central to the web as Google is now. The next day, one of Calce's rivals took down Buy.com. Calce responded by DDoSing eBay the following day. Then someone in one of Calce's IRC chats suggested that CNN would be difficult to DDoS because its network was so advanced. So Calce successfully targeted CNN, then Dell, and then Amazon.

Law enforcement was hot on Calce's trail. As Calce told NPR: "You know, I'm a pretty calm, collected, cool person, but when you have the president of the United States and attorney general basically calling you out and saying 'We're going to find you'… at that point I was a little bit worried. I started to notice this utility van that was parked at the end of my street at, like, Sunday at 4 a.m."

On September 12, 2001, as a 17-year-old high school senior, Calce was sentenced (*https://oreil.ly/PMAun*) to eight months in a youth detention center. Not long after, many American jurisdictions improved their cybercrime laws (*https://oreil.ly/WF-Jy*)—and eBay, CNN, and Yahoo! improved their defenses against DDoS attacks.

Calce published a memoir in 2009.[1] Since 2015, he has run his own penetration-testing firm, Optimal Secure (*https://oreil.ly/RS9bj*).

See also "Cybersecurity" on page 68,"Denial-of-service (DoS, DDoS) attacks" on page 81, "Exploit" on page 101, "IRC (Internet Relay Chat)" on page 147, "Penetration testing" on page 196, "Yahoo!" on page 277

Cama, Amat

Amat Cama (1992–) is an innovative hacker and cybersecurity researcher from Senegal who is best known for discovering (*https://oreil.ly/EFE1S*) critical security vulnerabilities in the Tesla Model 3 electric car's onboard computer system. He was introduced to Capture the Flag (CTF) hacking competitions in 2012, while studying computer science and math at Northeastern University.

Hundreds of CTF events happen every year, hosted by tech companies, cybersecurity events, technical schools, and academic institutions around the world. Cama got experience at CTF events, and those skills helped him with bug hunting. After winning many different CTF competitions over the years, Cama and fellow hacker Richard Zhu participated in Pwn2Own, a biannual bug-hunting event hosted by Trend Micro since 2007. Competing as "Team Fluoroacetate," Cama and Zhu proved unstoppable for three events in a row in 2018 and 2019.

In an interview with Catalin Cimpanu for ZDNet (*https://oreil.ly/mYEqO*), Cama discussed the significance of his Pwn2Own event to his security research career:

> *Winning Pwn2Own three times in a row is definitely something that I am proud of. At one point in time, I viewed even getting a single entry in the contest as an unattainable goal, so it is pretty satisfying to have won the competition three times in a row. However, I wouldn't call it as the*

---

1 Michael Calce with Craig Silverman, *Mafiaboy: How I Cracked the Internet and Why It's Still Broken* (Penguin Canada, 2009).

pinnacle of my career as a security researcher. In this field, there is always something more, something else or something better you can do.

Bug hunters like Cama find security vulnerabilities so that tech companies can improve the security of their products and services. The bug Cama discovered is a just-in-time compiler vulnerability *(https://oreil.ly/Kq7M4)* in the car's onboard internet browser. I honestly don't think it's a good idea to build an internet browser into a car in the first place—it seems like a totally unnecessary expansion of the car's cyberattack surface—but good for Cama for discovering it! He and Zhu won $35,000, and they got to keep the car. Cama now works as a principal security researcher for Vigilant Labs *(https://oreil.ly/I2XWr)*.

See also "Bug" on page 37, "Capture the Flag" on page 42, "Cybersecurity" on page 68

Captain Crunch (John Draper)

John "Captain Crunch" Draper (1943–) is a well-known *phreaker* (slang for "phone hacker") whose name derives from the popular sugary breakfast cereal Cap'n Crunch and its cartoon naval officer mascot.

As the son of a former US Air Force engineer, young Draper was able to acquire a lot of discarded electronics and radio equipment! He used it to build an unlicensed home radio station. Draper enlisted in the Air Force in 1964. By 1968, while stationed at Charleston Air Force Station in Maine, he launched a pirate radio station that he dubbed WKOS, for "chaos." (Authentic call signs are designated by formal radio licensing authorities.) The nearby legally licensed radio station, WDME, didn't like WKOS very much and managed to get authorities to shut it down.

In the late 1960s and early 1970s, Draper worked two jobs in Silicon Valley: as an engineer for National Semiconductor, and as an engineer and disc jockey for the (lawful) radio station KKUP in Cupertino, California. He continued his pirate radio hobby in his spare time.

From the 1870s until the US phone system became digitized in 1988, the technology that was used to route and transmit phone calls was completely analog. (Today it has the retronym POTS, for "plain old telephone service.") Long-distance calls could be very expensive, and phone companies used inaudible high-pitched tones while routing call connections to indicate that a long-distance call was authorized.

Draper discussed phreaking with other phreakers on his pirate radio station, including the famous blind phone hacker Josef Carl "Joybubbles" Engressia Jr.

(1949–2007), who was great at imitating precise tone pitches with his voice. Draper, meanwhile, discovered that a plastic whistle toy distributed in boxes of Cap'n Crunch cereal made a sound of 2600 hertz: the correct pitch for fooling the POTS network into treating a long-distance call as authorized. (This became the origin of Draper's nickname as well as of 2600 magazine, the top print publication in the hacker community since January 1984.)

Some might consider such an act to be stealing from the telecommunications industry. In 1972, Draper was sentenced to five years' probation for telephone fraud. But he got the attention of Steve Wozniak and Steve Jobs, and the three of them started a business selling blue boxes for phreaking a few years before founding Apple in 1976.

Captain Crunch wouldn't stop phreaking. He served prison sentences in 1976 and 1978 for phone fraud. In 1977, between prison stints, he joined the newly formed Apple Computers as an independent contractor.

See also "Apple" on page 13, "Cybersecurity" on page 68, "Ham radio" on page 127, "Jobs, Steve" on page 150, "Phreaking" on page 199, "2600 (Twenty-Six Hundred): The Hacker Quarterly (magazine)" on page 250, "Wozniak, Steve" on page 269

Capture the Flag

In the old-fashioned children's game Capture the Flag, there are two teams. Each team gets a different colored flag. Each team is tasked with hiding its flag within its zone. Then players run into the opposing team's zone, pushing and shoving to find the other team's flag. The first team to grab the other team's flag and move it to their own side of the field wins.

The hacker version of Capture the Flag (*https://oreil.ly/9GCAh*) (CTF) is conceptually similar (*https://oreil.ly/ucyu6*). One or more digital "flags" (such as a file, or a line of text within a file) are hidden in an application, virtual machine, or virtualized network. Hackers use their hacking skills to find the flag(s). Depending on how the game is organized, whichever individual or team finds the flag or all of the flags first wins.

Most hacker CTF games are operated by cybersecurity events, hacker spaces, colleges and universities, and online training platforms like Hack The Box (*https://oreil.ly/2RVPP*). *CTFTime.org* (*https://oreil.ly/J5ySy*) is one of the best resources to learn about upcoming CTF events around the world. If you hope to hack professionally as a penetration tester or vulnerability researcher, participating in CTF games is a great idea; you'll learn hacking skills in a fun environment, and you can include your participation on your resume or CV.

See also "Cybersecurity" on page 68, "Penetration testing" on page 196

Carnegie Mellon University

Carnegie Mellon University (*https://oreil.ly/Leiy3*) (CMU) has played an important role in the development of computer science. Stanford and MIT get a lot of attention for their roles in the history of hacker culture, and rightfully so, but CMU shouldn't be overlooked.

CMU was founded in 1900 in Pittsburgh, Pennsylvania, as Carnegie Technical Schools, with funding from steel tycoon Andrew Carnegie. (Carnegie funded dozens of institutions and 2,509 libraries (*https://oreil.ly/rOwab*) between 1883 and 1929—to justify his vast money hoarding, I suppose.) It merged in 1967 with the Mellon Institute of Industrial Research to form CMU. By the time CMU's School of Computer Science was formed in 1988 (*https://oreil.ly/QJXC7*), the university had performed decades of direct and indirect computer science research.

In 1956, Carnegie Institute of Technology acquired an IBM 650 computer (*https://oreil.ly/zuZXT*), which was placed in the basement of the Graduate School of Industrial Administration to help social scientists (*https://oreil.ly/KrmL8*) compute complex logistics problems. The IBM 650 was compact by the standards of the day: a read-punch unit the size of two kitchen stoves, a console unit the size of a few refrigerators stacked together, and a second unit of the same size, all with vacuum tubes. It could process 200 punch cards per minute and, if it had a processing error, could automatically repeat portions of the processing by restarting at a breaking point. In 1958, Carnegie Tech offered the very first freshman-level computer-programming course in the US.

In the 1960s CMU received lots of Cold War-driven government funding to progress computer science research. The first $600,000 grant from the Defense Advanced Research Projects Agency (DARPA) in 1962 helped to start the Computation Center, headed by Pascal language creator and Turing Award winner Alan Perlis (*https://oreil.ly/e7ojS*), along with decision theorist and future Nobel laureate Herbert Simon (*https://oreil.ly/HKqGP*) and AI pioneer and Turing Award winner Allen Newell (*https://oreil.ly/fEoCX*).

See also "DARPA (Defense Advanced Research Projects Agency)" on page 72, "IBM" on page 139, "Massachusetts Institute of Technology (MIT)" on page 170, "Stanford University" on page 230

Carr, Iris

Iris Carr (ca. 1917–?)[2] was an African American woman and a brilliant and pioneering hacker and cryptographer, before hacker culture was an established phenomenon. In 1932 (https://oreil.ly/hIA1D), she earned a bachelor's degree in mathematics and English from Prairie View College in Texas. As a young woman, Carr worked as a schoolteacher for 12 years, but was denied a retirement plan (https://oreil.ly/LOXFo) because she was Black. She considered different career paths, and in 1944, she moved to Washington, DC, to look for better work with the federal government.

Carr's first job in DC was for the Office of the Recorder of Deeds. Soon after, she got a job teaching mathematics and business English at Hilltop Radio Electronics Institute, a Black-owned technical school. There she met Bernice Mills, a member of the Russian Plaintext Office at the National Security Agency (NSA). Thanks to that fortunate encounter, the NSA hired her in 1950 to intercept and crack encrypted radio messages from the former Soviet Union.

Cryptography gave Carr's mathematical genius an opportunity to shine. Despite the NSA's history of racist hiring practices, she was optimistic for its future. She said, "I was so involved in what the Agency stood for, and I wanted it to be better. I had a feeling that things were going to get better."

In 1958, Carr was promoted to personnel officer for the NSA's Office of Collection. She kept cracking codes and advancing our understanding of digital cryptography until she retired in 1971. She is now deceased. She's a great example of a bright mind who forged her own path in life despite the limited professional opportunities offered to women of her generation.

See also "Cryptography" on page 63

The Cathedral and the Bazaar (1999 book)

Eric S. Raymond's book The Cathedral and the Bazaar: Musings on Linux and Open Source by an Accidental Revolutionary (https://oreil.ly/i5aiv) (O'Reilly, 1999) is, in my opinion, one of the best books ever written about the culture of computing and hacker culture.

---

2 Sadly, because her career existed and finished before the internet and also because she was an underappreciated technological innovator, I was unable to find her birth and death years. We know that she was 33 in 1950 and that she gave an interview (https://oreil.ly/D_oiB) to NSA oral historians in 1991. See Jeannette Williams with Yolande Dickerson, The Invisible Cryptologists: African-Americans, WWII to 1956 (Center for Cryptologic History, National Security Agency, United States Cryptologic History series V, vol. 5, 2001).

Raymond compares two open source software development models. In the "Cathedral" model, software is created by an exclusive group of programmers. The source code is released publicly after each release, but in between releases the code in progress is kept private. The "Bazaar" model is a freer, more inclusive model in which the source code is freely available on the internet at all stages of development. Anyone who makes changes that the community accepts gets to be one of the authors of that software. Richard Stallman's development of GNU Emacs is an example of Cathedral development, and Raymond credits Linus Torvalds as the pioneer of the Bazaar model of development.

Torvalds initiated Linux to create an open source UNIX-like operating system, but its massive success is largely due to the contributions of thousands of open source collaborators. That's why there isn't simply one operating system called Linux, but hundreds of Linux distributions, all developed and maintained by different groups of people. There is a Linux kernel that all of those operating systems use, and its contributions include both individual eccentric nerds and big corporations. (For instance, Google's Android operating system is based on a Linux kernel for ARM processors.)

Raymond argues that the Bazaar model is usually the most effective at creating software that works well and has minimal bugs. He also considers it very important to release code early and often, so the hacker community can make improvements and so users can share their feedback. If you haven't read *The Cathedral and the Bazaar* yet, please do!

See also "Android operating system" on page 11, "Emacs" on page 97, "Linux" on page 161, "Open source" on page 189, "Stallman, Richard" on page 229, "Torvalds, Linus" on page 246

Certificates (cryptography)

The word *certificate* is used in two very different ways in cybersecurity. This entry is about machine identities that are used in public-key cryptography.

Martin Hellman, Ralph Merkle, and Whitfield Diffie presented the concept (*https://oreil.ly/CQ49u*) of public-key cryptography at Stanford University in 1976. Before, all digital cryptography used private keys only. So you'd have to be within the cryptographic system, such as within an internal network, to be able to encrypt and decrypt data. Private keys can be symmetrical, meaning that the decryption key is just the encryption key in reverse. So if the encryption key was "× 3 × 2 + 11," the decryption key would be "−11 ÷ 2 ÷ 3."

In public-key cryptography, the key used to encrypt data is available publicly and only the decryption key is used privately. And for the private key to remain private and secure, the cipher has to be asymmetrical, unlike in private key cryptography. In 1977 (*https://oreil.ly/-N7xl*), Ron Rivest, Adi Shamir, and Leonard Adleman built on Diffie, Hellman, and Merkle's work to invent Rivest-Shamir-Adleman (RSA) cryptography, which made public-key cryptography a lot more feasible to implement.

When my web browser visits an HTTPS-encrypted website (almost all web pages these days), the destination web server gives it a public key. Then a certificate is sent to my web browser from the web server's public-key infrastructure that certifies that the public key is correct and authentic. My browser can use the key in good faith, and when my browser sends data, the server decrypts that data with its private key. The certificate itself isn't the key; the certificate *certifies* the key. It's sort of like an airline ticket; it contains information about the user and the web page, and confirms that the web page is the proper destination for the user's browser. As with airline tickets, forging a certificate is a big no-no!

There are two kinds of identities in cryptography: a machine identity and a user identity. My user identity can be the username and password that I use to log into a web application, identifying me as a user. A certificate is a machine identity, so it identifies a machine—in this case, a web server.

See also "Cryptography" on page 63, "Cybersecurity" on page 68, "Diffie, Whitfield" on page 83, "Diffie-Hellman key exchange" on page 84, "Hellman, Martin" on page 128, "Key" on page 156, "Rivest-Shamir-Adleman (RSA) cryptography" on page 215, "Stanford University" on page 230

Certificates (professional credentials)

The word *certificate* is used in two very different ways in cybersecurity. This entry is about a credential that's supposed to prove someone's technical skills and know-how in cybersecurity. Job seekers often pursue certifications to make them more employable. From the employer's perspective, a certification proves that an employee or job candidate has particular skills and knowledge without the employer having to directly train them in that area.

There are two types of certifications: vendor and vendor-neutral. Some big tech companies, such as Microsoft and Cisco, offer certifications for their own technologies. Those are *vendor certifications. Vendor-neutral certifications* are supposed to demonstrate knowledge and skills in particular areas of computing, but they aren't tied to any specific vendor. For instance, the Computing Technology

Industry Association (CompTIA) offers a long-running A+ certification that covers how to maintain computers that use an x86-64 CPU architecture; CompTIA is independent of the two companies that make x86-64 CPUs, Intel and Advanced Micro Devices (AMD). There are hundreds of certifications in cybersecurity and even more in IT in general, both vendor and vendor-neutral.

Now it's time for my opinion. Are they worthwhile?

Some prestigious people in the cybersecurity industry pretty much winged it to the top without certifications. If you're looking to enter the industry, or if you're unhappy working in tech support and want to be a cloud administrator, for example, I strongly recommend searching postings for the kinds of jobs you're curious about. If those postings mention the same few certifications over and over again, it would be prudent for you to work on acquiring them. If you're lucky, your employer might even cover the expense of study materials, courses, and exam fees.

As to whether or not certifications actually demonstrate the skills they're supposed to prove, it varies. I think using certifications for gatekeeping in hiring is a huge problem: the cost alone keeps poor people out of the industry, because study materials and exam fees can be quite expensive. For example, the Certified Information Systems Security Professional (CISSP) certification is relatively difficult to get. To even arrange a CISSP exam (*https://oreil.ly/nUoN3*), candidates must have a minimum of five years' cumulative paid work experience in at least two of eight knowledge domains. It's an advanced certification that's best suited for executive roles—yet lots of job postings demand CISSPs (*https://oreil.ly/LZ5tH*) for *entry-level cybersecurity jobs*. Certifications can be useful sometimes, but ultimately people's skills should be assessed based on what they can demonstrate.

See also "AMD (Advanced Micro Devices)" on page 9, "Cybersecurity" on page 68, "Intel" on page 144, "Microsoft" on page 174

ChatGPT

ChatGPT (*https://oreil.ly/xraNj*), short for Chat Generative Pre-trained Transformer, is an AI program released in 2022. It is designed to respond to text questions (*https://oreil.ly/8XoG8*) with intelligent text answers. Its companion program, DALL-E (*https://oreil.ly/eL6oX*), generates images based on text prompts. Both were developed by OpenAI (*https://oreil.ly/toa8B*), a company founded in 2015 by a group of Silicon Valley bigwigs (including Y Combinator alumni Sam Altman and Jessica Livingston, as well as Peter Thiel and Elon

Musk). Microsoft has invested billions of dollars (*https://oreil.ly/Lk-W1*) in the company.

The Turing test is a prominent concept in computer science, and it's also the paradigm of artificial intelligence (AI): if a computer can convince a human that it is human, it passes the Turing test. The Turing test is based on computer-science pioneer Alan Turing's work.[3]

ChatGPT is changing the minds of researchers when it comes to the philosophical question of what an effective Turing test really is. The now famous AI chatbot is great at simulating human-like conversations, but research published by *Nature* (*https://oreil.ly/52P-W*) in July 2023 suggests its thinking isn't so human-like when it comes to solving some visual logic puzzles. The report added:

> Rather than the Turing test, researchers instead typically assess AI systems using benchmarks intended to evaluate performance on specific capabilities, such as language ability, common-sense reasoning and mathematical capacity. Increasingly, teams are also turning to academic and professional examinations designed for people.

ChatGPT uses language models and machine learning (with both supervised and reinforcement techniques) to respond to human questions intelligently in natural English. ChatGPT has no humanlike physical avatar. I decided to give ChatGPT a try for the purposes of this book and asked, "What is hacker culture?" It replied:

> Hacker culture refers to a subculture of individuals who are interested in computer programming and technology, and who often use their skills to find and exploit vulnerabilities in computer systems. The term 'hacker' originally referred to someone with a high level of technical expertise who used their skills to push the boundaries of what was possible with computers. Over time, the term has also come to be associated with individuals who use their skills for illegal or unethical purposes, such as stealing sensitive information or disrupting computer systems. However, in the original sense, a hacker is a person who enjoys exploring the details of

---

3 Alan Turing, 1950, "Computing Machinery and Intelligence (*https://oreil.ly/S5HUE*)," *Mind*, 59 (236): 433–60, quoted in the *Stanford Encyclopedia of Philosophy*, "Turing test (*https://oreil.ly/JdJGW*)," revised 2021.

programmable systems and how to stretch their capabilities—as opposed to most users, who prefer to learn only the minimum necessary.[4]

ChatGPT is not without controversy. My career and livelihood entirely revolves around researching information, interpreting that information, and writing about it. I really hope AI doesn't replace my job. Stephen Hawking, the late physicist, was asked on Reddit (*https://oreil.ly/lbNow*) what he thought of technological unemployment. He replied,

> *If machines produce everything we need, the outcome will depend on how things are distributed. Everyone can enjoy a life of luxurious leisure if the machine-produced wealth is shared, or most people can end up miserably poor if the machine-owners successfully lobby against wealth redistribution. So far, the trend seems to be toward the second option, with technology driving ever-increasing inequality.*

I wouldn't be quite as concerned about ChatGPT taking my job if it weren't for capitalism. For my own sake, I hope AI does for my profession what Hatsune Miku (*https://oreil.ly/gDpFg*) has done as a pop star: Miku is a pop star, but real human pop stars are definitely still a thing.

See also "Artificial intelligence (AI)" on page 17, "Microsoft" on page 174, "Turing, Alan" on page 248

CIA (Central Intelligence Agency)

See "Assange, Julian" on page 18, "Manning, Chelsea" on page 168, "Snowden, Edward" on page 227, "Stuxnet" on page 232, "WikiLeaks" on page 266

CIA triad (confidentiality, integrity, availability)

The CIA triad is one of the most important concepts in cybersecurity. It has nothing to do with the Central Intelligence Agency, at least to the best of my knowledge: CIA is an acronym for confidentiality, integrity, and availability. All cyberattacks and threats harm at least one of these data properties.

Confidentiality is about making sure that only authorized people and entities can access data. If criminals steal your credit card number, that's an attack on confidentiality.

---

4 ChatGPT, prompt: "What is hacker culture?" March 2023.

Integrity is about making sure only authorized people and entities can alter or modify data. For example, you can configure your account on an operating system to launch certain applications upon booting. I have my copy of Windows 11 configured to launch Steam, Firefox, and LibreOffice when I boot into it. If a cyberattacker modifies the Windows partition on my hard drive to make my Windows account also boot their nasty malware, that's an attack on integrity.

Availability is about making sure data is accessible when authorized entities and people need to use it. For instance, from the 2000s to 2015 or so, attackers often used ransomware that would maliciously encrypt data on a victim's hard drive or other data storage. The attacker, who had the decryption key, would extort their victim, demanding they pay huge sums of money to get their data back. That's an attack on availability.

Today, ransomware that targets enterprises attacks both availability *and* confidentiality. Typically it threatens to publicly breach the victim's data, not just encrypt it. That's because businesses have gotten a lot better at maintaining data backups, so encrypting the data on the infected disk isn't enough motivation to make them pay a ransom. But backups can't prevent the tremendous harm that breaching sensitive data can do to a company!

Some cybersecurity educational curriculum, such as study material for ISC2's CISSP certification, also mentions the DAD triad, the yin to the CIA triad's yang. The DAD triad describes the bad things cyberattacks can do to data—*disclosure* (in contrast to *confidentiality*), *alteration* (in contrast to *integrity*), and *destruction* (in contrast to *availability*).

See also "Cybersecurity" on page 68, "Malware" on page 167

CISSP

See "Certificates (professional credentials)" on page 46

C languages

See "Programming" on page 204, "Ritchie, Dennis" on page 214

Cleartext

Cleartext refers to text that's never going to be encrypted. Cleartext (*https://oreil.ly/ tRhYh*) can be ASCII and Unicode characters (like the ones in this book), computer programming code, hexadecimal code, or binary code.

The terms *cleartext* and *plain text* are often used interchangeably, but there's a difference: plain text is unencrypted data that's then encrypted. The encrypted output is called *ciphertext*. When ciphertext is decrypted, the output is plaintext again.

Cleartext and plain text are data in its immediately readable form. You're reading this as plain text right now, whether you're reading the ebook or paperback version of this book. It's not technically cleartext, because its content was originally written in Microsoft Word files, and those files became encrypted when I shared them through the internet with my editor. (Hi, Sarah!) It went through more encryption and decryption when the O'Reilly production team worked on its layouts, illustrations, and more. Amazon, Apple, Google, Barnes & Noble, and other ebook retailers encrypt their products, so while you can read this as plain text, it's technically not cleartext.

See also "Cryptography" on page 63, "DRM (Digital Rights Management)" on page 89

Closed source software

See "Proprietary software" on page 205

Cloud

In the context of the internet and hacker culture, *cloud computing* (*https://oreil.ly/5x6b4*) (or "the cloud") refers to a computer network deployed through the internet that deploys a variety of different IT services to endpoints and users around the world. The term was coined in 1996 in one of Compaq's internal documents (*https://oreil.ly/NNArB*). Cloud computing started to become popular in the 2000s and 2010s.

Before that, businesses and enterprises could either run servers on their own premises ("on premises" or "on prem") or use a simple internet hosting provider to run servers for their email and websites. A lot of companies had intranets (*https://oreil.ly/sVyV2*)—websites and networked applications that were designed to only be used internally, by people within the organization. Intranets are not a part of the internet, so they usually had to be deployed through on-premises servers. These days, most companies deploy their own pseudo-"intranet" through a cloud provider with encryption and restricted authentication, often referred to as "private cloud" (*https://oreil.ly/GHtXp*).

Computer scientist J. C .R. Licklider is referred to as the Father of Cloud Computing (*https://oreil.ly/yVaaj*), because he led the research and development of ARPAnet, precursor to the modern internet, and was probably the first to conceptualize cloud computing. He died in 1990 and probably didn't get to see the web as we know it.

Amazon Web Services (*https://oreil.ly/4zdGi*) (AWS), one of the top three cloud platforms, began operating in its current form in 2006 and was one of the first platforms to really popularize cloud services. The other two, Google Cloud Platform and Microsoft Azure (*https://oreil.ly/1o-dj*), followed in 2008. Salesforce, Oracle, IBM, and Alibaba also have major cloud platforms.

Salesforce (*https://oreil.ly/9mqAD*) popularized the concept of *software as a service* (SaaS). Instead of running on your local computer, an SaaS application is deployed on demand through a network, most often the internet. The major cloud platforms operate their own SaaS. They also make it possible for anyone to deploy their own developed SaaS applications on the cloud providers' platform and infrastructure. In platform as a service (PaaS), you deploy your own applications through the cloud provider's application programming interfaces (APIs) and virtual machines. With infrastructure as a service (IaaS), you only use the cloud platform's infrastructure (like servers and networking equipment) but use your own code and create any virtual machines yourself.

The cloud is responsible for widely expanding how we use the internet.

See also "Amazon Web Services (AWS)" on page 8, "ARPAnet" on page 17, "Azure" on page 28, "Google Cloud Platform (GCP)" on page 117

Comic-Con

Imagine a Venn diagram that contains hackers in one circle. If we make another circle of people who are into nerdy pop culture—comic books, science fiction, fantasy, anime, video games, tabletop gaming—the two circles will almost completely overlap. Or at least, the hacker circle will be almost completely inside the nerdy pop culture circle even if a lot of the pop culture nerds aren't hackers.

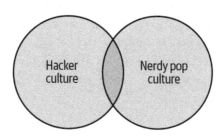

Understanding nerdy pop culture is key to understanding how hacker culture types have fun when they're not making contributions to the Linux kernel code base or configuring their own virtual private network (VPN) servers.

In the English-speaking world, there's no bigger event in nerdy pop culture than San Diego Comic-Con. Big Hollywood film studios and video game publishers go there to promote their upcoming movies, TV shows, and games. More than 200,000 people attend the San Diego and New York Comic-Cons (*https://oreil.ly/B12Tf*) each year.

The phenomenon started with small groups of science fiction fans getting together for a chat (*https://oreil.ly/o22RR*) at Philadelphia's annual Philcon (*https://oreil.ly/M21dd*), founded by the Philadelphia Science Fiction Society in 1936. The event grew over the decades, and in the 1940s and 1950s, there were several annual gatherings of science fiction and fantasy fans, with maybe a few hundred people per event. Science fiction had a renaissance in the 1960s, and comic books enjoyed a similar growth in popularity. Both spurred major growth in nerdy fan conventions.

Then, in 1970, San Diego held its first Comic-Con (*https://oreil.ly/wN48r*). Initially it focused entirely on comic books, but today it includes "genre fiction" movies and TV, anime and manga, and video games, with appearances from stars and creators. Today there are lots of Comic-Cons and similar events (*https://oreil.ly/1WArx*) all over the world.

See also "Cyberpunk" on page 67, "Dungeons & Dragons (game franchise)" on page 90, "Roleplaying games (RPGs)" on page 218

Commodore

In 1988, when I was 4, my 19-year-old half-brother Anthony got a Commodore 64. It intrigued me to no end. The CRT screen glowed in pretty colors. The keyboard had all the letters of the alphabet I was eagerly learning, plus fascinating square symbols on the sides of the keys (*https://oreil.ly/nhyjb*). I wanted it! "I wanna use com-poo-der! Now! Pwease?" I grew up to be a hacker, cybersecurity researcher, and computing historian. Anthony grew up to be a construction foreman.

Commodore started making typewriters in the 1950s but became integral to the popularity of PCs in the last quarter of the 20th century and was a force in the PC market well into the 1990s. Commodore also has an absolutely bonkers history (*https://oreil.ly/Vj-TY*).

Founder Jack Tramiel (*https://oreil.ly/xUBim*) was born Idek Trzmiel in 1928 in Łódź, Poland. He was Jewish, and in 1939, with Poland under Nazi occupation, he and his parents were sent to Auschwitz. He and his mother survived, but his father was murdered there.

In 1947, Tramiel emigrated to the United States. He joined the US Army not long after, and discovered his talent for repairing mechanical typewriters. In 1952, he moved to the Bronx in New York City and worked in a typewriter repair shop. Later, he set up his own shop, while supplementing his income by working as a taxi driver.

In 1955, Tramiel moved to Toronto and founded Everest Office Machine Company (Canada) Limited (*https://oreil.ly/OBhN9*). His new business designed and manufactured typewriters, but the actual manufacturing was done in what was then Czechoslovakia. In 1958, he renamed the business Commodore Portable Typewriter Company Limited. It was a popular typewriter brand.

In the late 1960s, in response to a rapidly evolving tech industry, Commodore transitioned from making adding machines to making calculators (*https://oreil.ly/OBhN9*). In 1976, Commodore bought MOS Technology (*https://oreil.ly/WAk6-*), a calculator company that was already making processors. Along with MOS it got Chuck Peddle (*https://oreil.ly/_pFgu*), who had helped design Motorola's groundbreaking 6800 CPU. Peddle helped to develop the MOS 6502 CPU and convinced Jack Tramiel that personal computers were the way of the future—and could be built with the MOS 6502 CPU.

Commodore's very first personal computer was built with the same CPU as the Apple I, the MOS 6502. Also in the mid-1970s, the pioneering microcomputer Altair 8800 debuted. The Homebrew Computer Club was founded soon after, initially to show off the Altair 8800, and inspired Steve Jobs and Steve Wozniak to start Apple Computers. Apple chose the MOS 6502 for its first product, the Apple I. (Commodore was interested in buying the new company, but Tramiel didn't want (*https://oreil.ly/_pFgu*) to pay their asking price of $150,000!)

Peddle needed to find a high-level programming language for Commodore computers. At the time (*https://oreil.ly/_pFgu*), Microsoft's language BASIC (for Beginner's All-Purpose Symbolic Instruction Code) was very popular. Bill Gates preferred proprietary, closed-source software to free, open source software and didn't like other hackers using BASIC for free, so he wrote an angry letter (*https://oreil.ly/GHgWq*) accusing the Homebrew Computer Club of theft. Peddle decided to play nice and negotiated a deal with Gates that granted Commodore a perpetual BASIC license for cheap—partly because Gates didn't think Commodore PCs would be profitable.

The Commodore PET's (*https://oreil.ly/iRBfg*) 1977 launch was a smash success, bringing personal computing to the masses. By 1980 (*https://oreil.ly/c4H_q*), Commodore was one of the three largest microcomputer makers in the world. Take that, Bill Gates!

Commodore also developed a graphics processor and a computer to use it: the VIC-20 (*https://oreil.ly/CDAtM*), an inexpensive full-color personal computer. It was the first PC to sell for less than $300 (*https://oreil.ly/WkeR7*) (about $1,000 in 2023 dollars) and the first (*https://oreil.ly/7diO6*) to sell more than a million units.

The Commodore 64 hit the market in 1982 for $595 (about $1,900 in 2023 dollars) and sold a jaw-dropping 500,000 units (*https://oreil.ly/rj1M8*) in just a few months. Top software developers were making games and productivity software for it.

On a Friday the 13th in 1984,[5] Tramiel had a big fight with Irving Gould, a major investor in Commodore. As the *Digital Antiquarian* (*https://oreil.ly/mH1tX*) reports: "Tramiel stormed red-faced out of the meeting and sped away in the new sports car he'd just gotten for his 55th birthday, [and] it was clear that this was not just the usual squabbling.... He would never darken Commodore's doors again."

Tramiel wanted a company that his sons could inherit, so he bought the consumer division of Atari Inc. from Warner Communications (*https://oreil.ly/IMGoY*).

The first Commodore Amiga, which debuted in 1985 (*https://oreil.ly/T6uqB*), has its own entry in this book; it launched within a month of Tramiel's rival Atari ST. Both were based on the Motorola 68000 CPU. The Amiga line did way better commercially, but by 1994, Commodore was in serious trouble. Under Tramiel, Commodore had dominated the PC market by selling their computers as widely and cheaply as possible. Under Gould and Jay Miner, Commodore sold powerful but expensive PCs that weren't easy enough to buy. The company's assets were liquidated through the mid-1990s.

See also "Amiga" on page 10, "Apple" on page 13, "Atari" on page 22, "Homebrew Computer Club" on page 136, "Personal computers" on page 196

---

5 It was literally the day I was born, January!

Common Vulnerabilities and Exposures (CVE)

CVE stands for Common Vulnerabilities and Exposures, a publicly available database (*https://oreil.ly/hcH6m*) of most known cybersecurity vulnerabilities in software, inspired by a 1999 whitepaper.[6] Not all CVEs can be exploited through the internet, but the internet radically changed how cybersecurity professionals share information about and respond to vulnerabilities.

In cybersecurity, we talk about responsible disclosure (*https://oreil.ly/pHkxR*). In short: if a ("good") hacker discovers a *zero-day vulnerability*—a specific software vulnerability that isn't publicly known—what should they do? It would be unethical and dangerous for them to immediately post about it on Reddit or StackExchange: "Look at this cool vulnerability I found! Here's how I exploited it!" That would make it easy for anyone to use that information to do bad stuff.

As a safe alternative, most software companies have responsible disclosure procedures—usually a dedicated email account where anyone who finds a bug can report it privately. Many companies also have *bug bounty* policies that offer payment for privately reporting vulnerabilities. Once someone reports a bug, it's the company's responsibility to develop a patch or otherwise address the vulnerability. That process usually takes months. Once the company addresses the vulnerability, they might give the hacker permission to announce it publicly or announce it themselves. They then work with the hacker to create a new record in the CVE database. Only recognized CVE Numbering Authorities (*https://oreil.ly/Un1Lv*) (CNAs) can add records.

The idea is for security professionals to keep up with additions to the CVE database, so that any time their system is impacted by a known vulnerability, they can release patches immediately. In practice, however, most cyberattacks exploit known vulnerabilities. As a cybersecurity researcher, I've seen firsthand that lots of catastrophic data breaches and advanced persistent threats exploit vulnerabilities that have been in the CVE database for five years or more! It's astonishing and disturbing.

CVE records have a particular format. Each one is assigned an ID number that starts with CVE, then the year, then a unique five-digit number, like "CVE-2022-23627" (*https://oreil.ly/DQxJs*). There is also a title, such as "GitHub (maintainer security advisories)." The record includes a highly technical description of the vulnerability and its consequences, plus a list of any online references

---

6 David E. Mann and Steven M. Christey, "Towards a Common Enumeration of Vulnerabilities (*https://oreil.ly/AfNU7*)," MITRE Corporation, 1999.

to it. Then the CNA is named; in this case it's "GitHub (maintainer security advisories)." Finally, the date the record was created is listed (*not* when the vulnerability was discovered or disclosed).

Outsiders often assume that cybersecurity is all hacking and penetration testing. Cybersecurity experts sometimes say, as a joke, "You think you're so good at cybersecurity? Where are your CVEs?!" Only people pretending to understand cybersecurity say that with a straight face. Few people personally discover any zero-day vulnerabilities, but the world also needs thousands upon thousands of people to do defensive security and IT work. A lot of the most important but least celebrated cybersecurity work is done by people like network administrators who remember to deploy patches and check their application firewall logs.

See also "Advanced persistent threat (APT)" on page 4, "Bug" on page 37, "Cybersecurity" on page 68, "Git/GitHub" on page 113, "Zero day" on page 279

Consumer Electronics Show (CES)

The Consumer Electronics Show (CES) is an annual event that showcases new technology. The first CES took place in New York City (*https://oreil.ly/uxCaO*) in 1967, drawing 17,500 attendees. The 117 exhibitors included 3M, Memorex, Motorola, Panasonic-Matsushita, Philips, RCA, Sanyo Fisher, Sharp, Sony, Toshiba, Westinghouse, and Zenith. Shiny new color televisions were among the featured products, alongside hi-fi stereo components, stereo receivers, and record turntables. Between 1978 and 1994 (*https://oreil.ly/pk4eA*), the CES was held twice per year; today there is one show per year, in Las Vegas every January.

See also "Electronics" on page 95

Copyleft

See "Open source" on page 189

CPU (Central processing unit)

What's central to hacker culture? Computers. And what's central to all computers? The *central processing unit* (CPU)! It's the part of your computer that does the actual computing. Sometimes you'll also hear it called the *processor* or *microprocessor*.

All computers have at least one CPU: PCs and MacBooks, smartphones and tablets, ATMs and elevator interfaces, server machines in datacenters and industrial control systems in factories, smart thermostats, game consoles, and the International Space Station. There are also specialized CPUs designed for high-quality graphics processing.

While early computers like ENIAC used vacuum tubes to make calculations, every CPU today is an integrated circuit (*https://oreil.ly/vNTxr*): a small piece of silicon with thousands upon thousands of tiny transistors. (That's where Silicon Valley gets its name.) The transistor was invented by John Bardeen, Walter Brattain, and William Shockley at Bell Labs in 1947, and the first working integrated circuit (*https://oreil.ly/nJGiG*) was developed in 1958 by Robert Noyce of Fairchild Semiconductor and Jack Kilby of Texas Instruments—pioneering companies built by hackers.

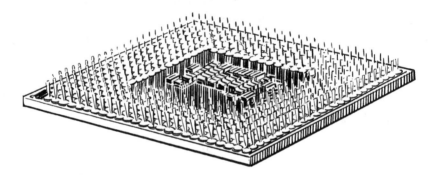

If the physical functioning and design of computers and CPUs really stirs your curiosity, check out Noam Nisan and Shimon Schocken's book *The Elements of Computing Systems: Building a Modern Computer from First Principles* (MIT Press, 2021).

See also "Bell Labs" on page 31, "Electronics" on page 95, "Fairchild Semiconductor" on page 103, "Texas Instruments" on page 242

Cray, Seymour

Seymour Cray (*https://oreil.ly/XgpSG*) (1925–1996) led the development of what's now considered to be the world's first supercomputer, the CDC 6600. Born in Chippewa Falls, Wisconsin, Cray was interested in electronics (*https://oreil.ly/PrGE_*) from an early age. After a brief US Army career, in 1950 Cray graduated from the University of Minnesota with a bachelor's degree in electrical engineering. He was soon employed by Engineering Research Associates (ERA) to help develop computers. He went on to help found Control Data Corporation (CDC) and develop the CDC 1604, one of the first computers to replace vacuum tubes with transistors.

In 1964, Cray led the development of what's now considered to be the world's first (and, at the time, fastest) supercomputer, the CDC 6600 (*https://oreil.ly/XgpSG*). It beat the 7094 developed by IBM, CDC's rival and a way larger and more established company. IBM chairman Thomas J. Watson apparently berated his staff over how CDC beat them with only 34 people, "including the janitor."

Cray also wanted to be able to work on his own without interruption (*https://oreil.ly/8fTPy*), yet middle managers wanted to meddle with his work and use him as a sales tool. So in 1971, Cray left CDC and formed his own company, Cray Research. Its first product, the cool-looking Cray-1 supercomputer (*https://oreil.ly/XgpSG*), released in 1976, could perform 240 million calculations per second. That year, Cray sold Cray-1 technology to the Los Alamos National Laboratory and the National Center for Atmospheric Research. And in 1986, David H. Bailey used the Cray-2 (*https://oreil.ly/MzDYM*) to calculate π to 29,360,111 decimal places.

One of Cray-2's customers called Seymour Cray to their site to fix a problem that baffled their engineers. After being in the room with the machine for six hours, Cray figured out how to fix the problem. He pointed to a single wire that needed to be replaced (*https://oreil.ly/PrGE_*).

Cray Research went bankrupt in May 1995, and Cray formed SRC Computers soon after, but in 1996 he died in a car accident (*https://oreil.ly/8fTPy*). What an incredible life he lived; may he rest in peace.

See also "IBM" on page 139, "Supercomputers" on page 233

Creative Commons licenses

Copyright law gives a person or an entity exclusive commercial rights to an intellectual property, such as a book, film, piece of music, or video games: creative works in various mediums. The original creator of a work has the copyright by default, but creators often sell the rights to their work to corporations. For most commercially published books, the author retains copyright but grants a publisher an exclusive license to publish and generate revenue from their work for a certain period of time. I have the intellectual property rights to some of my body of work, but not all of it. My situation is typical of most professional writers from the 20th century on.

In 1998, Congress passed the Sonny Bono Copyright Term Extension Act (*https://oreil.ly/ZtGUR*), which mandates that under US law, an author's estate retains their copyright for 50 to 70 years after the author's death.

Retired computer programmer Eric Eldred (*https://oreil.ly/EIhlJ*), whose hobby was publishing public-domain books on the web, challenged the law with help from his lawyer, Lawrence Lessig. They formed a group (*https://oreil.ly/R8uja*) called Creative Commons. In 2003, the US Supreme Court ruled against Eldred and Creative Commons ultimately lost their case.

But Creative Commons announced its own form of license, inspired by the GNU Public License, that gives creators a way to share and redistribute their work in a way that fits the spirit of hacker culture. Lessig's friend, the late hacker hero Aaron Swartz, created its technical architecture (*https://oreil.ly/4DS4-*). There are several different Creative Commons licenses (*https://oreil.ly/bemDi*), most of which allow "reusers to distribute, remix, adapt, and build upon the material in any medium or format, so long as attribution is given to the creator," with different versions specifying different terms (such as noncommercial use only).

See also "Open source" on page 189, "Swartz, Aaron" on page 235

Crunch time

Your manager posts a message in your development team's Slack channel: "We've got to start crunch time early. Instead of leaving at 6 p.m., I need you all to stay here until at least midnight to get our early alpha build ready for the quality assurance team. But to thank you all for being such *rockstar ninja code masters*, I'm ordering everyone pizza! What are your favorite toppings?"

No pizza is so tasty that it's worth the psychological and physical stress of *crunch time*: when tech workers are expected to work extra-long hours, extra hard, to hurry the development of a product. Often, that product is a video game: perhaps a AAA game the development studio wants released by November for the Christmas season, or a playable demo in time for the Electronic Entertainment Expo (E3) in June. When their corporate overlords throw in pizza as a "treat," hackers tend to view it as a bribe to get them to give up on having any life outside of work.

Take This (*https://oreil.ly/5RLvV*), a nonprofit organization focused on mental health in the tech industry, released a report in 2016 called "Crunch Hurts" (*https://oreil.ly/-aYxY*), detailing crunch time's harmful effects on workers. It notes that "employees who are dealing with the stress of tight deadlines, lack of sleep, and long hours are generally less productive, more likely to fall ill or suffer from mental health issues (and therefore call in sick), and less likely to remain in their current jobs."

Crunch time also has a negative effect on game quality:

Games produced under crunch conditions also suffer, with more bugs and lower Metacritic scores to show for all those extra hours. Studios incur the costs of sick, fatigued employees and their lost productivity. The industry as a whole loses developers to early burnout, and they take their talents, experience, and expertise with them.

Investigative journalist Jason Schreier wrote in 2015 (*https://oreil.ly/-p-ci*) about a game development team whose boss organized a pizza and bowling party to celebrate wrapping up testing: "After a few hours of everyone enjoying themselves, the VP asks for everyone's attention...begins to thank them for their hard work and has the leads hand them their termination papers."

Cryptocurrency

When you hear someone say "crypto," what do you think? In a room full of computer nerds in 2005, "crypto" would certainly refer to cryptography, the art and science of scrambling data through a cipher so it cannot be understood without the means to decipher. Cryptography predates computer technology by centuries, and as applied to computer data, it's a vital cybersecurity tool.

Since the advent of Bitcoin in 2009 (*https://oreil.ly/dw7DR*), "crypto" has come to mean something else to large numbers of people: cryptocurrency. Cryptocurrency is a medium of exchange that many people consider to be money, a means of investment (like buying shares in a company), or both. It uses digital cryptographic technology to prove that its monetary value is "real," by either "proof of work" or "proof of stake." New cryptocurrencies are launched with initial *coin* offerings (ICOs).

Bitcoin was the first cryptocurrency, but many other cryptocurrencies have been invented ever since. Monero is frequently used in darknet markets; Ethereum has the blockchain that most nonfungible tokens (NFTs) use; Dogecoin was a "credible" cryptocurrency while Elon Musk was tweeting to raise its price. That "credibility" ceased when he tweeted to crash it (*https://oreil.ly/dNcvq*). (A "credible" cryptocurrency is like an honest politician. Everything's relative, I suppose.) However, the vast majority of cryptocurrencies have had shorter life spans than an ice cream cone in a heatwave (*https://oreil.ly/RUEUA*). After all, money and financial investments only have value because people have decided that they do. If everyone collectively decided that money was worthless, money would become worthless.

Most cryptocurrencies use a *blockchain*: a long ledger of transactions that uses cryptography to assure the integrity of each transaction while keeping the parties to it anonymous, except for a lengthy identifier for each cryptocurrency wallet. When new Bitcoin, Monero, or Ethereum is "created," a new transaction must be added to the ledger.

Cryptocurrencies are generated through complex cryptographic math as "proof of work" (*https://oreil.ly/8ol_b*) through a process called *cryptomining*. Here's the only way to explain it without getting incredibly technical: computers have to solve lots and lots of complex math problems. The longer the blockchain gets, the more complex the math gets. Harder math requires more computing power. In the early days of Bitcoin (say, before 2011), it was feasible to do a respectable amount of cryptomining with just a Raspberry Pi. But today there's no way to generate any significant amount without leveraging the computing power of massive datacenters or botnets.

The problem with that? Computers consume electricity, and the kind of computing power needed for cryptomining consumes a *lot* of energy. Some cryptocurrency blockchains have consumed as much electricity as an entire nation. And electricity is still mainly generated in ways that cause pollution, like oil and coal-burning power plants.[7] So the lust for cryptocurrency has been worsening our massive climate change problem.

Proponents of crypto argue that their currencies are "going green" by transitioning from "proof of work" to "proof of stake" (*https://oreil.ly/6Pee3*), a method that uses consensus mechanisms between blockchain users and validators to promise the authenticity of a record in the ledger. While that method is less energy-intensive, prominent cryptocurrency skeptic Stephen Diehl (*https://oreil.ly/83WxX*) notes that

> *its staking model is necessarily deflationary, is not decentralized, and thus results in inevitably plutocratic governance which makes the entire structure have a nearly identical payout structure to that of a pyramid scheme, that enriches the already wealthy. . . . The externalities of the proof of stake system at scale would exacerbate inequality and encourage extraction from and defrauding of small shareholders.*

I interviewed computer scientist Nicholas Weaver about his objections to cryptocurrency, which he describes as "a self-assembled Ponzi scheme full of

---

7 Nuclear power doesn't generate much air pollution, but it does generate spent uranium and plutonium rods and comes with some significant risks. Clean energy sources, like solar, wind, and hydroelectric power, exist but are not yet anywhere close to supplanting dirtier generation methods.

Ponzi schemes and other frauds, intent on speed-running half a millennium of various financial failures over and over and over again." In addition to fraud, Weaver argues, crypto "enables ransomware, a global pestilence doing tens of billions of dollars in damage to the global economy."

Weaver echoes Diehl on the waste involved in cryptomining: "What the miners are doing is literally wasting tons of electricity to prove that the record is intact, because anybody who would want to attack it has to waste that similar kind of electricity."[8]

Between massive crashes in value and the problems I've noted here, what is keeping cryptocurrency going? Crime. Crypto is the currency of the darkest parts of the darknet: it's used in transactions that involve drugs, child abuse material, and ransomware. Even on the clearnet, though, it's involved in plenty of old-fashioned financial scams made hip through Silicon Valley marketing language.

See also "Cryptography" on page 63, "Dark Web/darknet" on page 71, "Non-fungible tokens (NFTs)" on page 186

Cryptography

Cryptography is the art and science of scrambling data through a cipher so it cannot be understood without a key (a means to decipher it). Some laypeople may be surprised to learn that cryptography predates electronic computers by centuries (if not longer). Ciphers can be applied to digital data and analog data alike.

Here's a very simple example of an analog cipher. In the early 1990s, when I was about 8, a neighbor girl who was about 12, and thus very impressive and wise, took me under her wing. One day she announced, "Kim! We can write secret messages to each other in our own special code!"

"Really? Show me!"

On a piece of paper, she wrote down this cipher, one of the most basic analog ciphers used in the Latin (or Roman) alphabet (*https://oreil.ly/nlitc*):

1	2	3	4	5	6	7	8	9	10	11	12	13
A	B	C	D	E	F	G	H	I	J	K	L	M
14	15	16	17	18	19	20	21	22	23	24	25	26
N	O	P	Q	R	S	T	U	V	W	X	Y	Z

---

8 From an interview of Weaver by Nathan J. Robinson in Current Affairs (*https://oreil.ly/Mb3wp*).

In response, I must have written something like:

20-8-9-19 9-19 19-15 3-15-15-12!

8-5-25, 20-8-5 14-5-23 19-9-13-16-19-15-14-19 5-16-9-19-15-4-5 9-19 15-14
20-15-14-9-7-8-20.

23-5 19-8-15-21-12-4 5-14-10-15-25 9-20, 13-9-7-8-20 2-5 3-1-14-3-5-12-12-5-4
19-15-15-14!

In the ninth century, Arab mathematician Al-Kindi (*https://oreil.ly/NJnMt*) found the deciphering key for another code used by Roman soldiers that was about as simple: just shifting one letter of the alphabet to another. The same concept is used in cryptogram puzzles. Here's a cryptogram I made just for you:

B ZJ NQWQ!

The words I used are some of the most common in the English language. The only one-letter words in English (unless you're using an alphabet letter as a noun) are "a" and "I." You might also work out that Q probably stands for a vowel, based on how it's repeated in the four-letter word (which I promise isn't profane). Working from that and a lot of letter-letter substitution trial and error, you'll eventually solve the puzzle. "I am here!"

Let's zoom forward to the 20th century. Alan Turing, one of the earliest and most important computer scientists, has his own entry in this book, so I'll just cover one of his most notable works: the Enigma machine (*https://oreil.ly/OD5U7*). Enigma was a mechanical cryptographic device invented in Germany near the end of World War I. It looked like an old-fashioned typewriter with some extra mechanical features. It was used commercially between the wars. During World War II, Nazi Germany relied heavily on it for encrypted communication. In the 1930s, Polish mathematicians and French spies discovered some vulnerabilities in Enigma. And in 1939, the UK put its best people on cracking Enigma, including Turing. Digital cryptography hadn't been invented yet, so completely cracking Enigma would leave the Nazis without their main means of secret communication. Turing and his team managed it, and the Allies were able to decode German messages, gleaning intelligence that would be crucial to the war effort.

Today, whether you know it or not, you use digital cryptography every day. One system commonly used in email is Pretty Good Privacy (PGP). You might also see public PGP keys in the various hacker-dominated corners of the internet.

Another is Transport Layer Security (TLS), the successor to Secure Sockets Layer (SSL), a cryptography system developed for Netscape (*https://oreil.ly/i1EZO*) by Taher Elgamal in 1995. TLS is used on the web through the HTTPS protocol, as well as for email, VoIP (Voice over Internet Protocol), and a number of other internet services. Digital certificates, a public-key infrastructure, and the Diffie-Hellman key exchange (*https://oreil.ly/ykVBN*) are some of its major technological components. It uses a stream cipher (*https://oreil.ly/w2ub2*), which works well for encrypting data in transit as it's streaming. (All data moving through computer networks is streaming—not just Netflix and YouTube!)

Different digital encryption technologies are used to encrypt data in storage: usually a block cipher. You might already be using disk encryption with an Advanced Encryption Standard (AES) cipher (*https://oreil.ly/rDACh*) built right into your operating system, like BitLocker (*https://oreil.ly/LMkjI*) in Windows, FileVault (*https://oreil.ly/C_arP*) in macOS, full disk encryption (*https://oreil.ly/kSnwU*) in Android, or Data Protection (*https://oreil.ly/C_arP*). If you have permission to change your OS settings, you can turn disk encryption on.

Comprehensive explanations of most of the digital encryption technologies we use these days would take multiple books. But in understanding cryptography and its importance to hackers and in cybersecurity, a few basic ideas remain as technology evolves.

Specific ciphers and specific cryptographic implementations often depreciate when they're several years old, because threat actors get better at cracking them. Newer encryption standards, often with longer key bit lengths, will always need to replace older encryption standards. Quantum computers may be in (enterprise) production in the next decade or so, and when that happens, they're likely to crack the vast majority of the binary encryption systems we use now in seconds. Anticipating this, companies like IBM have been developing quantum-safe cryptography (*https://oreil.ly/RmblT*) for years.

Today, it's common cybersecurity wisdom that you should encrypt as much of your data as possible, both in storage and in transit—even if you don't think it's very sensitive. Good encryption won't make you invulnerable to cyberattacks, any more than wearing a seatbelt can guarantee that you'll survive a car accident. But in both cases, the security they provide definitely improves your odds.

See also "Carr, Iris" on page 44, "Certificates (cryptography)" on page 45, "Cryptocurrency" on page 61, "Cybersecurity" on page 68, "Diffie-Hellman key exchange" on page 84, "Key" on page 156, "Pretty Good Privacy (PGP)" on page 203, "Quantum computing" on page 207, "Rivest-Shamir-Adleman (RSA) cryptography" on page 215, "Turing, Alan" on page 248

Cult of the Dead Cow (cDc)

The first hacktivist group to target Scientology was not, as many people think, Anonymous. In fact, that honor goes to Cult of the Dead Cow (cDc), founded in Lubbock, Texas, in June 1984 (*https://oreil.ly/ITCl5*). The group's name comes from the original location of their meetings: an abandoned cattle slaughterhouse (*https://oreil.ly/ow3n5*)!

cDc operated a series of BBSes that engaged in pranks, jokes, and ASCII art (*https://oreil.ly/dMGvZ*). It originated a lot of the artistic elements in today's hacker culture, including l33tspeak (*https://oreil.ly/FN8RD*). And in 1995, many cDc members were posting criticism of the Church of Scientology on the Usenet group alt.religion.scientology. The Church's lawyers tried to force Usenet to remove the group. The cDc didn't like that one bit, and declared war on the Church in a hyperbolic, tongue-in-cheek public statement (*https://oreil.ly/Iomtn*).

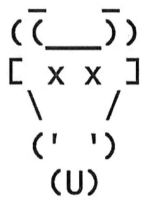

The cDc ran the first cybersecurity conference, HoHoCon (*https://oreil.ly/fnDJW*), for five events in the early 1990s.

It also gained notoriety for pointing out vulnerabilities in popular software. For instance, group member Sir Dystic developed the application Back Orifice (*https://oreil.ly/k_D6U*), a malicious remote-access Trojan horse that could grant a user remote administrative access to Windows 9x operating systems. Dystic presented it at DEF CON 6 in 1998 to demonstrate Windows' vulnerabilities.

Dozens of people under l33t usernames have participated in cDc over the years, including some who are now quite prominent, like former member of Congress and 2020 US presidential candidate Beto O'Rourke (*https://oreil.ly/P1oKa*) and Peiter "Mudge" Zatko (*https://oreil.ly/6WIDJ*), who advised Bill Clinton on cybersecurity and today plays a major role in the US Defense Advanced Research Projects Agency (DARPA). I'm just scratching the surface of cDc's participation in the Washington military-industrial complex. Despite their anti-authoritarian spirit, prominent cDc members aren't really fighting "The Man": they are "The Man." A hacker with a security clearance really contradicts the spirit of hacker culture itself.

See also "Anonymous" on page 12, "Bulletin board systems (BBSes)" on page 37, "Cybersecurity" on page 68, "DARPA (Defense Advanced Research Projects Agency)" on page 72, "DEF CON" on page 80, "Hacktivism" on page 125, "Usenet" on page 255

Cyberpunk

We are living in a cyberpunk world right now, whether you're reading this in 2023, 2024, 2028, or 2037: our world is dominated by a few powerful mega-corporations, climate change is quickly making much of the earth uninhabitable, pandemics are decimating society, and cyberattacks regularly shut down hospitals (*https://oreil.ly/1hLs5*). As William Gibson (1948–), author of the cyberpunk novel *Neuromancer*, once said (*https://oreil.ly/qowi4*), "The future's already here— it's just not very evenly distributed."

Bruce Bethke (*https://www.britannica.com/art/cyberpunk*) coined the term *cyberpunk* in 1982, by combining the words *cybernetics* and *punk*. My simplified definition of *cybernetics* is the art of substituting or augmenting facets of humanity with technology. (You can find more complex definitions at the American Society for Cybernetics (*https://oreil.ly/wphXX*).) That's a vague definition that can encompass lots of ideas. The punk subculture and music genre emerged in the UK in the late 1970s, created by young people whose hope for a peaceful and prosperous future had been stolen from them. Its values include disobeying authority, thinking critically, fighting for marginalized people, being creative with what you have, and trying to have a good time despite having very little.

So, in a cyberpunk world, elements of humanity and society are being augmented by technology, and a hostile political system that requires disobedience, critical thought, and making do with what you have. In cyberpunk fiction, hackers are often the heroes: protagonists with a chaotic good moral alignment who use their intellectual curiosity and technical skills to fight the good fight.

If you'd like to get into cyberpunk fiction, here are some of my picks:

- William Gibson, *Neuromancer* (Ace Books, 1984; updated edition Penguin Galaxy, 2016)
- Rudy Rucker, *Software* (Eos, 1987)
- Pat Cadigan, *Mindplayers* (Gateway, 1987)

Cybersecurity

Cybersecurity is computer security: the practice of protecting computers and their data from threats. Hackers are very useful in cybersecurity, as people who find novel uses for technology.

The most obvious career path for a hacker in cybersecurity is being a *penetration tester* (pentester): someone who conducts simulated cyberattacks with the permission of the target's owner. They think like an attacker to understand them better and find security vulnerabilities that can't be found through other means.[9]

Pentesting is an offensive security practice, but defensive security specialists are important too. They harden networks' security based on pentest reports' findings. Defensive security roles include digital forensics and threat intelligence specialists, incident response, and analysts and managers of security operations centers (SOC). SOCs and computer security incident response teams are departments within larger organizations focused on monitoring security and responding to threats, and usually include cybersecurity and general IT practitioners, plus people like lawyers and PR specialists to handle the legalities and media management aspects of incident response. Some companies have a chief information security officer (CISO) on their board of directors as well.

You can also specialize in secure application development and the secure systems development lifecycle. It's now common wisdom that every stage of application development should be cybersecurity-minded to prevent software vulnerabilities that threat actors can exploit.

---

9 I coauthored one of the most popular pentester career guides: Phillip L. Wylie and Kim Crawley, *The Pentester BluePrint* (Wiley, 2021). Also see Kim Crawley, *8 Steps to Better Security* (Wiley, 2021), a holistic business cybersecurity guide.

Governance, risk, and compliance (GRC) is a related area of specialization. GRC specialists advise companies on risk analysis and management, while security and regulatory compliance auditors make sure companies are compliant with data security regulations and standards.

On the academic side, social-engineering specialists study how cybercriminals exploit human psychology to conduct cyberattacks.

But most of the practice of cybersecurity is actually quite tedious and not at all sexy, like it's portrayed on TV. I'm sorry to break it to you like that. But hacker culture and cybersecurity intersect, and the cybersecurity industry is always in need of hackers.

See also "Airgapping" on page 5, "CIA triad (confidentiality, integrity, availability)" on page 49, "Denial-of-service (DoS, DDoS) attacks" on page 81, "Exploit" on page 101, "Malware" on page 167, "Metasploit Framework" on page 173, "Penetration testing" on page 196, "Phishing" on page 198, "Phreaking" on page 199, "Spyware" on page 228, "Stuxnet" on page 232, "Threat actor" on page 243, "Virus" on page 258, "Worm" on page 269, "Zero day" on page 279

4

D

Dark.Fail

Dark.Fail is a vital directory service on the Tor network. While Google has used *google.com* since 1998 and Amazon has used *amazon.com* since 1994, that sort of consistency and reliability is seldom seen on what many refer to as the Dark Web. Tor network domain names change frequently (sometimes multiple times a day), so Dark.Fail's clearnet (the regular internet outside of the Dark Web) site, *dark.fail*, is a constantly updated directory of Dark Web URLs on the Tor network and I2P, the two most popular encrypted proxy networks.

The anonymizing nature of proxy networks makes them a popular medium for illegal activity. Dark.Fail lists many illegal darknet markets, but it also lists Tor websites for mainstream entities such as the *New York Times*, the BBC, and Facebook. In most countries outside of China, the Tor network and its accompanying browser are perfectly lawful, and so is simply visiting darknet markets. The moment you buy or sell illegal goods and services, that's when you've broken the law.

See also "Dark Web/darknet" on page 71, "Invisible Internet Project (I2P)" on page 147, "Tor (The Onion Router)" on page 245

Dark Web/darknet

The darknet (*https://oreil.ly/m7cya*) is a part of the internet that is only accessible through a particular proxy network, usually Tor or I2P. The web component of the darknet is called the Dark Web (*https://oreil.ly/D1PYz*). For simplicity, all of the Dark Web is part of the darknet, but not all of the darknet is the Dark Web. In most of the world, it's lawful to use the darknet as long as you're not breaking other laws while doing so. (The term *clearnet*, by contrast, refers to the ordinary internet.)

To access the darknet, you need to install Tor Browser or an I2P client (*https://oreil.ly/vIUov*) on your PC or mobile device, make sure that your firewalls don't block Tor or I2P, and connect to the internet. You can't access Tor with an I2P client, and you can't access I2P through the Tor Browser, but you can still access the clearnet through Tor and I2P.

Here's how proxy networks work: your endpoint (PC or phone) sends packets to a Tor or I2P entry node. That node sends packets to the next node, and so on, until the packets go through the exit node and to the internet server you're communicating with. Each node in the route only knows the IP addresses for the nodes it's sending or receiving from, and only the entry and exit nodes know your endpoint's IP address or the server's IP address. There's end-to-end encryption throughout the Tor or I2P route, so you're anonymous (unless someone spies on your packets through an exit node).

The Dark Web, and the darknet in general, are often portrayed as solely evil places. A technology designed for anonymous communication will inevitably be used for crime (*https://oreil.ly/2HUZI*), and darknet markets do sell illegal drugs, malware, cyberattack services, sensitive stolen data, and other kinds of illicit goods and services. Criminals and threat actors often plan their crimes on darknet forums and chat services, and law enforcement agencies access the darknet to monitor those plans and investigate crime. Many such markets have been shut down, but it would be very difficult to eliminate the darknet completely.

But the fact that a medium can be used for crime doesn't mean that medium shouldn't exist. The darknet is also a crucial means for investigative journalists, whistleblowers, and hacktivists to communicate for the benefit of society, while protecting their anonymity from hostile governments, militaries, and other such powerful entities.

See also "Cybersecurity" on page 68, "Dark.Fail" on page 71, "Dread forums" on page 88, "Exploit" on page 101, "Hacktivism" on page 125, "Malware" on page 167, "Invisible Internet Project (I2P)" on page 147, "Silk Road" on page 225, "Tor (The Onion Router)" on page 245

DARPA (Defense Advanced Research Projects Agency)

The Defense Advanced Research Projects Agency (DARPA) is a US government agency under the US Department of Defense (DoD) that was founded in 1958 (*https://oreil.ly/TOlwP*). There have been periods where it was named the Advanced Research Projects Agency (ARPA)—between 1958 and 1972, and again during Bill Clinton's presidency from 1993 to 1996. ARPAnet, the technological precursor to the modern TCP/IP-based internet, was launched in 1969.

DARPA and the National Aeronautics and Space Administration (NASA) have a common origin: both were responses to the Soviet space program (*https:// oreil.ly/t58DR*) launching the Earth's first artificial satellite, Sputnik, in 1957. It was the height of the Cold War, and American ingenuity would not be outdone by those communist Soviets! So the Space Race commenced. NASA focuses on advancing American space exploration and research, while DARPA develops new technologies for the military.

DARPA doesn't have its own research facilities or laboratories—unusual for the DoD. It has minimal bureaucracy, and its leaders typically serve (*https:// oreil.ly/ETwwg*) only about three to five years. DARPA recruits the "best and brightest" to conduct bold and innovative (and usually secretive) projects during their short terms of employment. It saddens me that war is such a driver of computer technology, but war is one of America's top financial priorities!

There's at least one direct connection (*https://oreil.ly/OuLE8*) between DARPA and Cult of the Dead Cow (cDc), the notorious hacker culture pioneering hacktivist group: after Michael "MafiaBoy" Calce's infamous series of DDoS attacks, DARPA recruited cDc member Peiter "Mudge" Zatko in 2000 to help prevent future such attacks. At DARPA, Mudge created a program to offer grants to hackers (*https://oreil.ly/v9wQm*) to help improve the US government's security posture.

The most important technological advance that came out of DARPA is surely ARPAnet, which has its own entry in this book. Others include:

- DARPA's oN-Line System (*https://oreil.ly/1ykBn*) (NLS), unveiled in 1968, which is ARPAnet's father, the internet's grandfather, and the World Wide Web's great-grandfather. The very first computer mouse, raster-scan video monitors, screen windowing, and hypertext links, and some very rudimentary computer networking, were all invented for NLS.

- The NAVSTAR Global Positioning System (GPS), which began development in 1973.

- The Personalized Assistant that Learns (PAL) (*https://oreil.ly/89sgr*) artificial intelligence program started at DARPA in 2002 with the goal of designing "cognitive computing systems to make military decision-making more efficient." Its voice interaction functions became a part of the creation of Siri in 2007.

- The High-Productivity Computing Systems (HPCS) (*https://oreil.ly/8bHur*) program, launched in 2002, gives grants to IBM, Cray, Hewlett-Packard, Silicon Graphics, and Sun Microsystems to develop better-performing and more affordable (relatively speaking) supercomputers.

See also "ARPAnet" on page 17, "Artificial intelligence (AI)" on page 17, "Calce, Michael "MafiaBoy"" on page 39, "Cult of the Dead Cow (cDc)" on page 66, "Internet" on page 145, "Supercomputers" on page 233, "TCP/IP (Transmission Control Protocol/Internet Protocol)" on page 239

Data

See "Azure" on page 28, "Binary" on page 35, "CIA triad (confidentiality, integrity, availability)" on page 49, "Cleartext" on page 50, "Common Vulnerabilities and Exposures (CVE)" on page 56, "Cryptography" on page 63, "Cybersecurity" on page 68, "Dark Web/darknet" on page 71, "Denial-of-service (DoS, DDoS) attacks" on page 81, "Diffie-Hellman key exchange" on page 84, "Floppy disk" on page 105, "Ham radio" on page 127, "Hexadecimal numbering" on page 133, "Hopper, Grace" on page 137, "Internet" on page 145, "Key" on page 156, "Networking" on page 183, "Packet switching" on page 193, "Piracy" on page 200, "Pretty Good Privacy (PGP)" on page 203, "Quantum computing" on page 207, "Ransomware" on page 211, "Rivest-Shamir-Adleman (RSA) cryptography" on page 215, "Zettabyte Era" on page 279

Da Vinci, Leonardo

Leonardo da Vinci (1452–1519), born in Florence, Italy, (*https://oreil.ly/AOw1r*) is probably the most famous person from the 15th-century Italian Renaissance, and certainly the earliest historical figure with an entry in this book. He's someone I think of as being a "hacker" before being a hacker was a thing. (I would say being a hacker has been "a thing" since the 1950s at MIT's Tech Model Railroad Club.)

Of course, da Vinci painted the most famous piece of visual art in history, the *Mona Lisa*, as well as *The Last Supper* and many other masterpieces. His drawing *The Vitruvian Man* is still seen in countless medical anatomy textbooks and classrooms.

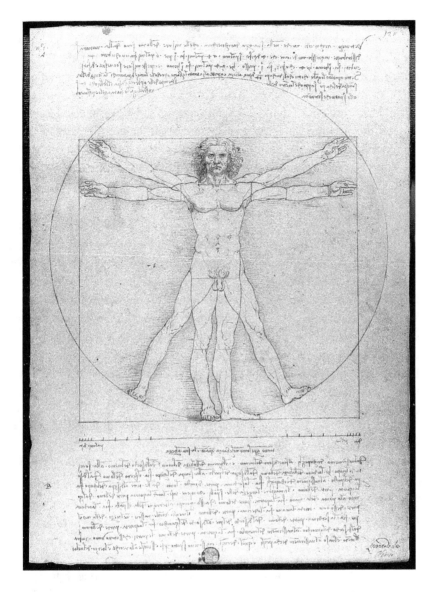

The term STEM (science, technology, engineering, and mathematics) didn't exist in da Vinci's era, but he was highly accomplished in all four of those areas. *The Vitruvian Man* (*https://oreil.ly/uXo3v*) combines da Vinci's fascination with human anatomy and proportion with concepts he learned from the architect Vitruvius Pollio.

Da Vinci was also famed for his inventions (*https://oreil.ly/HvWzD*). Some were precursors to modern aircraft, but couldn't be built without motor engines, which didn't exist yet. He was truly thinking centuries into the future.

Imagine what could have happened for hacker culture if we could put da Vinci in a room with Ada Lovelace, Alan Turing, and Hedy Lamarr! Perhaps that room could be a meeting of the Tech Model Railroad Club or the Homebrew Computer Club. It would make a great holodeck simulation for Captain Picard and Commander Data.

See also "Homebrew Computer Club" on page 136, "Tech Model Railroad Club" on page 240

Debian

Debian (*https://oreil.ly/2Fm36*) is one of the oldest and most popular Linux kernel-based operating systems. Pre-Alpha Debian Linux 0.01 (*https://oreil.ly/E-NhT*) was released in September 1993, and the first public beta, Debian Linux 0.90, was released in January 1994. Beta development took quite a long time, because the first stable release, Debian 1.1 (*https://oreil.ly/p5M_i*) didn't come out until June 1996. As of November 2022, the latest Debian release is the Alpha 1 version of Debian 12.0 (*https://oreil.ly/_srUC*).

Debian is maintained by the Debian Project (*https://oreil.ly/rZoAE*), which describes itself as "an association of individuals, sharing a common goal: We want to create a free operating system, freely available for everyone. Now, when we use the word 'free', we're not talking about money, instead, we are referring to software freedom." Now that's hacker culture!

Interestingly enough, people use Linux distributions based on Debian (*https://oreil.ly/3v3s2*) even more often than "vanilla" Debian. The nature of the open source community, where code is freely shared, means that developers are welcome to develop their own forks of other applications and operating systems. (A *fork* is a copy of an existing software project to which another entity has added their own modifications.)

It's difficult to find reliable usage statistics for open source operating systems on consumer PCs, but many web servers run Debian and forks of Debian. According to W3Techs.com (*https://oreil.ly/j5LDD*), as of 2022, 6.1% of websites were using web servers in Debian and 12.6% of websites were using web servers in Ubuntu (*https://oreil.ly/oKomb*), one of the most popular Debian forks. There are also forks of Ubuntu that use different graphical user environments. For instance, Kubuntu (*https://oreil.ly/gw2vM*) combines Ubuntu with the KDE user environment. Linux Mint (*https://oreil.ly/Jil5G*) is another popular Debian fork.

See also "Git/GitHub" on page 113, "Linux" on page 161

DEC (Digital Equipment Corporation)

Digital Equipment Corporation (DEC) was an innovative underdog computer maker that dominated enterprise computing from the 1960s through the 1980s. Its machines, mainly minicomputers, looked as serious as the competing products that IBM was making, and its leadership and corporate culture were progressive—a David to IBM's Goliath. Hackers in the 1960s loved DEC's computers, including MIT's Tech Model Railroad Club.

Ken Olsen and Harlan Anderson (*https://oreil.ly/CyvAc*), colleagues at MIT's Lincoln Laboratory in the 1950s, noticed that students preferred computers that were easier to interact with than punch-card machines like the IBM 650 (*https://oreil.ly/7bS_n*) and that could provide real-time feedback.

Olsen and his brother Stan (*https://oreil.ly/BoonF*) founded a company to produce a user-friendly computer, but initially had difficulty securing financing; investors were wary of investing in computer companies (*https://oreil.ly/5xNTP*), which mostly didn't last long. Olsen and Anderson were advised to not use the word "computer" in their name. They named the company Digital Equipment Corporation and planned to market their products as laboratory equipment, which brought in enough funding to get the company up and running in a former 19th-century wool mill in Maynard, Massachusetts.

In 1961, DEC produced its first proper computer, the PDP-1. PDP stood for "programmable data processor," to avoid the dreaded C-word. The PDP-1 model sold for $120,000 (about $1 million today), but Olsen gave one to MIT (*https://oreil.ly/5xNTP*), where the Tech Model Railroad Club used it to create Spacewar! (*https://oreil.ly/MJ_MX*), widely considered to be the first video game ever.

To sell to more businesses and institutions, DEC produced relatively more affordable computers, all things being relative: 1962's PDP-4 was "only" $65,000, or about $640,000 in 2023 dollars. It was similar in capability to the PDP-1 (*https://oreil.ly/oSknN*), but slower.

In 1970, the PDP-11 was DEC's big breakthrough in minicomputers (which meant it was the size of a home appliance, not a room or a building floor). It used 8-inch floppy disk drives and memory that was physically similar to the memory our PCs use today. It was so popular that DEC sold technologically upgraded versions (*https://oreil.ly/Pprmd*) of it through 1996.

Olsen was a popular and very progressive leader whose employees actually enjoyed working for him. He made an effort to employ female and racially marginalized engineers and even offered employees home mortgages. One employee, Jerry Bernath (*https://oreil.ly/4GmMY*), quoted Olsen's often-used refrain: "Do what's right and do the right thing!'"

DEC had the foresight to register the dec.com domain name in 1985, several years before the World Wide Web, and its machines could network with ARPAnet in the 1970s and the TCP/IP-based internet in the 1980s.

By 1990, DEC was number two in global computer sales (*https://oreil.ly/Mt3JJ*), second only to IBM. But the early 1990s recession was hard on DEC, and they lost market share to Hewlett-Packard and Sun Microsystems. In 1992, Olsen retired. His replacement, Robert B. Palmer (*https://oreil.ly/VWaS8*), was very unpopular with DEC employees. A former DEC employee (*https://oreil.ly/3piDi*) explains that "GQ Bob," known for driving a Porsche 911 to work, "was never one of us, and he never wanted to be one of us."[1]

DEC launched AltaVista (*https://oreil.ly/oSknN*), a popular web search engine, in 1995 (three years ahead of Google). In 1998, DEC was acquired by Compaq for a whopping $9.6 billion, the biggest computer industry acquisition (*https://oreil.ly/naO4Y*) at the time. But Compaq couldn't understand how to leverage DEC's international market, and in 2002, Hewlett-Packard bought Compaq. The DEC brand had disappeared by 2004. I truly believe that if Ken Olsen had been replaced with a leader with an equally progressive, employee-friendly mindset, DEC would still exist today.

See also "ARPAnet" on page 17, "Hewlett-Packard (HP)" on page 131, "Minicomputers" on page 176, "Tech Model Railroad Club" on page 240, "World Wide Web" on page 268

Deep Web

People sometimes confuse the Deep Web with the Dark Web. The Dark Web is part of the Deep Web (*https://oreil.ly/A4joo*), but the vast majority of the Deep Web is on the clearnet (the ordinary internet, which isn't locked behind proxy networks like Tor or I2P). The definition of the Deep Web is everything on the web that isn't indexed by mainstream search engines. Search engines like Google and Bing (you might use Bing and not even know it, it's the search engine

---

1 Quoted in Steven Levy, *Hackers: Heroes of the Computer Revolution: 25th Anniversary Edition* (*https://oreil.ly/GYad7*) (O'Reilly, 2010).

underneath DuckDuckGo) have web crawler bots that survey the web by going to a web page, and then going to as many links in those web pages as possible. A web page that isn't linked effectively to web crawled web pages is going to be missed.

If you have a web browser handy, go ahead and visit *https://www.oreilly.com*. That's the website for O'Reilly Media. It's on the clearnet, because you were able to visit the site without using Tor or I2P. Google Search results (*https://oreil.ly/AA3Y-*) for "O'Reilly Media" show O'Reilly's official website as the top search result. That's clear evidence that the O'Reilly Media site is part of the Surface Web (*https://oreil.ly/uEubF*) and not the Deep Web.

Some of the Deep Web is very old content, and some consists of things like databases and parts of web applications (like your Gmail inbox) that shouldn't be search-engine indexable for security reasons.

As of this writing, the URL for Dark.Fail is:

http://darkfailenbsdla5mal2mxn2uz66od5vtzd5qozslagrfzachha3f3id.onion

You need to use Tor Browser in order to access that website. So it's on the Dark Web, not the clearnet, and everything on the Dark Web is also on the Deep Web. So Dark.Fail isn't Surface Web either.

Simple, eh?

If you want to try finding Deep Web content that's Deep Web because it's old, one of the best resources is Wayback Machine (*https://oreil.ly/UTxUy*) at Internet Archive. Wayback Machine is constantly taking snapshots of pages all over the web, both user-generated and automated.

There's a Save Page Now web form (*https://oreil.ly/SNo8T*) on the home page. Enter the URL of any webpage you want, and it'll snapshot it for you. The snapshots Wayback Machine stores can be explored like regular web pages. Most of the time, you can even click on links in the snapshots, and it'll load a snapshot of the web page that was intended to be linked. Wayback Machine's snapshots go all the way back to the 1990s. If there's a very old web page that probably isn't hosted on its original web server anymore, that's the best place to find it. Thank you, Internet Archive, for this valuable service!

See also "Dark.Fail" on page 71, "Dark Web/darknet" on page 71, "Internet" on page 145, "World Wide Web" on page 268

DEF CON

DEF CON (*https://oreil.ly/A9S3-*) is a cybersecurity and hacking conference that has taken place every year since June 1993 (*https://oreil.ly/sNUIX*). Now it happens every August in Las Vegas. Though the conference is not a military event, its name is a reference to the US Military's Defense Readiness Condition (*https://oreil.ly/wK1We*) system, as mentioned in the 1980s hacker movie *WarGames* (*https://oreil.ly/uFa7Y*), which uses five threat levels. DEF CON 5 is the lowest perceived threat level, and DEF CON 1 indicates the maximum threat level and the need to prepare for war.

Jeff Moss (*https://oreil.ly/fk2xo*), otherwise known as Dark Tangent, founded DEF CON when he was 18 years old. In a video from 2007 (*https://oreil.ly/3A_dl*), he discussed DEF CON's roots in phone phreaking:

> I just happened to have a bulletin board set up, and I had an OK job. So I paid my phone bill, unlike most back then, everybody else was phreaking [phone hacking] the connections. And so I became a big hub for eleven of these international networks...all these different networks from back in the day, and because of that, I was connected to pretty much all the communication that was going on in the underground that was active in those days.

DEF CON holds smaller events year round, such as movie nights over Discord and in-person security training sessions.

See also "Cybersecurity" on page 68, "Phreaking" on page 199, "WarGames (1983 film)" on page 263

Demoscene

The *demoscene* (*https://oreil.ly/jQ7nU*) is where hacker culture meets art and music, as hackers explore the visual and musical potential of computers old and new. Many of the demoscene's most prominent demogroups started in the late 1990s and early 2000s, and the earliest demos were made in the 1980s. Demogroups often maintain older PCs and operating systems as tools for their art, like the Commodore Amiga, Atari ST, Commodore 64, MS-DOS, ZX Spectrum, and Amstrad CPC. Most of the demoscene videos I've watched look like trippy synthwave (*https://oreil.ly/Dd2gc*) music videos.

Demoscene.info (*https://oreil.ly/RDplt*) states: "Demo-making is teamwork.... Graphicians and musicians create suitable pieces of art, the programmers fit all the parts together in an extensive amount of detail work to finally make it an executable program: the demo."

The precursor to the demoscene was the "display hacks (*https://oreil.ly/Y8Xny*)" of the 1950s: programs "with the same approximate purpose as a kaleidoscope: to make pretty pictures" and explore what a computer's display output can do, according to *The Cathedral and the Bazaar* author Eric S. Raymond.

Some of the better-known demogroups include Conspiracy (*https://oreil.ly/D3wAt*), MFX (*https://oreil.ly/k_4Gd*), Farbrausch (*https://oreil.ly/zAV4L*), Haujobb, and Kolor (*https://oreil.ly/a9iGa*). Demogroups often enter their demos in competitions, where they're judged for their artistry and technical proficiency.

See also "The Cathedral and the Bazaar (1999 book)" on page 44

Denial-of-service (DoS, DDoS) attacks

Denial-of-service (DoS) attacks are one of the most common cyberattacks. They target the A in the CIA triad of cybersecurity: availability. A DoS attack (*https://oreil.ly/mVgGY*) overwhelms a networked target with so many packets of data that it shuts down.

A *distributed denial-of-service* (*https://oreil.ly/N7dlL*) (DDoS) *attack* uses a network of synchronized computers to perform a DoS, which is often more effective than a DoS attack which uses just one. DDoS attacks are most often performed by botnets (*https://oreil.ly/-b6k7*), in which a cyberattacker commands a network of zombie malware-infected computers to engage in attacks. A computer may be infected by zombie malware without the user noticing.

Web servers (*https://oreil.ly/WO89z*) are frequent targets of DoS and DDoS attacks, although any kind of networked computer can be a target. Sometimes networking devices such as routers (*https://oreil.ly/Mij6A*) can be targets as well.

Here are a few types of DoS attacks:

Ping of Death
Ping of Death DoS attacks involve sending malicious ping packets to a server that go over that server's data size limit, causing it to crash.

UDP flood
Some internet protocols use User Datagram Protocol (UDP) packets instead of the more common Transmission Control Protocol (TCP) packets. A UDP packet doesn't contain a header to guide its sequence. In a UDP flood DoS attack, a mass of UDP packets are sent to a bunch of random IP ports on the same target. That forces the target to repeatedly

check for the application listening at each port. When it finds none, the targeted server can crash.

HTTP flood attacks

In an HTTP flood attack, one of the most common ways to DoS attack, the attacker floods a web server with a large number of HTTP GET or POST requests that look legitimate but aren't, until the server crashes.

Low Orbit Ion Cannon

Low Orbit Ion Cannon (LOIC) (*https://oreil.ly/ZoRue*) may be one of the most infamous DDoS attack tools. It was developed by Praetox Technologies for legitimate penetration testing purposes but has been abused by cyberattackers many times.

See also "CIA triad (confidentiality, integrity, availability)" on page 49, "Cybersecurity" on page 68, "Malware" on page 167, "Networking" on page 183, "Packet switching" on page 193, "Ping" on page 200

Developers

See "Crunch time" on page 60, "Git/GitHub" on page 113, "Programming" on page 204, "Whiteboard interviews" on page 265, "World Wide Web" on page 268

DevOps

DevOps is one of the most commonly used methodologies for deploying applications, both through cloud platforms and through internal enterprise networks. It's all about combining the development team (the programmers) with the operations team (the IT department) to deploy and maintain responsive applications. To understand DevOps (*https://oreil.ly/3jdPT*) properly, first you must understand Agile development.

Applications and software projects deployed through the Agile methodology release new code and new features in small pieces to be responsive to changing client needs, rather than as fewer, larger updates. An Agile application (*https:// oreil.ly/ex3cg*) updates in lots of little ways continuously, rather than going from version 1.5 one year to version 1.6 the next year. Ideally, this means it is always relevant and functional according to whatever the client's needs are at any given time.

In DevOps, all of the work is as synchronized, frequent, and up to date as possible. Developers and operations work and collaborate simultaneously at each stage of development. IT people monitor the network's usage and operation and share information with the developers, who are constantly working on patches and new features. It's a way to apply hacker ingenuity to big corporate software needs. And the development of the application is a constant process. As soon as a patch or new feature is tested to be stable, it's deployed!

DevOps and Agile development emerged around 2007 and 2008 (*https:// oreil.ly/G_IrG*) and are considered an improvement on other application development methodologies, particularly the older, slower "waterfall" style.

The common wisdom in the cybersecurity industry now is that security testers must continuously audit and test code for security vulnerabilities in every step of the application development process. When security is implemented that way into DevOps, it's called DevSecOps (*https://oreil.ly/97uOt*).

See also "Bug" on page 37, "Cybersecurity" on page 68, "Penetration testing" on page 196

Diffie, Whitfield

Did you buy something online today? Did you input your credit card number without it being breached by cyberattackers? One of the people you can thank is Whitfield Diffie (1944–), one of the founders of public-key cryptography.

Diffie loved math and started reading about cryptography in his youth. As a young man, he joined the MITRE Corporation, partly motivated by his desire to avoid being drafted to fight the Vietnam War. He also worked as a guest researcher at MIT's Artificial Intelligence Laboratory, co-founded by AI scientist John McCarthy. McCarthy left MIT for Stanford University, and in 1969, Diffie followed, joining the Stanford Artificial Intelligence Laboratory.

Reading David Kahn's *The Codebreakers: The Story of Secret Writing* (McMillan, 1967) fueled Diffie's passion for digital privacy. He was especially interested in one-way functions, which would be important to developing cryptography technology with a public vector.

Public-key cryptography, which is necessary for encrypting internet communications, uses *asymmetric* keys. With symmetric keys, the math for the decryption key is the encryption key in reverse; that's good for private-key cryptography because it's all in a contained system. But the internet is public. If the encryption key sent to your web browser can be used to calculate the decryption key, that renders the cryptography pointless. It's like leaving your house key right outside your front door.

In 1974, Diffie began collaborating with fellow cryptographer Martin Hellman, and the following year they were joined by cryptographer and puzzle-maker Ralph Merkle, from the University of California, Berkeley. Merkle's puzzles influenced the development of the technology Diffie and Hellman would become known for: the Diffie-Hellman key exchange.

Diffie and Hellman introduced the Diffie-Hellman key exchange in a groundbreaking 1976 paper.[2] Today it is used in RSA cryptography, which makes it part of all kinds of data-in-transit encryption.

I asked Diffie how the internet might be different if not for the advent of public key cryptography. He replied, "I assume it would depend far more on verified email addresses, in the way you currently prove that an email address is yours by receiving a PIN at the address and typing it into a website. I couldn't have made a living fighting over whether encryption should be trapdoored; the police would be able to read everything."

Diffie says quantum-safe public-key cryptography could be possible, but he does not believe the Diffie-Hellman key exchange could be applied to it. He does believe that quantum-safe public-key cryptography can be possible. He pointed me to the National Institute of Standards and Technology's (NIST) Post-Quantum Cryptography (*https://oreil.ly/WFmlJ*) project.

Diffie is now a consulting scholar at Stanford's Center for International Security and Cooperation (*https://oreil.ly/einjL*). He was inducted into the US National Security Agency's Hall of Honor (*https://oreil.ly/5FXdN*) in 2020.

See also "ARPAnet" on page 17, "Berkeley, University of California" on page 32, "Cryptography" on page 63, "Diffie-Hellman key exchange" on page 84, "Hellman, Martin" on page 128, "Key" on page 156, "Massachusetts Institute of Technology (MIT)" on page 170, "Quantum computing" on page 207, "Rivest, Ron" on page 214, "Rivest-Shamir-Adleman (RSA) cryptography" on page 215, "Stanford University" on page 230

Diffie-Hellman key exchange

Whitfield Diffie and Martin Hellman invented the Diffie-Hellman key exchange in 1976, during ARPANet's heyday. To secure data in a computer network, it needs to be encrypted while in transit. ARPAnet was the largest computer network in history at that point and needed that sort of security. The solution

---

2 Whitfield Diffie and Martin Hellman, "New Directions in Cryptography," (*https://oreil.ly/KqJgs*) *IEEE Transactions on Information Theory* 22, no 6 (November 1976): 644–54.

is public-key cryptography, which uses an asymmetric cipher. To encrypt data, users must receive a public key. Then the server on the receiving end uses a private key to decrypt the data. The cipher must be asymmetrical, meaning that knowing the public key doesn't reveal the private key. The key exchanges must be kept secret in order to be secure. That's where the Diffie-Hellman key exchange (*https://oreil.ly/LZTgw*) comes in.

Diffie and Hellman published a whitepaper in which they explained their goal: to "minimize the necessity of secure key distribution channels and supply the equivalent of a written signature."[3]

They were inspired by cryptographic puzzles (*https://oreil.ly/VfaZz*) created by Berkeley computer scientist Ralph C. Merkle. Interestingly enough, RSA cryptography co-inventor Ron Rivest was one of the editors of Merkle's paper.

See also "ARPAnet" on page 17, "Cryptography" on page 63, "Diffie, Whitfield" on page 83, "Hellman, Martin" on page 128, "Key" on page 156, "Rivest, Ron" on page 214, "Rivest-Shamir-Adleman (RSA) cryptography" on page 215

Disk, disc

See "Floppy disk" on page 105

DOOM (video game)

DOOM (1993) was a groundbreaking first-person shooter video game that left its mark on hacker culture. A whole franchise of *DOOM* games have been released since, but this entry focuses on the original, which debuted for MS-DOS with the shareware release of its first episode, *Knee-Deep in the Dead* (*https://oreil.ly/kbDCv*), through the University of Wisconsin's FTP server.

id Software's John Carmack developed the *Doom engine* (*https://oreil.ly/5yXyh*), which was eventually released as open source software under the GNU Public License. That opened the door for fans to develop a massive collection of fan levels and mods. *DOOM* has also been ported to just about every video game system and platform in existence (I think only *Tetris* can hold a candle to *DOOM* in that department). Some are quite obscure, like Symbian (a mobile operating system by Nokia that was never commercially successful), Flipper Zero (*https://oreil.ly/yZ5n7*) (a recently released penetration testing device for cybersecurity

---

3 Whitfield Diffie and Martin Hellman, "New Directions in Cryptography," (*https://oreil.ly/RwX6g*) *IEEE Transactions on Information Theory* 22, no. 6 (November 1976): 644–54.

hackers), and Texas Instruments TI-84 Plus graphing calculators. *DOOM* has even been run on ATMs and DSLR cameras (*https://oreil.ly/1a-aG*).

If this inspires your hacker spirit, you should know that Android runs on a lot of the embedded systems in Internet of Things devices. Just find a way to port the Android 25th anniversary release (*https://oreil.ly/p9AHG*), and you could be the first person to play *DOOM* on a smart refrigerator!

See also "Android operating system" on page 11, "DOS (Disk Operating System)" on page 86, "Open source" on page 189

DOS (Disk Operating System)

DOS stands for Disk Operating System. DOS operating systems generally have an ASCII text-based user interface, rather than a graphical user interface (GUI). The name DOS has been used for many operating systems over the years, but most of the time, when an old nerd talks about DOS, they're referring to the Microsoft (MS-DOS) or IBM (PC-DOS) versions. Until 2001, every consumer version of Windows ran on top of MS-DOS.

The story of DOS starts with Gary Kildall (*https://oreil.ly/teKsV*) and his company, Digital Research. In 1974, Kildall developed CP/M, an innovative operating system for the business market, designed for 8-bit microcomputers. It processed basic input and output tasks through hardware, so that applications would mainly interface with the operating system. This made it much easier to support a variety of 1970s microprocessor hardware from different vendors. It probably also made application development easier, since you could simply develop an application to run in CP/M rather than creating separate applications for specific models of business microcomputers. (A similar sort of broad hardware and vendor support would make Microsoft a smash success, with MS-DOS and Windows for "IBM compatible" PCs.)

If you want to try using DOS today, check out FreeDOS (*https://oreil.ly/rhRwr*), an GNU Public License open source project. If you need to run a supported OS directly on legacy hardware that ran PC-DOS/MS-DOS, FreeDOS is the way to go. If you want to play classic DOS games or emulate DOS utilities on a modern Windows, macOS, Linux, or BSD/UNIX-based PC, go for DOS Box (*https://oreil.ly/x6_O7*), an MS-DOS emulator which runs as its own application.

DOS games

Younger generations may not realize what a popular gaming platform MS-DOS was. Hundreds of games were developed for DOS, and the majority of them are now abandonware. *Abandonware* is software that used to be proprietary and commercial but is now a type of freeware, because the intellectual property rights on it have expired.

The hacker spirit holds that knowledge must be free, and hackers have taken full advantage of the abandonware status of most DOS games by lawfully sharing them online for free. You can download each game you want and execute it in the DOSBox emulator or in your web browser, which is even more convenient. Check out the MS-DOS game collection on the Internet Archive (*https://oreil.ly/XHaIc*).

If you do, here are a few DOS games that illustrate the medium well:

Zork
> *Zork* (*https://oreil.ly/pM5XY*) (1984) is a series of text adventure games. The Internet Archive (*https://oreil.ly/lg7zb*) also has *Zork II, Zork III, Beyond Zork, Zork Zero*, and the series' graphical entry, *Return to Zork* (*https://oreil.ly/Lmzaq*). Text adventure games were one of the first popular computer-game genres, and they continued to be popular throughout the 1980s. They also inspired the visual novel (*https://oreil.ly/v6xyl*) genre, which continues to be popular in Japan and has niche fan communities in the English-speaking world.

Where in the World Is Carmen Sandiego?
> I have fond childhood memories of the Carmen Sandiego (*https://oreil.ly/sjERS*) series, graphical adventure games designed to teach children geography and history. You play a detective from the Acme Agency who travels the world, time, and/or space to catch criminals from V.I.L.E., the Villains' International League of Evil, run by Carmen Sandiego. You can also find *Where in Time is Carmen Sandiego?* and *Where in Europe is Carmen Sandiego?* on the Internet Archive.

Lemmings
> The Lemmings (*https://oreil.ly/DaF2F*) series is a fast-paced puzzle game where you guide lemmings through dangerous environments.

The lemmings will just continuously walk forward to their deaths if you don't give them instructions! Inevitably, some of your lemmings will have to die to save the others.

DOOM

If you're looking for something with even more action and violence, the DOS versions of the DOOM (*https://oreil.ly/WhO3l*) series are on the Internet Archive, as are lots of fan games made with the *Doom* engine.

See also "DOOM (video game)" on page 85, "IBM" on page 139, "Microcomputers" on page 173, "Microsoft" on page 174, "Open source" on page 189, "Shareware/freeware/abandonware" on page 223

Draper, John

See "Captain Crunch (John Draper)" on page 41

Dread forums

Dread is a website on the Dark Web that's modelled on Reddit and can only be opened via Tor.[4] Anyone can make their own subdread (the Dread version of a subreddit) based on an area of interest. Moderators control what types of posts are allowed and can ban users who break their rules. Most subs never become popular, but a handful can have millions of active users. The most popular subdreads focus on darknet markets (*https://oreil.ly/-RfB3*) and how to engage in cybercrime.

There is *no* connection or affiliation between Reddit and Dread. When Reddit cracked down on cybercrime subreddits in 2018, anonymous founder HugBunter simply replicated its model.

Dread was offline in early 2023 when I first researched this entry, but as of October 2023, it's back online. That's the nature of the darknet: sites are often subject to DDoS (distributed denial-of-service) attacks from law enforcement and other cybercriminals (*https://oreil.ly/BNidv*), and are thus unreliable.

---

4 This entry is adapted from a blog post (*https://oreil.ly/AhThU*) I wrote for *Hack the Box* in 2021.

See also "Dark Web/darknet" on page 71,"Denial-of-service (DoS, DDoS) attacks" on page 81, "Reddit" on page 212, "Tor (The Onion Router)" on page 245

DRM (Digital Rights Management)

DRM, which stands for digital rights management (*https://oreil.ly/jppq9*), is a controversial form of software code used to ensure that only paying customers have access to particular digital content. DRM is applied to a wide range of media, including music, videos, video games, software applications, paywalled websites and web apps, digital journals and periodicals, and ebooks. It is designed to restrict intellectual property rights under a capitalist system, and thus DRM goes against the spirit of hacker culture, wherein "knowledge should be free." As the Free Software Foundation's anti-DRM campaign, Defective By Design (*https://oreil.ly/Mz4Wy*), describes it:

> *DRM creates a damaged good; it prevents you from doing what would be possible without it. This concentrates control over production and distribution of media, giving DRM peddlers the power to carry out massive digital book burnings and conduct large scale surveillance over people's media viewing habits.*
>
> *If we want to avoid a future in which our devices serve as an apparatus to monitor and control our interaction with digital media, we must fight to retain control of our media and software.*

In fact, DRM often prevents paying consumers (*https://oreil.ly/OlKh8*) from using media in ways that are within their legal rights: it can interfere with using public library books, accessing public-domain media, making backup copies, and using media for nonprofit or educational purposes, as outlined under the "fair use" or "fair dealing" (*https://oreil.ly/wtZDw*) exemptions in copyright laws.

If you're reading an ebook version of this very book, there could well be DRM on it, depending on where you bought it. While O'Reilly doesn't place DRM on its ebooks, sellers like Amazon Kindle, Google Play, and Apple can and often do. If you pirated this book, you or the pirate likely cracked that DRM.

See also "Creative Commons licenses" on page 59, "Piracy" on page 200

Dungeons & Dragons (game franchise)

Dungeons & Dragons (*https://oreil.ly/ocFKG*) (DnD) was the first popular tabletop roleplaying game (RPG) and is still hugely popular. It was invented by Gary Gygax and David Arneson and was first published in 1974 by Gygax's company, Tactical Studies Rules (TSR). Wizards of the Coast, a subsidiary of Hasbro, bought the rights to DnD from TSR in 1997. DnD's long-lived commercial success has inspired thousands of other tabletop RPGs (*https://oreil.ly/L9Q5t*). The common element in these games is that they tell a story in which players make decisions and roll dice for their characters, and they can be played without computers, in person (*https://oreil.ly/2gOJg*), as a social activity (though many players these days do play over the internet).

In the game, a small group of people (known as a "party") invent fantasy characters for themselves to play. Each player uses a paper character sheet to design their character's biography and statistics; optionally, they can also use a toy figure to represent their character. Each character is assigned a class (such as Rogue or Cleric) and a race (such as Elf or Human),[5] and these classifications influence the characters' skills, available spells, strengths, and weaknesses by modifying the results of their die rolls. Players use a set of seven dice (*https:// oreil.ly/YpdmA*), including a 4-sided die, a 6-sided die, an 8-sided die, a 10-sided die, a percentile die, a 12-sided die, and a 20-sided die.

The game is facilitated by a player called the Dungeon Master (DM), who tells the story and judges how players can implement game rules. Most DMs use official game books to guide character and world creation. The DM may provide a hand-drawn world map or physical props to represent the story's world.

Although DnD is the ultimate in nerdy, low-tech fun, it has many connections to hacker culture. A lot of hackers are into DnD, including innovators from the Silicon Valley scene. DnD has also inspired many, many video game RPGs and JRPGs. And in the fifth edition of DnD (the most recent as of this writing), players can even choose a Hacker subclass for their Rogue characters. As the DnD Wiki (*https://oreil.ly/LtH96*) describes it:

> As a hacker, you gain access to knowledge utilized to fade out of sight, infiltrate technology, and eventually even tap into the spellweave to block access to it. This is the common lot of a hacker, abusing technology to your whim, and with this nefarious capability, what a new world you can build....

See also "Roleplaying games (RPGs)" on page 218

---

5 Wizards of the Coast announced (*https://oreil.ly/mnH6S*) in 2022 that the "race" system will transition to "species" in new editions.

5

E

Electronic Arts

Electronic Arts (EA) is one of the most profitable brands in the video game industry. Its founder, William Murray "Trip" Hawkins III, was a hacker who started his career at Apple.

Hawkins told Jeffrey Fleming (*https://oreil.ly/mJxoU*) of *GameDeveloper.com* (*https://oreil.ly/n6ozu*) how he went from being an early Apple employee to launching one of the world's largest video game publishers:

> In the summer of 1975, I learned about the invention of the microprocessor and about the first retail store where a consumer could rent a time-sharing terminal to use from home. That very day I committed to found EA in 1982. I figured that it would take seven years for enough computing hardware to get into homes to create an audience for the computer games that I wanted to make. When I finished my education in 1978, I got a job at Apple. When I started there, we had only fifty employees and had sold only 1,000 computers in the history of the company, most of them in the prior year. Four years later, we were a Fortune 500 company with 4,000 employees and nearing $1 billion in annual revenue.

Sequoia Capital, of Menlo Park, California, was instrumental in setting up EA as a business, providing initial financing and even office space when the company first incorporated as Amazin' Software in 1982. Later that year, the company changed its name to Electronic Arts.

Hawkins envisioned his game developers as "software artists," and the earliest EA titles (like *Hard Hat Mack, Pinball Construction Set*, and *Archon*) were released with packaging to look like progressive rock albums in vinyl-record-style gatefold sleeves. (Is that The Alan Parsons Project or Electronic Arts on your shelf?)

In the 1980s, EA mainly targeted home computers and Atari 8-bit platforms. Its first game for a popular plug-into-the-TV-style game console was *The Immortal* in November 1990, for the Nintendo Entertainment System (NES).

EA Sports, launched in 1991, is still one of EA's most profitable divisions. It was founded largely due to the popularity of *John Madden Football* (1988). EA Sports has continued releasing Madden titles every year since, as of this writing, though the legendary football coach died in December 2021. The cover art of *Madden NFL 23* is a sort of eulogy to Madden, with a photo of him in his football coaching essence and a signature that says "Thanks, Coach." EA Sports expanded to other licensed professional-sports games that continue today, and popular series are based on hockey (*NHL*), soccer (*FIFA*), golf (*PGA Tour*), auto racing (*Formula 1*), and mixed martial arts (*UFC*).

EA has acquired many other notable game studios over the years, such as Bullfrog Studios, Criterion Games, Westwood Studios, Respawn Entertainment, and Maxis. EA acquired Maxis in 1997 on the strength of its hit game *SimCity*, a groundbreaking city-management simulator first released in 1989. *The Sims* series that followed, people and household simulators in which players control their characters' everyday lives, relationships, and careers, has been even more commercially successful than *SimCity*. EA also bought BioWare in 2007, largely motivated by the commercial success of the first *Mass Effect* game. Today Bio-Ware is best known for RPG series like *Baldur's Gate, Mass Effect, Dragon Age*, and *Star Wars: Knights of the Old Republic*.

See also "Atari" on page 22, "Nintendo" on page 185, "Roleplaying games (RPGs)" on page 218

Electronic Entertainment Expo (E3)

Electronic Entertainment Expo (E3) is a really important annual event in the video game industry. E3's existence is the product of the video game industry's emergence into commercial significance.

Through the 1980s and early 1990s (*https://oreil.ly/iw6V_*), only a minority of lucky kids had access to the internet, so we mainly learned about new games by word of mouth and through magazines like *GamePro* (which, fun fact, originated the term "pro tip"). The standard practice in the US at that time was for video game industry leaders like Atari, Nintendo (of America), and Sega to present their new and upcoming consoles, games, and peripherals at the New York

Toy Fair and the Consumer Electronics Show (CES). It wasn't clear yet whether games and consoles counted as toys, consumer electronics, or something else altogether, but it was clear that they weren't much of a priority at CES. Former Sega of America CEO Tom Kalinske writes (*https://oreil.ly/f9Vxe*):

> In the early nineties, CES was huge, but it treated the gaming industry poorly. We were put in the back, past the new gadgets, computers and stereos and TVs. One year we were in a tent, and it was raining. Our Genesis machines got wet and I said, "That's it, we're not coming back." We set out to form our own show with favored third parties. It became E3.

So the American video game industry joined forces and held the first Electronic Entertainment Expo (*https://oreil.ly/FKs3w*) at the Los Angeles Convention Center in May 1995. E3 has taken place at the same venue in May or June of most years ever since, attracting 10,000 to 75,000 people per event.

Up until the late 2010s or so, E3 was where game companies announced new consoles and upcoming titles. In 2011, however, Nintendo began publicly releasing its "Nintendo Direct" presentations (*https://oreil.ly/Zhke6*), with news about upcoming Nintendo products, services, and games. Nintendo Directs happen at least a few times per year in each regional market. In 2018, Sony followed suit, announcing that it would no longer participate in E3 and instead streaming a similar event called State of Play (*https://oreil.ly/KFL8-*). However, even in the age of COVID-19, E3 continues its annual in-person shows.

See also "Atari" on page 22, "Consumer Electronics Show (CES)" on page 57, "Nintendo" on page 185, "Sega" on page 221

Electronic Frontier Foundation (EFF)

See "Hacking Is Not a Crime" on page 124, "Lamarr, Hedy" on page 159, "Schneier, Bruce" on page 220

Electronics

Hacker culture wouldn't exist without computers, and each and every modern computer is a piece of electronics. Every motherboard can be written as an electronics schematic (*https://oreil.ly/pGg_H*). Even today's hackers enjoy making electronics, whether or not they're computing devices. Platforms like Arduino (*https://oreil.ly/MrsKp*) have made electronics hacking more accessible than ever before. So I want to briefly summarize what electronics are.

There's a difference (*https://oreil.ly/x_3v1*) between electrical devices (such as toasters) and electronics (such as digital alarm clocks and iPhones). Electrical devices simply manipulate electrical power to produce heat, energy, light, or radio waves (without signals). Electronics use more complex circuits to process information or signals through both electronic circuits and radio waves.

ENIAC, one of the first electronic computers, contained over 17,000 vacuum tubes (*https://oreil.ly/xYFHh*) at any given time, which had to be replaced constantly. The desire to overcome the fragile nature of vacuum tubes motivated the development of the transistor at AT&T Bell Labs. By the early 1960s, computers with vacuum tubes were being phased out in favor of computers with transistors. The next big breakthrough happened in 1958, when Texas Instruments engineer Jack Kilby (*https://oreil.ly/TwqxD*) invented the integrated circuit: a chip with lots and lots of tiny transistors on it. The CPUs in our modern computers are a type of integrated circuit.

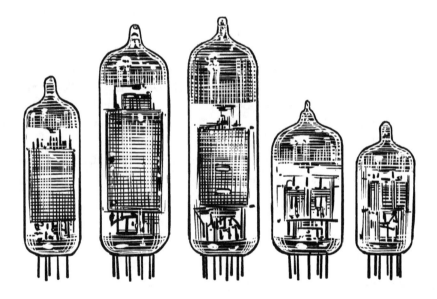

Many of the most influential hackers in history have come from electronics engineering backgrounds. Here are just a few examples (*https://oreil.ly/eco6q*):

Seymour Cray
    Supercomputer pioneer

Grace Hopper
    Legendary computer programmer

Bill Joy
: BSD/UNIX creator and Sun Microsystems cofounder

Jack Kilby
: Inventor of the integrated circuit, something all modern computers use

Robert Metcalfe
: Co-inventor of Ethernet

William Hewlett and David Packard
: Founders and namesakes of Hewlett-Packard

Steve Wozniak
: Cofounder of Apple

Innovations in electronics engineering spawned the computing revolution that permanently changed the world.

See also "Bell Labs" on page 31, "Binary" on page 35, "Cray, Seymour" on page 58, "ENIAC (Electronic Numerical Integrator and Computer)" on page 98, "Fairchild Semiconductor" on page 103, "Hardware" on page 128, "Hopper, Grace" on page 137, "Texas Instruments" on page 242, "Wozniak, Steve" on page 269

Emacs

Emacs is a completely free text editor that's popular with a lot of hackers, especially older hackers. Text editors are the quintessential software for hackers and programmers. If you want to write code or edit a configuration file, you need a text editor. You could use a text editor for noncode projects—it would be possible, if awkward, for me to write this book in Emacs—but a text editor has features designed for programming, such as color coding syntax. And, no, Emacs is not an Apple product.

Creator Richard Stallman is perhaps most famous for launching the GNU project in 1983, as well as his passionate and often controversial advocacy for the free software movement (also known as open source, but Stallman rejects that term). Years before GNU, though, in the 1970s, Stallman and Guy Steele wrote the first version of Emacs (*https://oreil.ly/mCpHa*). Stallman was working for MIT's AI Lab at the time, so he first developed Emacs for their Incompatible Timesharing System (ITS). In the 1980s, it was ported to UNIX operating systems, and by the '90s and beyond it was ported to Linux and even the "computer as a jail" operating systems Stallman hates, like Windows and macOS. It's still being updated and is available for most proprietary and open source operating systems. A number of forks have also been developed.

See also "Integrated development environment (IDE)" on page 143, "Open source" on page 189, "Stallman, Richard" on page 229, "vi" on page 257

Email

Email is older than most people assume. It's even older than the internet (if you define "internet" as a TCP/IP-based public network)! The first proto-email messaging system (*https://oreil.ly/YuLf3*) was designed for the AUTODIN military network in 1962. In 1965 (*https://oreil.ly/jHHi1*), MIT computer users could send human-readable messages to other computers by networking to a shared disk. And in 1971, Ray Tomlinson (*https://oreil.ly/NNHi9*) invented what we now call email for ARPAnet, the precursor to the modern internet. His version was the first to use the @ symbol!

By the 1980s, lots of academics and nerdy hackers had email addresses. And by the 1990s, email was widespread. Thanks in large part to massive marketing efforts (*https://oreil.ly/cl8Wj*) by America Online, even relatively computer-illiterate people began using email, complete with @aol.com email addresses.

Today, many of the most popular email services, like Gmail, offer webmail: email that users access with the web. Webmail uses email servers the exact same way email accessed through a client like Outlook uses them, with the same POP3, IMAP, and SMTP protocols. There are also webmail clients (*https://oreil.ly/pGMB6*) and email clients that run directly in the operating system (*https://oreil.ly/Ku3xL*) that you can use with email servers you could set up yourself. Email's standards are open, thank goodness. And when my editor (hi, Sarah!) has something to share with me, I'd better check my inbox!

See also "ARPAnet" on page 17, "Internet" on page 145, "Massachusetts Institute of Technology (MIT)" on page 170, "TCP/IP (Transmission Control Protocol/Internet Protocol)" on page 239, "World Wide Web" on page 268

ENIAC (Electronic Numerical Integrator and Computer)

The Electronic Numerical Integrator and Computer, known as ENIAC, was the first electronic computer in the United States. Like many 20th-century computer science breakthroughs, it was funded by the US Army for the purposes of World War II, a period that blurred the lines between civilian and military life, infrastructure, and technology. The Army's goal was to find a better way to calculate artillery firing tables for ballistic weapons.

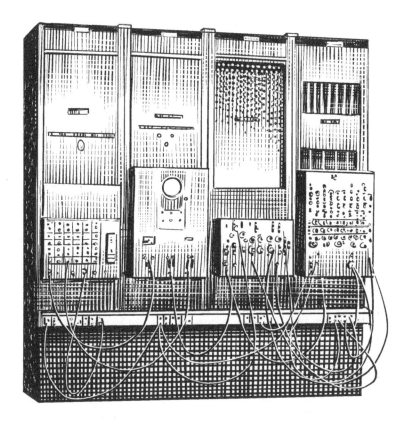

Work started in secret in 1943 at the University of Pennsylvania's Moore School of Electrical Engineering, where, according to co-inventor J. Presper Eckert, the massive computing machine occupied "a room that was 30 feet by 50 feet." ENIAC couldn't store any programs, nor did it have a proper CPU: it was programmed by arranging wires and setting thousands of switches to operate about 18,000 vacuum tubes to perform advanced calculations. The tubes frequently burned out and had to be replaced daily.

ENIAC was completed just as the war was ending. It was first used on December 10, 1945, to perform calculations for the development of John von Neumann's hydrogen bomb.

The army declassified ENIAC and announced it to the public in 1946. The *New York Times* described it as "an amazing machine that applies electronic speeds for the first time to mathematical tasks hitherto too difficult and cumbersome for solution." It added, "Leaders who saw the device in action for the first time heralded it as a tool with which to begin to rebuild scientific affairs on new foundations."

ENIAC's programming team consisted of six women: Jean Jennings Bartik, Marlyn Wescoff Meltzer, Betty Snyder Holberton, Ruth Lichterman Teitelbaum, Kathleen McNulty Mauchly Antonelli, and Frances Bilas Spence. (Before microprocessors emerged in the 1970s, most computer programmers were women!)

ENIAC was last used in 1956. Its components are on display at museums (*https://oreil.ly/I8wjy*) around the world.[1]

See also "Assembly" on page 20, "Binary" on page 35, "Hardware" on page 128, "Programming" on page 204, "Supercomputers" on page 233

Enigma

See "Turing, Alan" on page 248

"Ethical" hacking

The phrase "ethical hacker" (*https://oreil.ly/XeEIY*) is used often in the tech industry, but it's a controversial term that doesn't quite fit with the ethos of hacker culture. Here's why.

Hackers are basically people who invent new ways to use technology. This book is full of real-life hackers and their creations, from operating systems to programming languages to patented electronics and computing devices. Within the context of cybersecurity specifically, a *hacker* is usually someone who finds a way to exploit software and hardware. The "bad guy" threat actors are hackers, yes, but so are the bug hunters and penetration testers who help make computers more secure. Some call the latter "ethical hackers."

Hack The Box (*https://oreil.ly/NEM4P*) is a learning platform for people who want to improve cybersecurity. When I helped launch their blog in 2021, cofounder Aris Zikopoulos told me that he strongly dislikes the term "ethical hacker." Hack The Box community members and staff are simply called hackers. We don't call locksmiths "ethical locksmiths," after all, and we don't call surgeons "ethical surgeons"—even though locksmithing skills would be useful to burglars and surgeons would make very effective murderers.

---

1 As of this writing, that included University of Michigan in Ann Arbor; the Computer History Museum in Mountain View, California; the Heinz Nixdorf Museum in Paderborn, Germany; the United States Army Ordnance Museum at Aberdeen Proving Ground, Maryland; the Smithsonian in Washington, DC; the Science Museum in London; and the School of Engineering and Applied Science at the University of Pennsylvania in Philadelphia.

The term "ethical hacker" was popularized by the International Council of E-Commerce Consultants (*https://oreil.ly/KgVbW*), known as EC-Council. Many tech giants, such as Microsoft and Cisco, offer certification programs for people to demonstrate their skills in specific technologies. Vendor-neutral certifiers, like EC-Council and CompTIA (Computing Technology Industry Association), also offer certifications but are not tied to one particular technology vendor. EC-Council's certifications focus on cybersecurity, and the company is known for its Certified Ethical Hacker (*https://oreil.ly/qTl-P*) (CEH) program. A CEH may help you land a job in offensive cybersecurity, but be careful in using the term "ethical hacker."

See also "Bug" on page 37, "Certificates (professional credentials)" on page 46, "Cybersecurity" on page 68, "Hacker" on page 121, "Penetration testing" on page 196, "Whitehat hackers" on page 265

Exploit

In cybersecurity, an *exploit* is a way to attack a computer system, such as a script or application used to conduct a cyberattack. The darknet markets that cyberthreat actors frequent are full of exploits and exploit kits for sale (priced in cryptocurrency).

I'm an experienced Dark Web threat researcher. While writing this entry, I decided to go on the Dark Web and find an example of an exploit being advertised. So I launched Tor Browser—but I immediately got a pop-up from Malwarebytes, my antivirus client, that said, "Website blocked due to exploit." What an appropriate coincidence!

On AlphaBay Market, a Dark Web market, I navigated to the "Hacking & Spam" section, then to the "Exploits, Kits & Vulnerabilities" subsection. I found this typical example:[2]

Exploit Pack 15.07 2022 lifetime - Think like a hacker - be professional

Exploit Pack is a multiplatform exploitation framework including zero days and more than 39.000 PLUS exploits, post exploitation modules, undetectable and ready for your next target. Exploit Pack has been designed to be used by hands on security professionals to support their testing process.

---

2 Remember, folks, simply looking at this stuff is lawful in most of the world. Actually using an exploit kit to cyberattack another computer or network would be breaking the law.

39.000 PLUS exploits

Zero day exploits

Adversary simulations

Remote and local Fuzzer

Web attacks

Post-Exploitation

Remote control

Auto attacks

Network scanner

Targets management

Hexa editor

Reverse shells

Notice the phrase "for security professionals." It's true that a penetration tester could legally use this kit for testing, with permission from the owner of the computer being tested. But this wording is the darknet equivalent of the "for use with tobacco" signs that head shops used to post on their displays of bongs and pipes. Most of the people who bought those bongs used them for cannabis, and most of the people who buy these exploit kits are cyberthreat actors.

In the world of cybersecurity, you'll hear the word *exploit* used often. It's a more specific word than *hack*, which could refer to an exploit or to a nifty but innocuous technological trick.

See also "Dark Web/darknet" on page 71, "Cryptocurrency" on page 61, "Cybersecurity" on page 68, "Penetration testing" on page 196, "Threat actor" on page 243, "Tor (The Onion Router)" on page 245

6

F

Facebook

See "Meta" on page 171, "Zuckerberg, Mark" on page 280

Fairchild Semiconductor

William Bradford Shockley Jr. (1910–1989) was a brilliant inventor, but a terrible boss. In 1947 at Bell Labs, he helped to invent the transistor (*https://oreil.ly/F1wqR*), one of the most revolutionary inventions of the 20th century. It's used in all kinds of electronics, including televisions and radios, and it revolutionized electronic computers.

One of the earliest programmable electronic computers, ENIAC, started operating in 1945, and it used lots and lots of vacuum tubes that had to be replaced constantly. Transistors were the perfect upgrade. Like vacuum tubes, they make an electric signal go on (1 in binary) or off (0 in binary). But transistors are much smaller, much more efficient, and much more durable. They made electronics of all kinds more practical, smaller, and more affordable.

The next big revolution was to put lots and lots of little transistors on one chip—a type of semiconductor called an integrated circuit. (A CPU is a type of integrated circuit, and all of our modern computers are based on them.)

In 1955, Shockley founded (*https://oreil.ly/2KCvA*) Shockley Semiconductor Laboratory. He and his team were brilliant, but Shockley didn't know how to manage people. So eight of his employees—the "Traitorous Eight" (*https://oreil.ly/FSD_H*) (Gordon Moore, Robert Noyce, Julius Blank, Victor Grinich, Jean Hoerni, Eugene Kleiner, Jay Last, and Sheldon Roberts)—decided to form their own semiconductor company. With their combined financial contributions and a loan from Fairchild Camera and Instrument, they founded Fairchild Semiconductor (*https://oreil.ly/GTFoO*) in 1957.

Robert Noyce at Fairchild Semiconductor and Jack Kilby at Texas Instruments unknowingly spent 1958 working on the same invention: the integrated circuit. Kilby got there first, and when Noyce learned about Kilby's work, he was careful to make Fairchild's integrated circuit different enough to be worthy of its own patent (*https://oreil.ly/HSG6S*), granted in 1961. Kilby was later credited for his work, but as far as the US Patent Office was concerned, the early bird didn't catch the worm. (Another source (*https://oreil.ly/FSD_H*) says that Texas Instruments and Fairchild fought in court, with a ruling resulting in a 1966 cross-licensing agreement.)

During Fairchild's apex in the 1960s and 1970s, it launched some important innovations. For example, the resistor logic integrated circuit helped NASA's Apollo program put the first men on the moon. The Fairchild F8 (*https://oreil.ly/u2R9Y*) microprocessor (CPU) in 1975 was one of the early influential 8-bit CPUs and by some accounts the first purpose-designed 8-bit microcontroller (*https://oreil.ly/fkunz*). And while 1976's Fairchild Channel F (*https://oreil.ly/Xk9tz*) wasn't the very first video game console (the Magnavox Odyssey is slightly older), it *was* the first to use cartridges, thanks to the brilliant work of Fairchild's Jerry Lawson.

Fairchild was also known for its "Fairchildren" (*https://oreil.ly/QyuAR*): tech companies that made integrated circuits and similar technologies, including Intel (founded by Robert Noyce and Gordon Moore (*https://oreil.ly/FSD_H*) in 1967), AMD, Exar, and more. Fairchild struggled to compete against its Fairchildren (*https://oreil.ly/GTFoO*). It shrank, was acquired by other companies, spun off on its own, and was acquired by ON Semiconductor in 2016.

See also "AMD (Advanced Micro Devices)" on page 9, "Bell Labs" on page 31, "CPU (Central processing unit)" on page 57, "ENIAC (Electronic Numerical Integrator and Computer)" on page 98, "Intel" on page 144, "Lawson, Jerry" on page 160, "Moore's law" on page 180, "Texas Instruments" on page 242

Floppy disk

Floppy disks were a primary medium for hackers from the 1970s well into the 1990s and helped to popularize personal computing. According to IBM (*https://oreil.ly/vYHEt*), where the first floppy disks were invented, floppy disk sales peaked in the mid-1990s, then were eventually replaced by CD-ROM drives.

These days, you might still encounter floppy disk drives in legacy PC and server machines. If you find a floppy disk from the 1980s or 1990s that was stored carefully, it might still be readable, according to the nerds on StackExchange (*https://oreil.ly/Sydgo*). They should be kept away from sources of magnetic energy, because floppy disks are a magnetic storage medium. (I was warned as a fifth-grader not to leave Commodore 64 disks on top of the disk drive, because the data on them could disappear!)

In 1967, IBM assigned a group of engineers led by David L. Noble to develop a new removable data storage medium (*https://oreil.ly/RALUz*) for mainframe computers, to replace punch cards and tape reels. They invented the 8-inch floppy disks, which were seen in corporate and institutional environments in the early 1970s but never became popular in the consumer market. Each disk could store 80 kilobytes of data, equivalent to 3,000 punch cards. Now a single 8-inch floppy could barely contain the text on this page.

A member of that IBM team, Alan Shugart, left IBM to found his own company, Shugart Associates. In 1975 the company developed a new, more practical format: the 5.25-inch floppy drive. Shugart employee George Sollman showed one to the Homebrew Computer Club, where it impressed Steve Jobs. Shugart Associates ended up manufacturing the 5.25-inch floppy drives for the Apple II, which helped to widely popularize its use in PCs.

Sony introduced the 3.5-inch floppy disk format in 1980. These disks had harder bodies than the 5.25-inch format, which were literally "floppy," but the name had stuck. The first 3.5-inch floppies could store 720 kilobytes of data, but IBM's "high-density floppy disk" (introduced in 1984), could store 1.2 megabytes—huge back then!

See also "Apple" on page 13, "Hardware" on page 128, "Homebrew Computer Club" on page 136, "IBM" on page 139, "Jobs, Steve" on page 150

Form factor

Form factor defines the shape and size of computer hardware components (*https://oreil.ly/g8xwC*) like memory cards, PC tower cases, power supplies, and disk drives. These sorts of hardware components are designed to be modular, but form factors must be aligned for the modularization of PC hardware components to be compatible. It is an important consideration for hackers who build their own computers, because if you get the form factor wrong, your components won't fit into each other properly.

See also "Electronics" on page 95, "Hardware" on page 128

Freenet

Freenet is a peer-to-peer online communication platform that's designed to be private and resistant to censorship. It has been in continuous development (*https://oreil.ly/PPM5C*) since 2000. Its genesis was a 1999 school paper by University of Edinburgh student Ian Clarke, who published it as a collaborative paper (*https://oreil.ly/7Gnl3*) in 2001.

Peer-to-peer networks are defined by their serverless implementation, and Freenet uses a serverless network with encryption throughout, with fragments of files scattered across peers (a bit like BitTorrent). It also supports browsing and publishing "freesites" (*https://oreil.ly/vOe8P*) on its network and has a chat forum system. As Freenet Classic's documentation (*https://oreil.ly/UNn6j*) describes it:

> *Freenet can be thought of as a large storage device. When you store a file in it, you receive a key which can be used to retrieve the file. When you supply Freenet with a key, it returns the appropriate file (if it is located). The storage space is distributed among all connected nodes on Freenet. Freenet is a peer-to-peer network which is both decentralized and anonymized. The nodes that you connect to only know their nearest neighbors and have no idea about how the network as a whole is structured.*

So your anonymity, privacy, and freedom from censorship on Freenet are technologically protected by decentralization and robust cryptography.

You can download free software for using Freenet (Classic) (*https://oreil.ly/fHtgT*) for Windows, macOS, desktop Linux, and POSIX. An improved version of Freenet codenamed "Locutus" (*https://oreil.ly/aSxqN*) is in development as of this writing in March 2023. The original Freenet has been renamed Freenet Classic.

See also "Cryptography" on page 63, "Hacktivism" on page 125, "Networking" on page 183, "Peer-to-peer (P2P) networks" on page 195, "Shareware/freeware/abandonware" on page 223

Free Software Foundation (FSF)

See "DRM (Digital Rights Management)" on page 89, "Emacs" on page 97, "Open source" on page 189, "Shareware/freeware/abandonware" on page 223, "Stallman, Richard" on page 229

Freeware

See "Open source" on page 189, "Shareware/freeware/abandonware" on page 223

FUD

FUD is an acronym for two different phrases: "Fear, uncertainty, and doubt" (*https://oreil.ly/mXNhu*) and "fully undetectable."

"Fear, uncertainty, and doubt" is a tactic sometimes used in marketing, public relations, politics, and cults. *The Cathedral and the Bazaar* author Eric S. Raymond describes how this meaning of FUD (*https://oreil.ly/vp4Mo*) was used to sell computer hardware back in the day:

> The idea, of course, was to persuade buyers to go with safe IBM gear rather than with competitors' equipment. This implicit coercion was traditionally accomplished by promising that Good Things would happen to people who stuck with IBM, but Dark Shadows loomed over the future of competitors' equipment or software. After 1991, the term has become generalized to refer to any kind of disinformation used as a competitive weapon.

Something bad could happen! We aren't quite sure of the full extent of the bad that can happen, but I doubt it'd be anything good! That's fear, uncertainty, and doubt in a nutshell.

When I worked in cybersecurity research and writing, my employer advised me to avoid engaging in FUD: "Kim, just give our readers the plain facts. No 'cyberattacks can kill!' kind of stuff."

The other common meaning of FUD is "fully undetectable." This is the meaning I was first familiar with. I saw FUD in Dark Web forums where cyberattackers sold crypters to make their malware undetectable by various antivirus software platforms. "Use this latest crypter! McAfee? FUD! AVG? FUD! Malwarebytes? FUD! Avast? FUD! Kaspersky? FUD!"

FUD malware can strike your computer network at any time! We aren't quite sure of the full extent of the bad that could happen, but I doubt it'd be anything good!

7

G

Game Developers Conference (GDC)

Some tech industry events feature shiny new electronic devices to show off to the media, like the Consumer Electronics Show (CES). Some industry events feature upcoming video games and gaming hardware with the same sort of eagerness for media coverage, like the Electronic Entertainment Expo (E3). But there's one big event in the gaming scene that's popular with hackers where the media coverage is just a bonus. The Game Developers Conference (GDC) (*https:// oreil.ly/01BYe*) is really just a huge annual meeting of video game developers, with gaming-industry business leaders and fans coming along for the ride.

GDC was started by Atari game developer Chris Crawford (*https://oreil.ly/ QEAGf*) in 1988 as a social event called the Computer Game Developers Conference; it took place in his home, and 27 people attended. GDC grew steadily, fulfilling game developers' need to discuss their art and craft. Today GDC is based in San Francisco and draws thousands of participants, and even holds international events (*https://oreil.ly/cxUPL*) in places like Cologne, Germany, and Shanghai, China. The Independent Games Festival and the Game Developers Choice Awards are also part of GDC.

See also "Atari" on page 22, "Consumer Electronics Show (CES)" on page 57, "Electronic Entertainment Expo (E3)" on page 94

Gates, Bill

William "Bill" Henry Gates III (*https://oreil.ly/9BYux*) (1955–) is the founder of Microsoft and one of the most famous (or infamous) Silicon Valley billionaires. There's a popular myth that Gates (and many other tech moguls) all started from nothing and founded multitrillion-dollar tech giants in their quaint suburban garages (*https://oreil.ly/NEV8N*). (The subtext of this story is usually something like: "Why aren't you rich? Go learn to code and start a company in your garage like they did. You have no excuse!")

The garage aspect of this myth is true. Hewlett-Packard, Apple, Google, Amazon, and Microsoft were all technically started in garages. But none of their founders started from nothing. Gates came from a wealthy, connected family in Seattle. His father, William Henry Gates Jr., (*https://oreil.ly/eVlm_*) was a powerful attorney who hoped his son would also attend law school. But Gates the Third had access to a DEC PDP-10 (*https://oreil.ly/d9u5F*) at the private school he attended, Lakeside School, and spent countless hours learning to program it. One biography (*https://oreil.ly/eVlm_*) claims that Gates might even have created the first computer virus! The young Gates helped to debug a program used by a local utility, Bonneville Power Administration.

At Lakeside, Gates befriended another rich nerdy kid who loved computers: Paul Allen. Together they founded Traf-O-Data, a small business based on software that analyzed local vehicular-traffic patterns. The teens were paid thousands of dollars for that work.

In 1975, while Gates was at Harvard University, MITS (Micro Instrumentation and Telemetry Systems) released the Altair 8800 (*https://oreil.ly/5y5TH*), one of the earliest microcomputers. Gates called MITS (*https://oreil.ly/1sKpX*) and offered to develop software for it. Gates and Allen founded a new company, Micro-Soft, and MITS paid them $3,000 plus royalties for the programming language they helped to develop, Altair BASIC.

Gates and Allen were never members of the Homebrew Computer Club, and didn't subscribe to its hacker ethos of "knowledge should be free." He wrote a confrontational letter to the club in 1976, "Open Letter to Hobbyists (*https://oreil.ly/HXSG6*)," now the stuff of legends. He argues that the time he, Allen, and their one employee spent developing BASIC was worth at least $40,000. However, he wrote:

Most of these "users" never bought BASIC.... The amount of royalties we have received from sales to hobbyists makes the time spent on Altair BASIC worth less than $2 an hour.

Why is this? As the majority of hobbyists must be aware, most of you steal your software. Hardware must be paid for, but software is something to share. Who cares if the people who worked on it get paid? Is this fair? One thing you don't do by stealing software is get back at MITS for some problem you may have had. MITS doesn't make money selling software. The royalty paid to us, the manual, the tape, and the overhead make it a break-even operation. One thing you do do is prevent good software from being written. Who can afford to do professional work for nothing?

The open source software movement was soon founded, and many hackers much less wealthy than Gates did indeed write software for free. It's also worth noting that the original version of BASIC (*https://oreil.ly/tofIQ*) was developed by John G. Kemeny and Thomas E. Kurtz in 1963 and 1964.

Gates as a young man wasn't quite as business-savvy as he would become later on. He licensed Microsoft BASIC to Commodore for cheap (*https://oreil.ly/KkSSy*), initially for the Commodore PET, but the perpetual license meant that Commodore could use it for the VIC-20 and Commodore 64 without paying any extra fees.

In 1977, Gates took a second leave of absence from Harvard, and in 1979, he moved Microsoft's headquarters to Bellevue, Washington (*https://oreil.ly/Xe85C*), near Seattle.

The story of MS-DOS (Microsoft Disk Operating System) is also legendary. Gates's mother, Mary Gates, was a member of United Way's board (*https://oreil.ly/bsq2M*), along with IBM chairman John Opel. In 1980, Opel mentioned IBM's need for an operating system for the personal computer they were developing. Mrs. Gates told Opel about her son's little business, and that family connection got Bill's foot in the door.

Gates probably learned from his parents how crucial it is for a wealthy person to cloak their exploitation by engaging in "philanthropy." In 1994, Gates founded (*https://oreil.ly/ym8R7*) the William H. Gates Foundation, renamed the Bill & Melinda Gates Foundation in 1999. The foundation's vaccine work was a backdoor for pharmaceutical companies to maintain intellectual property rights to vaccines, which made vaccines even less accessible in the developing world (*https://oreil.ly/BBZLa*), and played a major role in preventing developing countries from obtaining sufficient COVID vaccines. The foundation has also funded destructive changes to the US public education system (*https://oreil.ly/loe26*).

In 2000, Steve Ballmer (*https://oreil.ly/Thk8M*) took over from Gates as CEO, and for pretty much the entirety of the 21st century, Gates's official job has been running his foundation.

A few years ago, Gates got into a pretty massive scandal I won't detail here (you can look it up!). In May 2021, Melinda Gates divorced Bill; I suspect that the scandal I won't describe was a major factor. Gates gave a very awkward television interview (*https://oreil.ly/XepII*) in an attempt to save his image, and it did not go well. Ever since, he's been living very privately on his own island, Grand Bogue Caye in Belize (*https://oreil.ly/F6JPy*).

See also "Commodore" on page 53, "Crunch time" on page 60, "DOS (Disk Operating System)" on page 86, "Microsoft" on page 174, "Personal computers" on page 196, "Pirates of Silicon Valley (1999 film)" on page 202, "Proprietary software" on page 205, "Silicon Valley" on page 224

Gibson, William

See "Cyberpunk" on page 67

Git/GitHub

Git is the most popular version-control system. It was initially developed (*https://oreil.ly/ootYf*) by Linux creator Linus Torvalds in 2005.

Most applications are developed by more than one person. If one person makes a change to a script, another person makes another change, and those changes aren't synchronized, disaster can strike![1]

Git provides a platform for developers to keep track of all the changes they've made to all of the scripts in their applications, so everything's in sync. Torvalds understands the importance of version control because he pretty much pioneered coordinating open source application development between large groups of people.

GitHub (*https://oreil.ly/zYOPZ*), which is a way to deploy Git through a web interface, was founded by Chris Wanstrath, P. J. Hyett, Tom Preston-Werner, and Scott Chacon in 2007 and launched in 2008. Most open source applications these days use GitHub for development collaboration, and so do most hackers who do coding or application-development work.

In June 2018, Microsoft CEO Satya Nadella acquired GitHub, contradicting Gates and Ballmer's long-standing hostility to Linux and open source development.

See also "Linux" on page 161, "Microsoft" on page 174, "Programming" on page 204, "Torvalds, Linus" on page 246

GNOME

GNOME, first released in March 1999, is an open source desktop environment that can be used with a variety of Linux and UNIX-based operating systems. The name is originally an acronym for "GNU Network Object Model Environment." (It should not be confused with another similarly named 1990s operating system, the now-defunct GNO Multitasking Environment.) It is licensed under the GNU Public License (GPL).

GNOME is one of the most popular and widely supported desktop environments in the world of Linux operating systems, most notably vanilla Debian, Ubuntu, Red Hat Enterprise Linux, Fedora, Tails, and SUSE. In the UNIX world, it's usually used as the desktop environment for Solaris.

---

1 Ask my editor Sarah Grey how confused we were when we worked on the edits and revisions for the first batch of entries in this book. We both had multiple versions of the same core document with different edits! Then I said, "I'll just respond to your edits in Google Docs." That made our work much easier.

A desktop environment is the main user interface (UI) of a graphical operating system. It affects any fundamental application part of an operating system that can be clicked on with a mouse or tapped on with a touchscreen. It affects how windows are displayed, how menus are presented, what the desktop looks like overall, and even what the mouse cursor looks like.

The dominant commercial desktop operating systems today are Microsoft Windows and Apple's macOS. Microsoft and Apple computers use these proprietary desktop environments unless the user hacks their operating system to modify (or "mod") it with a different UI, which Microsoft and Apple discourage. In contrast, in the mainly open source world of Linux and UNIX, users are allowed and even encouraged to choose a desktop environment of their liking.

Anyone may make changes to GNOME or implement it in their own developed operating system free of charge, on the condition that the GPL is written somewhere in the comments of the source code, and that the full source code used and altered is also made open and freely available.

As of this writing, GNOME 42.3 is the most recent stable version, released in July 2022. There are no GNOME versions 4 through 39. GNOME 3.38 was succeeded by GNOME 40 in March 2021, ushering in a new numbering standard.

See also "Debian" on page 76, "Linux" on page 161,"Graphical user interface (GUI)" on page 117, "Open source" on page 189, "Proprietary software" on page 205, "UNIX" on page 253

GNU (software collection)

See "Emacs" on page 97, "Open source" on page 189, "Stallman, Richard" on page 229, "UNIX" on page 253

Go

See "Programming" on page 204

Goldstein, Emmanuel

See "2600 (Twenty-Six Hundred): The Hacker Quarterly (magazine)" on page 250

Google

Google is a tech giant that started as a search engine. Founded by Larry Page and Sergey Brin, it was a parentless corporation for most of its history, but has been the crown jewel of conglomerate Alphabet Inc. since its founding in October 2015.

In the 1990s, a number of different web search engines (*https://oreil.ly/ c_RzI*) competed for users, including Excite, AltaVista, Webcrawler, Lycos, and HotBot. Yahoo! was super popular, but it was technically a web directory, not a search engine, at the time. (Yahoo! provided users with actual web search using Google's search engine (*https://oreil.ly/vG4KH*) from 2000 to 2004, and then again from 2015 onward.)

They were at exactly the right place at the right time: Stanford University's computer science department in 1995, just as Silicon Valley was booming. Brin was tasked with showing Page around campus in 1995. They didn't get along well at first (*https://oreil.ly/Z4a3Y*), but started working together in 1996.

Page had a school project which initiated the research and development of what would become Google search. Page's bright idea (*https://oreil.ly/_Esf6*) was that web search could deliver more relevant results not only by looking for a search string in a web page's contents, but by augmenting a site's search-result relevance based on how frequently other web pages linked to it. Brin, who had more math expertise, collaborated with Page to implement his new PageRank algorithm into a new search engine, and in August 1996 they made a beta version of their search engine, originally named BackRub, available to students. Thankfully, before their search engine became popular, they renamed it Google (a misspelling of *googol*, which is a really massive number).

Sun Microsystems cofounder Andy Bechtolsheim, (*https://oreil.ly/8ZzC4*) seeing its potential, invested $100,000 in Google in 1998. Soon, friends, family, and other investors pitched in until Google had about $1 million. The company incorporated on September 4, 1998 (*https://oreil.ly/_Esf6*), and moved its operations to Susan Wojcicki's home garage. (Wojcicki eventually became the CEO of YouTube, a position she held until recently.)

Page and Brin were lucky in other ways: they launched a search engine before the 20th century ended and managed to acquire initial funding before the infamous dot-com bubble (*https://oreil.ly/sgbgj*) burst from about 2000 to 2002 (*https://oreil.ly/-4sBH*). In the late 1990s, lots of big-money investors, afraid of missing out, had impulsively poured billions into branded internet-based startups, most of which failed (that was the bust). Had Google incorporated during the bust or in the few years after, it may have never taken off. But Google survived the bust, indicating that its service and business model had staying power.

In 2001 (the middle of the bust), Page and Brin—both twenty-something computer-science students—recruited Eric Schmidt (*https://oreil.ly/_Esf6*), CTO of Sun Microsystems and CEO of Novell, to run Google. Brin self-deprecatingly referred to Schmidt's role as "adult supervision." Schmidt handed the Google CEO position (*https://oreil.ly/y9yTX*) to Larry Page in 2011, when I suppose Page finally considered himself to be an "adult."

In July 2003, Google moved into its famous Googleplex headquarters (*https://oreil.ly/_Esf6*) in Mountain View, California. In 2004, Google was handling 200 million (*https://oreil.ly/8ZzC4*) web searches a day. By 2011, that number was up to three billion.

Google has launched and acquired a tremendous number of products and services over the years. It has also retired quite a few. The website Killed By Google (*https://oreil.ly/ZTCfk*) (which is definitely *not* operated by Google) covers all of the products and services for which Google has dropped support, like the Stadia gaming platform, the Google+ social media platform, and Google Hangouts messaging.

But a few products and services that began in the 2000s are still strong today:

- Gmail launched in 2004 and is now the basis of user identifiers for the whole Google ecosystem.

- Google Maps launched in 2005 and quickly beat its competitors.

- Android was acquired by Google in 2005; the first Android phone, the HTC Dream, launched in 2008.

- YouTube was acquired by Google in 2006.

- Google Cloud Platform launched in 2008.

- Alphabet Inc. was created in 2015 as a conglomerate holding company for Google and some Google-adjacent businesses.

If I've left any details out of this entry, I trust that you can Google them.

See also "Alphabet Inc." on page 8, "Android operating system" on page 11, "Google Cloud Platform (GCP)" on page 117, "Page, Larry" on page 194, "Pirates of Silicon Valley (1999 film)" on page 202, "Silicon Valley" on page 224, "Smartphone" on page 226, "Stanford University" on page 230

Google Cloud Platform (GCP)

Google Cloud Platform (GCP) is, well, Google's cloud platform. (Out of all the major cloud platforms, Google wins the prize for most generic name!)

Two things made GCP's creation inevitable. The first was the 2006 launch of Amazon Web Services (AWS), which quickly became the standard bearer for how tech giants should provide services and infrastructure in the emerging cloud computing market. The second was the growth of Google's networking infrastructure, which was very large by the mid-2000s. Hot competition plus similar resources equals new market-sector entry.

The launch of App Engine in April 2008 was basically GCP's trial run (*https://oreil.ly/whZ7J*), though the GCP name wasn't being used yet. App Engine (*https://oreil.ly/TrBqm*) is still an important application in GCP's ecosystem, but it predates GCP as a whole, much like how Google predates its parent company Alphabet Inc. App Engine is a service that customers can use to deploy and run web applications on Google's infrastructure. And unlike the old-fashioned web-hosting providers of the 1990s, App Engine scales an app's data storage and bandwidth capacity as its usage grows. That's now the standard way cloud services work, but it was groundbreaking in 2008.

Today, GCP offers dozens of services and applications (*https://oreil.ly/WlgUh*); like its competitors AWS and Azure, it has lots of options for software as a service (SaaS), platform as a service (PaaS), and infrastructure as a service (IaaS).

See also "Amazon Web Services (AWS)" on page 8, "Azure" on page 28, "Cloud" on page 51, "Google" on page 114

Governance

See "Cybersecurity" on page 68

Graphical user interface (GUI)

The graphical user interface (GUI)[2] makes computing more accessible to the masses by representing what's happening in the computer graphically, so that users don't have to enter all commands through the command line. GUIs generally use input devices like a mouse or touchscreen.

---

2 Although hackers debate whether "GIF" (the image file format) should be pronounced with a hard G, as in "gift," or with a soft G, as in "giraffe," we've almost universally agreed that GUI should be pronounced "gooey." (For the record, GIF is pronounced as "jiff"!)

The command line in nearly all popular operating systems is a preferable way of doing things like searching for a string, *if* you can remember a bunch of commands and think like a computer programmer. But even the nerdiest nerds spend lots of time in GUI computer environments. Personal computers probably wouldn't have become popular if GUIs hadn't been invented.

The GUI and mouse have older origins than most people think. Vannevar Bush, as director of the US Office of Scientific Research and Development, conceptualized (*https://oreil.ly/lI6bp*) the GUI in 1945 (the year ENIAC was completed). In an essay titled "As We May Think," Bush also conceptualized hyperlinks and the web, theorizing that people would one day access the world's information through computer devices he called "memex," which would graphically present information with connections to other information.

Bush's essay inspired Douglas Engelbart (*https://oreil.ly/bTNO_*), who worked at the Stanford Research Institute and created the first computer mouse in 1964 as part of building the oN-Line System (NLS) for DARPA. NLS, which became public in 1968, was called the "Mother of All Demos." It had the very first functioning GUI, was networked to other computing devices, and supported document collaboration and hypertext links. It prefigured the Xerox Alto, Apple Macintosh, Tim Berners-Lee's World Wide Web, and Google Docs, all in one go.

In 1973, Xerox (fearing a paperless future) introduced its first personal computer prototype, the Xerox Alto. It had a mouse and a GUI-driven operating system.[3] The mouse cursor's position on the screen was represented by a bitmapped image that changed its X and Y axis positions as a user moved the mouse.

In 1979, during the early development of the Apple Lisa and Macintosh, Xerox offered Steve Jobs and other members of the Apple team a tour (*https://oreil.ly/CSdJX*) of its research and development—in exchange for $1 million in Apple stock. Jobs was blown away by the Alto and knew immediately that its user interface was the best kind for Apple's products. The Macintosh (*https://oreil.ly/eheni*), launched in 1984 also had a GUI operating system and a mouse.

Microsoft recruited Xerox PARC's Charles Simonyi and Scott MacGregor (*https://oreil.ly/9L886*) in 1981 and released its first GUI operating system, Windows 1.0, in 1985. By the early 1990s it had become obvious that GUIs and mice were the new computing paradigm.

---

3 Both the Xerox Alto and NLS also had keyboards, if you're curious.

See also "DARPA (Defense Advanced Research Projects Agency)" on page 72, "Jobs, Steve" on page 150, "Personal computers" on page 196, "Stanford University" on page 230, "World Wide Web" on page 268, "Xerox" on page 273

8

H

Hacker

When you opened this book, was your first thought, "I wonder what the 'hacker' entry says?" If so, kudos to you.[1]

Hacker is a word with a lot of baggage. Laypeople think hackers are the bad guys doing bad things to computers, often reading the word as a synonym for *cyberattacker, cybercriminal,* or *threat actor.* I blame the mainstream media for that misconception, given how often we see headlines like "Hackers break into Sony's private network" or "Hackers send ransomware to cookie factory." The organization Hacking Is Not a Crime (*https://oreil.ly/QoGFV*) promotes positive uses of the word *hacker,* while discouraging people from using it to mean *cyberattacker.*

But hackers are actually people who find innovative new uses of technology. Hacking can be reverse-engineering software and then inserting your own code. It can be combining a Raspberry Pi with your own custom software and robotics to make a sassy robot rodent that distracts your cat. Some of the earliest hackers were members of MIT's Tech Model Railroad Club in the 1960s, who found clever new ways to use their school's PDP-1 and TX-0 computers.[2] My earliest "hack," when I was about nine, was making my dad's Windows 3.1 OEM PC usable faster from boot by removing several lines in autoexec.bat using Notepad.

This book is dedicated to hacker culture: that is, notable hackers, their computers, and the phenomena, concepts, art, media, programs, organizations, political movements, and so on that surround them.

---

1 This entry is adapted from my essay, "What Do Ordinary People Think a Hacker Is?" published in the Winter 2014-2015 issue of 2600 magazine (*https://oreil.ly/JajFe*).

2 Steven Levy, *Hackers: Heroes of the Computer Revolution* (O'Reilly, 2010).

See also "Hacking Is Not a Crime" on page 124, "Massachusetts Institute of Technology (MIT)" on page 170, "Tech Model Railroad Club" on page 240

Hackers (1995 film)

"Hack the planet!"

Hackers, directed by Iain Softley, was released in 1995, when home internet use was expanding quickly. Its aesthetic included lots of metaphorical cyberspace dreamscapes. The feature-length film, Softley's second, starred Angelina Jolie as Kate "Acid Burn" Libby and Jonny Lee Miller as Dade "Crash Override" Murphy. (Miller and Jolie fell in love while making the movie.)

The film's fictional plot begins with 11-year-old hacker Dade Murphy crashing 1,507 computer systems, causing the New York Stock Exchange to drop by seven points. Dade is fined $45,000 and banned from using computers and telephones (see "Swartz, Aaron" on page 235, to understand why this fictional punishment is relatively lenient). At 18, however, he cyberattacks a local TV station so he can watch an episode of *The Outer Limits*.

In school, Murphy begins using the handles "Zero Cool" and "Crash Override" and meets fellow hackers "Acid Burn" (Jolie), Emmanuel "Cereal Killer" Goldstein (Matthew Lillard), Paul "Lord Nikon" Cook (Laurence Mason), Ramón "The Phantom Phreak" Sánchez (Renoly Santiago), and Joey Pardella (Jesse Bradford). They get up to some l33t hijinks, and "their crime is curiosity."

Joey tries to prove his skills to the group by breaking into "The Gibson," a big corporation's supercomputer, gets into a fast-typing hacking battle with a Secret Service agent, and steals a file of what appears to be garbage code. Former hacker Eugene "The Plague" Belford, who had previously hacked the Gibson, realizes that the file Joey stole is one he had loaded: a worm designed to steal money from the corporation. The worm also contains the code to the "Da Vinci" computer virus, capable of doing great damage to the corporation's fleet of oil tankers.[3]

Joey gets caught, arrested, and released on bail, but he manages to hide a floppy disk containing the virus from law enforcement. Through a series of adventures, the hackers manage to keep the disk away from the Secret Service and expose "The Plague" as the author of the malware. "The Plague" is arrested and the hackers get to live freely.

---

3 The terms *virus* and *worm* describe types of malware that spread through computer systems in different ways. See the individual entries for those terms.

Although the film doesn't depict cyberexploitation with much technological accuracy, the spirit of hacker culture is all there: knowledge should be free, hack the planet, and don't trust the suits or the cops!

See also "Hacker" on page 121, "Swartz, Aaron" on page 235

Hackers: Heroes of the Computer Revolution (2010 book)

If you haven't read Steven Levy's *Hackers: Heroes of the Computer Revolution* (*https://oreil.ly/5pgrM*) (O'Reilly, 2010), you really ought to. Levy's writing has played a crucial role in our understanding of hacker culture and the impact that computer technology has on our lives. He's the editor at large (*https://oreil.ly/bLoMf*) for *WIRED* magazine and has written several books. (*https://oreil.ly/5RA_g*) *Hackers* was first published in 1984 and has since had multiple editions, most recently from O'Reilly Media (*https://oreil.ly/5pgrM*).

Hackers starts with MIT's Tech Model Railroad Club, the birthplace of hackerdom, and covers various interesting historical tidbits like the computer book publisher Dymax, the Altair 8800, the Homebrew Computer Club, and the fascinating story of BASIC. Its subject matter overlaps with this book, but Levy shares a lot of details you won't find here.

In an interview, Levy explained to me what inspired him in 1981 to write *Hackers*:

> The idea came from Jane Fonda's movie production company, which was giving ideas to writers, who would then write stories and option them for a possible movie. I did the story for **Rolling Stone** and was blown away by the hacking culture and the energy of the West Coast personal computer industry. I decided to keep writing about those subjects.

In fact, Levy was the first journalist to write about many of these topics. Take the Tech Model Railroad Club:

> As far as I know, not a single word in a general-interest publication was devoted to this before **Hackers**. My original plan was to have two sections—one about Homebrew Computer Club and the PC revolution, and the other about the game hackers. But as I researched it...I realized how important the MIT hackers were.... Every interview I did was pretty much the first time my subject had spoken to a journalist.

See also "Hacker" on page 121, "Hackers (1995 film)" on page 122, "Hacktivism" on page 125, "Homebrew Computer Club" on page 136, "Massachusetts Institute of Technology (MIT)" on page 170, "Tech Model Railroad Club" on page 240

Hackers on Planet Earth (HOPE)

Hackers on Planet Earth (*https://oreil.ly/3N7R7*) (HOPE) is a hacker conference founded in 1994 and run every other year by 2600 magazine founder Eric Corley (under the pseudonym Emmanuel Goldstein). It's full of hackers talking about hacking, digital rights, and cybersecurity. The 2008 conference included talks by Steven Levy, Kevin Mitnick, Steve Rambam, Jello Biafra, and Adam Savage.

However, 2018 was an embarrassing year for HOPE. "The conference is a magnet for anti-authoritarians of all stripes, a place where ACAB, not MAGA, is the four letter acronym *du jour*. If someone is brash enough to not only wear Trump gear to HOPE, but to harass and intimidate other attendees, they can expect to be expelled from the conference," *VICE* reported (*https://oreil.ly/ofOLd*). But that wasn't the case in 2018, "when an attendee wearing a MAGA hat who described himself as a 'nationalist' and said he marched at Unite the Right wasn't immediately removed." These sorts of controversies demonstrate that there are a lot of political differences among people who support hacker values (or at least say they do).

See also "Hacker" on page 121, "Hacktivism" on page 125, "Mitnick, Kevin" on page 177

Hacking Is Not a Crime

Hacking Is Not a Crime is a nonprofit organization dedicated to decriminalizing hacking and promoting positive media depictions of the hacker community. It discourages laypeople from using the term *hacker* to describe people who engage in cybercrime, arguing in its mission statement (*https://oreil.ly/4aPNb*) that such negative "stereotypes and narratives influenc[e] public opinion and legislation that create a pretext for censorship, surveillance, and prosecution."

Instead, the organization recommends using *hackers, researchers,* and *hacktivists* to describe those who perform positive acts, and calling the people who do harm *cybercriminals* or *threat actors.* It also discourages use of the terms *white hat* and *black hat.*

The organization is also affiliated with the Electronic Frontier Foundation, DEF CON, Amnesty International, and Citizen Lab (*https://oreil.ly/xPi2q*). Its members are a collective of people who work in cybersecurity and influential people in the hacking community, including Wirefall, Ted James, Filipi Pires, Lily Clark, and myself (*https://oreil.ly/xPi2q*).

See also "DEF CON" on page 80, "Hacker" on page 121, "Hacktivism" on page 125, "Whitehat hackers" on page 265

Hack the Box

See "Capture the Flag" on page 42, "Certificates (professional credentials)" on page 46, ""Ethical" hacking" on page 100, "Penetration testing" on page 196, "Ramachandran, Vivek" on page 210

Hacktivism

Hacktivism is the act of breaking computer technology for political reasons. Most cybercrime is motivated by profit, but hacktivists intend to break technology to make the world a better place (at least from their perspective). The word is a portmanteau of *hacking* and *activism*. A classic example of hacktivism would be an animal-rights activist vandalizing an online fur retailer's website to display the message "Fur is murder!"

Whether you think hacktivism is good or bad is entirely dependent on your political worldview. It generally isn't lawful. Let's look at two real stories of hacktivist actions.

In 2011, the hacktivist group LulzSec attacked the massive Sony corporation with two major data breaches. First it stole sensitive data from the PlayStation Network, one of the most popular video game services, including the usernames, passwords, credit card information, and home addresses of 77 million users. Then it targeted Sony Pictures for an even larger breach. In a statement, LulzSec said: "From a single [SQL] injection, we accessed EVERYTHING. Why do you put such faith in a company that allows itself to become open to these simple attacks?" Their political message was... "Hey, consumers, don't trust Sony"?

In 2008, the gossip site Gawker leaked an internal Church of Scientology video featuring Tom Cruise that many people found creepy. When the Church of Scientology sent Gawker a cease-and-desist letter, outraged members of the hacktivist group Anonymous decided to respond. They uploaded a video to YouTube titled "Message to Scientology" that featured an anonymized presenter wearing the Guy Fawkes mask (the symbol of Anonymous). Over the weeks and months that followed, Anonymous members held street protests in dozens of cities. Their campaign against Scientology included actions as simple as prank calls and as sophisticated as distributed denial-of-service attacks against Scientology websites. They also sent "black faxes" consisting of completely black pages, forcing the receiving fax machine to waste ink, time, and paper.

See also "Anonymous" on page 12, "Cult of the Dead Cow (cDc)" on page 66, "Denial-of-service (DoS, DDoS) attacks" on page 81, "Hacking Is Not a Crime" on page 124, "Invisible Internet Project (I2P)" on page 147, "Pirate Bay/Pirate Party" on page 202, "Snowden, Edward" on page 227, "Swartz, Aaron" on page 235, "WikiLeaks" on page 266

Hak5

Hackers love gadgets. But making your own electronic gadgets is a lot of work, even if you know how to do it, you can write custom code to firmware, and you have a RadioShack nearby.

Since 2005, Hak5 (*https://oreil.ly/sosHO*) has made a variety of devices that are useful to penetration testers and other hackers who want to test the security of their own computers and networks. Yes, they can also be used to engage in cybercrime—but the knives in your kitchen are also dangerous weapons in the wrong hands.

Here are some examples of Hak5's product line as of early 2023:

Shark Jack
> A cigarette-lighter-sized device that can physically plug into an Ethernet wall outlet. With the data it sends, you can identify the network transmissions and identifiers (such as IP addresses) that go through the outlet, and even simulate man-in-the-middle attacks with the right scripting.

Wifi Pineapple
> Looks like an ordinary wireless router, with three antennas, but it provides information about WiFi networks in its range and can be used for pentesting, including simulating man-in-the-middle attacks.

Bash Bunny
> A small device with a USB-A plug that you can plug into a computer to perform pentests with custom scripts.

See also "Cybersecurity" on page 68, "Penetration testing" on page 196

Ham radio

Ham radio is often called amateur radio, and amateur radio hobbyists sometimes call ourselves "hams."

There is considerable overlap between hams and hackers. Both hobbies/ disciplines require an enthusiasm for mastering technicalities and exploring new and innovative ways of using technology. It's also possible to transmit data packets over amateur radio frequencies, and to use computer hardware and software in an amateur radio station. Anyone with the right equipment in the right area can listen to any amateur radio broadcast! Nothing is private on ham radio.

The International Telecommunication Union (ITU) (*https://oreil.ly/8C27Q*) regulates and standardizes amateur radio around the world. You need an amateur radio license to lawfully broadcast amateur radio, but anyone may listen without a license. If data packets or any other sort of messages sent through amateur radio are encrypted, the decryption cipher must be publicly available. All licensed operators have call signs, which they must communicate by speech or Morse code, and must stay within the particular radio frequency band ranges reserved for them. Commercial use, such as advertising, is strictly forbidden, and discussing political or otherwise controversial matters is strongly discouraged. (Other designated frequency ranges include communications for emergency services, police, military, and meteorologists; nautical and aviation communications; commercial AM/FM radio and television; wireless computer networking; radio-controlled toys, models, and drones; CB radio and "walkie-talkies"; and shortwave commercial and military communications.

See also "Morse code" on page 180

Hardware

Before computers became commonplace, hardware generally referred to nails, wrenches, power tools, and the like. In the tech world, though, *hardware* refers to the physical objects involved in computing: like laptops, server towers, rackmount servers, supercomputers, smartphones and tablets, Internet of Things devices, and video game consoles. That includes the physical components of computers (motherboards, CPUs, memory cards, cooling fans), peripherals (mice, keyboards, printers, video game controllers, headphones), and physical data storage (hard drives, SD cards, and so on). By contrast, *software* refers to computer code and things made with computer code that our computers run.

Software gives our hardware a purpose, and hardware gives our software something to physically exist in. Hardware and software meet directly in the firmware that makes hardware operational, and the drivers that make it possible for an operating system to use hardware.

Some hackers prefer to tinker with hardware. They'll take out the devices plugged into a motherboard and then put a whole new set of devices in. That's called *hardware hacking*, not to be confused with software hacking.

See also "CPU (Central processing unit)" on page 57, "Electronics" on page 95, "Floppy disk" on page 105, "Form factor" on page 106, "Robotics" on page 216, "Smartphone" on page 226

Hellman, Martin

Martin Hellman (*https://oreil.ly/8NgwJ*) (1945–) is a professor emeritus at Stanford University, the Hellman in the Diffie-Hellman key exchange, and a 2015 Turing Award (*https://oreil.ly/dKkHR*) laureate. Public-key cryptography is essential to implementing encrypted data in transit on the internet and other computer networks. The Diffie-Hellman key exchange protects the transmission of encryption and decryption keys between two computers through a computer network to implement public-key cryptography.

I asked Hellman what would happen if the public-key exchange didn't exist. "If public-key exchange did not exist, we'd probably be using KDCs (key distribution centers)."

Hellman recognized the brilliance of Ralph Merkle's ideas. Merkle's paper "1974 CS244 Project Proposal" (*https://oreil.ly/nL7JK*), though rejected by his university, inspired Diffie and Hellman's key exchange. The two collaborated on other things (like this 1978 paper, "Hiding Information and Signatures in Trapdoor Knapsacks" (*https://oreil.ly/QIuf8*)). Hellman has always made sure that Merkle gets credit for his help in making their key exchange possible.

I asked Hellman about the significance of Merkle's puzzles.

Ralph Merkle's puzzle method was a "proof of concept" but not usable in practice, particularly in the 1970s and 1980s when communication was so expensive. While it has an n^2 to n work factor, the "n" is as much in communication as computation. If all of the "n" had been in computation, it might have been usable. Merkle's puzzles didn't figure directly in the invention of what is now usually called Diffie-Hellman key exchange, but I was trying to find a public-key cryptosystem (a concept that Whit and I had developed, and he first started it) and instead found a Merkle public-key distribution system. That surprised me, but worked. (It sounds like you know what both of those are, but if not, they are explained in "New Directions" (https://oreil.ly/DzUGE), which is searchable.)

The National Security Agency (NSA) wanted to classify the key exchange (*https://oreil.ly/y8yud*), but Hellman fought hard to make cryptography research available to the public. There was tension between Hellman and the NSA for years because of Hellman's hacker ethos of "knowledge should be free."

One of Hellman's current projects, called "Rethinking National Security" (*https://oreil.ly/MVKU8*), asks: "In this age of nuclear weapons, pandemics, cyberattacks, terrorism, and environmental crises, is national security becoming inseparable from global security? If so, how do our current policies need to change?"

Another project, and perhaps one of Hellman's most intriguing works, is *A New Map for Relationships: Creating True Love at Home and Peace on the Planet* (*https://oreil.ly/oJroq*), a love advice book written in collaboration with his wife Dorothie.

See also "Cryptography" on page 63, "Diffie-Hellman key exchange" on page 84, "Key" on page 156, "Rivest-Shamir-Adleman (RSA) cryptography" on page 215, "Stanford University" on page 230, "Turing, Alan" on page 248

Hello World

The function of a Hello World script is to print the words "Hello World" onto the screen. There's a long tradition of using these scripts to introduce new learners to programming languages. Pretty much every entry-level computer programming-language guide contains an example Hello World script. They show the language's correct syntax and how to use basic functions and text strings. Programmers also use Hello World scripts to test if a programming language works—for example, in an IDE, runtime environment, command line, or text editor.

One of the earliest examples of a Hello World script appears in Bell Laboratories' 1974 documentation for the language C, written by Brian Kernighan:

```
main( ) {
        printf("hello, world");
}
```

Here are a few examples of Hello World scripts in popular programming languages.

BASIC:

```
10 PRINT "Hello, World!"
```

Go:

```
package main
import "fmt"

func main() {
    fmt.Println("Hello, World!")
}
```

Java:

```
public class Main {
  public static void main(String[] args) {
    System.out.println("Hello, World!");
```

```
    }
}
```

HTML 5:

```
<!DOCTYPE html>
<html>
    <head>
        <!-- header content here -->
    </head>
    <body>
        Hello, world!
    </body>
</html>
```

x86 CPU architecture assembly languages:

```
SECTION .data
Msg: db "Hello world!", 10
Len: equ $-Msg

SECTION .text
global _start
_start:
    mov eax,4
    mov ebx,1
    mov ecx,Msg
    mov edx,Len
    int 80H

    mov eax,1
    mov ebx,0
    int 80H
```

See also "Bell Labs" on page 31, "Programming" on page 204, "Syntax" on page 236

Hewlett-Packard (HP)

Hewlett-Packard is the mother of all Silicon Valley startups. It originated many of the startup tropes: starting out in a garage, Stanford students, Palo Alto address, boundless optimism, military contracts. Some of the tech companies in this book are as powerful as they've ever been; others started with a bang and then faded away. As of 2023, HP's legacy is now two corporations, HP Inc. and Hewlett-Packard Enterprise, with much more complicated histories.

In the 1930s, Bill Hewlett (1912–2001) and David Packard (*https://oreil.ly/ J9JIT*) (1912–1996) were electrical engineering graduate students and football players at Stanford University. In 1934, they agreed to start a business together. They weren't exactly sure what their first product would be, but they knew it'd have something to do with electronics. Packard spent four years working for General Electric (GE) and learning about the emerging tech industry, and in 1938 took a leave of absence from GE and returned to Palo Alto to get serious about his shared aspirations with Hewlett. It was probably the very first time a Silicon Valley startup began in a garage: at 367 Addison Avenue in Palo Alto.[4]

Hewlett and Packard's first invention was the HP Model 200A oscillator, used to test sound equipment (*https://oreil.ly/FYmEO*). In their first business deal, Disney's 1940 animated feature *Fantasia* (*https://oreil.ly/esiHI*) used eight brand-new HP oscillators (*https://oreil.ly/yuwl3*) to make its musical score sound as good as possible. The Hewlett-Packard Company (*https://oreil.ly/-yxaC*) was officially born, and the oscillator helped to finance its move from the garage to a rented commercial space. Soon, the US Department of Defense (*https://oreil.ly/1CeYz*) was buying oscillators, wave analyzers, voltmeters (*https://oreil.ly/7Uooo*) and other electronic components for the war effort. Hewlett-Packard diversified its customer base in 1951 by introducing a high-speed frequency counter for the booming FM radio and television broadcasting industry (*https://oreil.ly/1CeYz*). Not long after that, in 1957, Hewlett-Packard made its public stock offering.

Throughout the 1950s and 1960s, Hewlett-Packard made a wide variety of industrial electronic devices and components for the public and private sectors. The United States' postwar global dominance helped the company open a factory in West Germany and start a joint business venture in Japan. Hewlett-Packard wasn't hesitant to work with Japanese technologists, unlike other American tech companies at the time, and benefited from their ingenuity.

IBM and Digital Equipment Corporation already had a foothold in the new computer industry, now driven by transistors and integrated circuits. By 1966, Hewlett-Packard was ready to enter that market with its HP 2100/1000 (*https://oreil.ly/3OOij*) line of minicomputers (which were about the size of a refrigerator). Its 1968 9100A Desktop Calculator (*https://oreil.ly/yz10X*) is considered the first personal computer and the first programmable scientific desktop calculator.

In 1976, Hewlett-Packard was looking for a way to enter the promising new home computer market. An engineering intern named Steve Wozniak (*https://oreil.ly/1CeYz*) showed his bosses a prototype of his personal computer, but they

---

4 Hewlett came from a rich family, refuting the popular myth that poor ordinary folks can become rich by "starting in a garage." See Malcolm Harris, *Palo Alto: A History of California, Capitalism, and the World* (Little, Brown, 2023).

turned him down. This encouraged Wozniak and his friend Steve Jobs to start Apple Computer, using the same prototype in the development of their first product, the Apple I.

Perhaps realizing this mistake, Hewlett-Packard created a Personal Computer Operation research and development department (*https://oreil.ly/ndPsf*), which in 1980 produced the HP-85 personal computer (*https://oreil.ly/IsdQJ*). It had a horizontal all-in-one form factor with a tiny screen built into the left-hand side, ran Microsoft's BASIC, and featured HP's proprietary Capricorn CPU. Soon after, 1983's HP-150 touchscreen (*https://oreil.ly/PueoA*) (cool!) personal computer came with MS-DOS preinstalled. (Perhaps they understood that the future of non-Apple personal computing lay in Microsoft.) The HP Pavilion "multimedia" personal computer line launched in 1995 with the HP Pavilion 5030 (*https://oreil.ly/RSAW8*), featuring the much hyped Windows 95, and the Pavilion line stayed strong until the mid-2000s.The 1980s also saw Hewlett-Packard rapidly expand into the home and small business printing market.

In 2001, not long after Hewlett and Packard died, Hewlett-Packard was under the leadership of future Republican presidential candidate Carly Fiorina. HP acquired computing giant Compaq (*https://oreil.ly/ndPsf*) for a whopping $25 billion and laid off about 15,000 workers (*https://oreil.ly/zgiik*). The company did its best to integrate the HP and Compaq product lines through the 2000s, but it was an awkward period. The Compaq brand had pretty much disappeared by 2013, and the quality of HP's consumer products was decreasing. (Around that time, my former partner and I acquired a relatively new HP laptop, and we were stunned to discover that its Intel x86 series CPU had no proper CPU fan.)

In 2014, HP would split in two: HP Inc. would focus on consumer PCs and printers, and Hewlett-Packard Enterprise would be dedicated to enterprise products. I think HP will continue to have an important foothold in the tech industry, but its glory days are behind it.

See also "Apple" on page 13, "IBM" on page 139, "Jobs, Steve" on page 150, "Silicon Valley" on page 224, "Stanford University" on page 230, "Wozniak, Steve" on page 269

Hexadecimal numbering

The most fundamental numbering system that computers use is binary—a base 2 system, where all numbers and values are based on combinations of 1 and 0. That's the form of data that's directly processed by the CPU. Hexadecimal is a base 16 numbering system (*https://oreil.ly/jonKk*) that computers often use one step before data is converted into binary. (The Arabic 0–9 numeral system we use most often in our everyday lives is base 10.)

Computers use hexadecimal numbers in many ways (*https://oreil.ly/mjX9C*), including:

- To write media access control (MAC) addresses, unique identifiers for devices that connect to the internet and other computer networks.

- To represent specific colors as hexadecimal codes in applications and development.

- In much of the low-level machine language (*https://oreil.ly/IRzHI*) computers use, such as Klein Computer 85's machine code (*https://oreil.ly/bUawa*).

- In hex editors (*https://oreil.ly/OcKUM*), programs that can open any kind of file and convert its data into hexadecimal code—frequently used for ROM hacking, or modifying ROM files of video games, and to find data hidden in files.

See also "Assembly" on page 20, "Binary" on page 35, "CPU (Central processing unit)" on page 57

Hidden Figures (2017 film)

The 2017 film *Hidden Figures* (*https://oreil.ly/sqEoX*), directed by Theodore Melfi and written by Melfi and Allison Schroeder, tells the story of three Black female hackers who worked for NASA—Katherine Johnson, Dorothy Vaughan, and Mary Jackson. The movie is based on Margot Lee Shetterly's nonfiction book *Hidden Figures: The American Dream and the Untold Story of the Black Women Mathematicians Who Helped Win the Space Race* (William Morrow, 2016).

Johnson and Vaughan were mathematicians, and Jackson was the very first female African-American engineer to work for NASA (*https://oreil.ly/gZYIK*).

Katherine Coleman Johnson (1918–2020) was such an intelligent (*https://oreil.ly/S2Msl*) child that she skipped ahead several grades in school. She began working as a math teacher in 1937, and briefly attended a newly desegregated West Virginia University as one of only three Black women graduate students. She worked as a human "computer" through the 1950s at the National Advisory Committee for Aeronautics (NACA), which became the National Aeronautics and Space Administration (NASA) in 1958. Her math equations were used in the Notes on Space Technology compendium (*https://oreil.ly/KlXD1*), which was part of a space technology course given at the Flight Research Division of the NACA Langley Aeronautical Laboratory in 1958. She conducted trajectory analysis for two early NASA missions, Alan Shepard's in 1961 and John Glenn's in 1962, as well as the 1969 Apollo 11 moon mission, and was responsible for bringing the crew of the aborted Apollo 13 moon mission home safely. She is played in the film by Taraji P. Henson.

Dorothy Vaughan (1910–2008) originally worked as a math teacher in Virginia. She joined the Langley Memorial Aeronautical Laboratory in 1943, where she did intense mathematical work to help the US war effort. After World War II, Vaughan joined Johnson at NACA and became its first Black supervisor. After NACA became NASA, she helped the Scout rocket launch satellites into Earth's orbit, and became known as a brilliant FORTRAN programmer. She is played by Octavia Spencer in the film.

Mary Jackson (1921–2005) was also from Virginia. Jackson earned her bachelor's degree in science from the Hampton Institute in Mathematics and Physical Science (now part of Hampton University) and went on to join NACA. There, she was one of the "human computers" in the all-Black West Area Computing section. Her work was integral to many of NACA and NASA's wind tunnel research and flight experiments. She is portrayed in the film by Janelle Monáe.

In a better world, Johnson, Vaughan, and Jackson would be as famous as Buzz Aldrin and Neil Armstrong. In my opinion, they were at least as crucial to NASA's success in the 20th century.

Homebrew Computer Club

Personal computing wouldn't be where it is today if it weren't for the Homebrew Computer Club. From the club's first meeting in March 1975 to its last in December 1986, it hosted legendary events in hacker culture.

The club mostly met in Menlo Park, California, the heart of Silicon Valley. Computer hobbyists and hackers Gordon French and Fred Moore used the first meeting to show off one of the earliest microcomputers, the groundbreaking Altair 8800, just two months after its release. Before microcomputers, computers ranged from the size of a refrigerator to taking up multiple rooms, so the Altair made hobbyists hopeful that computers could finally be used in homes and small offices. A cover feature in *Popular Electronics* magazine added to the buzz.

The Homebrew Computer Club's members were a "who's who" of the personal computer revolution of the 1970s—Apple founders Steve Jobs and Steve Wozniak, John "Captain Crunch" Draper, video game cartridge inventor Jerry Lawson, Osborne Computer's Adam Osborne, and educational computing pioneer Liza Loop (the club's first female member). In fact, Jobs and Wozniak got the idea to start Apple at the Homebrew Computer Club, and they debuted the first prototype of the Apple I (built by Wozniak) at a 1976 club meeting. The club's newsletter ran for 21 issues, from March 1975 to December 1977, and (in my opinion) was likely the inspiration for 2600 magazine.

See also "Apple" on page 13, "Captain Crunch (John Draper)" on page 41, "Jobs, Steve" on page 150, "Lawson, Jerry" on page 160, "Silicon Valley" on page 224, "Wozniak, Steve" on page 269, "2600 (Twenty-Six Hundred): The Hacker Quarterly (magazine)" on page 250

Hopper, Grace

Rear Admiral Grace Brewster Murray Hopper (1906–1992) was arguably the most revolutionary computer programmer in history. She was a technological innovator, a bold risk-taker, a glass-ceiling breaker, and a hacker par excellence, years before being a hacker was officially a thing. Hopper grew up privileged (*https://oreil.ly/OFNWn*) in a wealthy New York City family, but definitely didn't choose a *Great Gatsby* life.

She graduated from Vassar College in 1928 and earned her mathematics PhD at Yale in 1934. As the US joined World War II in the early 1940s, she was teaching at Vassar. Hopper enrolled in the US Navy's Women's Reserve in 1943. There she worked with one of the last great pre-ENIAC electromechanical computers, IBM's Mark I (*https://oreil.ly/A62b9*), and even wrote its 561-page user manual, considered (*https://oreil.ly/XloOa*) the "first extensive treatment of how to program a computer."

In computer programming, a *compiler* converts higher-level code into machine-readable code. Higher-level programming languages make it easier to create computer programs and for different machines to run the same program. Hopper invented the very first compiler (A-O, in 1949) and coined the term. She followed that with B-O, otherwise known as "Flow-Matic," the first English-language data-processing compiler, used in 1956 for the groundbreaking UNIVAC I and II computers.

While working in the private sector, Hopper was tasked with creating a new standardized programming language that could adapt to how rapidly computers were evolving. She created COBOL, based on her Flow-Matic work, in 1959.

Hopper was passionate about making computer programming more accessible to everyone. As she said in a 1980 interview (*https://oreil.ly/27E87*): "What I was after in beginning English language (programming) was to bring another whole group of people able to use the computer easily... I kept calling for more user friendly languages. Most of the stuff we get from academicians, computer science people, is in no way adapted to people."

In 1966, the Navy forced Hopper to retire; she called it the saddest day of her life. But just seven months later, the Navy practically begged her to rejoin: they needed her help to standardize their multiple compiler languages. She remained in active duty for another 19 years.

As the 20th century's pioneering computer programmer and inventor of the compiler, Hopper's life was full of medals and honorary degrees including the National Medal of Technology in 1991 as well as a posthumous 2016 Presidential Medal of Freedom. She has a Navy missile destroyer and a college at Yale named for her. But what she said she was most proud of was "all the young people I've trained over the years; that's more important than writing the first compiler."

See also "ENIAC (Electronic Numerical Integrator and Computer)" on page 98, "IBM" on page 139, "Programming" on page 204

HTML (HyperText Markup Language)

See "Programming" on page 204, "World Wide Web" on page 268

|

9

IBM

International Business Machines (IBM) is one of the most important corporations in the history of computing, with roots that predate the advent of electronic computers.

In 1889, Harlow Bundy founded Bundy Manufacturing Company, the first manufacturer of time clocks for shift workers. By 1900, it had evolved into the International Time Recording Company (*https://oreil.ly/qayeK*). In 1896, Herman Hollerith founded Tabulating Machine Company, which made mechanical devices for accounting and sold the New York Central Railroad "punched card" equipment for processing waybills. They merged to form the Computing-Tabulating-Recording Company (*https://oreil.ly/QxMD_*) in 1911.

Thomas J. Watson (*https://oreil.ly/pJlBQ*) became the general manager in 1914, but didn't like the name of the company very much. In 1924, he renamed the company's US and international operations to match the name of its Canadian operation: International Business Machines.

IBM got into computing in 1944 with a groundbreaking pre-electronic computer called the Automatic Sequence Controlled Calculator, or Mark I (*https://oreil.ly/VkDr8*), developed from years of research coordinated with Harvard University. It was a massive beast—and the first machine that could execute long computations automatically. (Its equally massive manual was written by none other than Grace Hopper!)

IBM's first properly electronic computer was the IBM 701 in 1952. ENIAC had proved the computational potential of vacuum tubes, and the 701 was full of them! The 1953 IBM 650 (*https://oreil.ly/e91WW*) Magnetic Drum Calculator became the most commercially successful computer of the 1950s (which meant that institutions used them). IBM also developed a major scientific programming language, FORTRAN, in 1957.

The System/360 (*https://oreil.ly/x-jd_*) line of computers, launched in 1964, brought the new ability to swap peripherals and software between computers, and IBM in the 1970s (*https://oreil.ly/1eVmF*) was defined by floppy disks (which they introduced in 1971), and the apex of minicomputers.

By the late 1970s, the personal computer revolution was well underway. IBM had always been focused on business customers, by its very name, but there was plenty of industry pressure for IBM to produce a consumer product.

Atari representatives (*https://oreil.ly/v_gfs*) proposed to design and build IBM's first PC for them. IBM chairman Frank Cary took the proposal seriously, as did Director of Entry Systems Bill Lowe, but IBM's management committee reportedly declared the proposal to be "the dumbest thing we've ever heard of." IBM's corporate culture had a reputation for conservative decision-making and bureaucracy—a potential liability when entering the innovative new PC industry. But some executives within IBM's dense corporate structure were open-minded about PCs, and with Cary's support, the management committee agreed to let Lowe form his own team within IBM to draft a new PC proposal—without Atari.

Lowe kept his internal IBM team small to replicate the way the newer PC upstarts did business. And in July 1980, IBM Head of Software Development Jack Sams contacted Microsoft about making an operating system to run on the IBM PC platform. They'd use the well-supported Intel 8088 CPU (*https://oreil.ly/wVdds*), and Microsoft would make a custom version of Seattle Computer Products' 86-DOS (*https://oreil.ly/YIype*), since IBM didn't give them enough time to develop something more original. That became Microsoft's first OS, released on the first IBM PC as PC-DOS but eventually renamed MS-DOS.

Microsoft worked out a clever deal with IBM that let them sell MS-DOS (*https://oreil.ly/hylIV*) to IBM's competitors. IBM was certain that the BIOS in the IBM PC would make it impossible to clone—about which they were famously wrong. Accidentally giving Microsoft control of the PC market was one of IBM's biggest mistakes. Windows 1.0 launched in 1985, and the rest was history. The consumer market was not IBM's forte, and it sold its PC division to Lenovo (*https://oreil.ly/YYWpr*) in 2005.

IBM's much prouder moments in recent decades have been in the realm of cutting-edge enterprise and scientific research computing (*https://oreil.ly/PkjJu*) —back to its roots, so to speak. IBM's Deep Blue (*https://oreil.ly/NkLYK*) supercomputer beat human chess champion Garry Kasparov in 1997. In 1998 the company launched Blue Pacific, the world's fastest computer at the time. It announced Linux for its System/390 mainframe line in 2000, and IBM's z/Architecture (*https://oreil.ly/_Yd2v*) line has dominated the mainframe market since. And in 2008, the Blue Gene supercomputer built on the foundation laid by Deep Blue.

IBM is known as "Big Blue" (*https://oreil.ly/nZYAs*). And Big Blue is now big where it's destined to be: in the world of big computers.

See also "Atari" on page 22, "CPU (Central processing unit)" on page 57, "DOS (Disk Operating System)" on page 86, "ENIAC (Electronic Numerical Integrator and Computer)" on page 98, "Floppy disk" on page 105, "Hopper, Grace" on page 137, "Intel" on page 144, "Microsoft" on page 174, "Personal computers" on page 196, "Supercomputers" on page 233

Indian Institute of Engineering Science and Technology (IIEST); Indian Institutes of Technology (IIT)

India is the second most populous nation on earth, and this entry looks at two of its most important technical school systems: the Indian Institute of Engineering Science and Technology (*https://www.iiests.ac.in*) (IIEST) Shibpur and the Indian Institutes of Technology (*https://oreil.ly/NGpa9*) (IIT).

IIEST is in Howrah in the eastern Indian state of West Bengal, not far from the India-Bangladesh border. Many of the brightest hackers in India's technology sector have been students and faculty there. It became Bengal Engineering College in 1857, under the rule of the British Empire, and the school has thrived in the decades since India's 1947 liberation.

One of IIEST's most famous alumni (*https://oreil.ly/DOM8-*) is Dr. Bimal Kumar Bose (*https://oreil.ly/ddvf9*), a prominent electrical engineer and artificial intelligence researcher. Most recently, he's worked as a professor at the University of Tennessee and as a member of the National Academy of Engineering, both in the United States.

Indian Institutes of Technology (*https://oreil.ly/NGpa9*) (IIT) is a collection of top technical schools, with 23 campuses all over India. Its origins date back to the establishment of IIT Kharagpur in West Bengal in 1950. As of 2022, the top-ranking IIT schools are IIT Madras, IIT Bombay, IIT Delhi, IIT Kanpur, and IIT Kharagpur.

Some of the IIT alumni most relevant to hacker culture include:

Sundar Pichai (https://oreil.ly/OSj8y)
> Alphabet Inc. and Google CEO (IIT Kharagpur)

Prith Banerjee (https://oreil.ly/eIFZw)
> Former HP Labs director (IIT Kharagpur)

Pranav Mistry (https://oreil.ly/A3ABh)
> Former Samsung Technology and Advanced Research Labs president (IIT Bombay)

Deepak B. Phatak (https://oreil.ly/IMltY)
> Smartcard technology innovator and computer scientist (IIT Bombay)

Pradeep Sindhu (https://oreil.ly/iV9do)
> Juniper Networks cofounder (IIT Kanpur)

Rajeev Motwani (https://oreil.ly/_3MZm)
> The late Stanford computer science professor (IIT Kanpur)

Abhay Bhushan (https://oreil.ly/gCOBF)
> File Transfer Protocol inventor (IIT Kanpur)

Jaishankar Menon (https://oreil.ly/JyNK6)
> IBM researcher and Redundant Array of Independent Disks developer (IIT Madras)

Vivek Ramachandran
> Pentester Academy founder and WiFi security expert (IIT Guwahati)

Krishna Bharat (https://oreil.ly/E9raB)
> Google principal scientist (IIT Madras)

Chandrasekaran Mohan (https://oreil.ly/Tk7GD)
> Multiple-award-winning IBM research scientist (IIT Madras)

See also "Artificial intelligence (AI)" on page 17, "Google" on page 114, "Hewlett-Packard (HP)" on page 131, "IBM" on page 139, "Ramachandran, Vivek" on page 210, "Stanford University" on page 230

Industrial control systems

Industrial control systems (*https://oreil.ly/IUBlR*) (ICSs) define the computer systems that help factories and utility plants in their everyday work by facilitating functions like automation and monitoring. Hackers and other technological innovators have put computers into schools, government agencies, hospitals, and homes. Factories and public utilities are operated with computers, too. And when computers and networks are designed to control the mechanical activities of factories and public utilities, they're called industrial control systems. You'll see ICS in automotive assembly plants, nuclear power stations, water treatment facilities, and oil extraction infrastructure, to name just a few.

ICSs take many different forms: an ICS in a toy factory will be different from an ICS in a hydroelectric generating station. Many of the computers in an ICS run modified versions of operating systems that many people are familiar with, such as Windows and UNIX.

There are different types of ICS. For example, Supervisory Control and Data Acquisition (*https://oreil.ly/xLrjN*) systems are used for monitoring, configuring, and logging rather than directly controlling automation. Their control is at the supervisory level, and they often contain very specialized components such as Programmable Logic Controllers. Distributed Control Systems (DCS) are used to control production systems in a single site (such as one factory location). If there's an operational fault in one part of the system, a DCS can reduce its impact on the system as a whole.

ICSs are often targeted by cyberattackers, especially in cyberwarfare! Perhaps the most infamous incident was the 2010 Stuxnet attack (*https://oreil.ly/bCilW*) on the Natanz uranium enrichment plant in Iran.

See also "Stuxnet" on page 232

Integrated development environment (IDE)

There are two types of applications that people use to develop software and write computer programming code: text editors and integrated development environment (*https://oreil.ly/A12_D*)s (IDEs).

A text editor is pretty simple: input text in individual files, use the correct syntax for the programming language, and you've got a script. Some text editors can display parts of your code in different colors to make it more readable, otherwise known as *syntax highlighting*.

An IDE has all of the functionality of a text editor, plus many other functions. For instance, you can load software development kits (*https://oreil.ly/ HXDjH*) (SDKs) for a wide range of specific platforms (such as Java or Nintendo Switch game development), computing systems, and programming languages. An IDE can also test your scripts for errors before they're compiled. They usually include debuggers (*https://oreil.ly/Ht9Vl*), local build automation (*https://oreil.ly/ muoVV*), and compilers. (A compiler (*https://oreil.ly/X2t2n*) makes higher-level programming code executable for computers by converting it to lower-level programming code, such as assembly languages.)

There's a wide range of IDEs out there. Some of the most popular (*https:// www.keycdn.com/blog/best-ide*) are NetBeans (for C++, HTML, Java, FORTRAN, and PHP), Visual Studio Code (for JavaScript, HTML, Markdown, C++, Python, and Java), Eclipse (Java, Perl, Ruby, PHP, C++), PyCharm (Python, HTML, JavaScript, Node.js), and Code::Blocks (C, C++, FORTRAN, assembly, Pascal).

See also "Assembly" on page 20, "Programming" on page 204, "Syntax" on page 236

Intel

Intel was founded in 1968 by former Fairchild Semiconductor (and Shockley Semiconductor) engineers Robert Noyce (*https://oreil.ly/B6AFz*) and Gordon Moore. Moore suggested that semiconductor memory (*https://oreil.ly/Hec3H*) could form the basis of a new company, and Noyce was sold. The companies made integrated circuits, which were lots of transistors on one chip. It was new and groundbreaking technology, and Intel learned to improve where Shockley and Fairchild had failed—because Intel's founders were the ultimate insiders.

Intel's first headquarters was in Mountain View, California, near the heart of Silicon Valley. Its very first product debuted in 1969: the Intel 3101 (*https:// oreil.ly/2YWYT*) static random-access memory (SRAM). This new memory product led to innovations that made integrated circuits cheaper, and it triggered an evolution that made PCs possible less than 20 years later.

Intel's first CPU was the world's first programmable microprocessor: the Intel 4004 (*https://oreil.ly/aYjhG*), released in 1971. The 8008 CPU, just a year later, had nearly twice the power of the 4004 (proving Moore's law (*https:// oreil.ly/nojiP*) to be accurate). The 1974 Intel 8080 (*https://oreil.ly/TpLN3*) microprocessor was smaller than an aspirin tablet and could work as a CPU without supporting chips, a major technological innovation. The 8080 powered the computer (*https://oreil.ly/Vr-2n*) that kicked off the personal computer revolution,

1975's Altair 8800, which inspired the Apple I and was the first commercial machine to run Microsoft's version of BASIC. Thus, the Intel 8080 CPU indirectly launched two Silicon Valley behemoths. The Intel 8088 (*https://oreil.ly/e1RKV*), made with the still-popular x86 architecture, was the CPU in the first IBM PC in 1981, which started to make Intel really big in the PC market.

Intel has launched some important CPUs for enterprise and institutional computing in the 21st century. A collaborative research effort with HP led to the 2001 launch of the Itanium (*https://oreil.ly/CG9PC*) series, with the IA-64 architecture. Intel debuted the Xeon 5500 (*https://oreil.ly/G_CDV*) CPU series for scientific computing in 2009. And in 2021 it completed the "Aurora with Intel" supercomputer (*https://oreil.ly/ZH8l7*), capable of a jaw-dropping *one quintillion* floating-point operations per second.

See also "CPU (Central processing unit)" on page 57, "Fairchild Semiconductor" on page 103, "Moore's law" on page 180, "Silicon Valley" on page 224, "Supercomputers" on page 233

Intellectual property

See "Creative Commons licenses" on page 59, "DRM (Digital Rights Management)" on page 89, "Open source" on page 189, "Proprietary software" on page 205

Internet

The internet! Where would hacker culture be without it? The internet is so ubiquitous that it revolutionized not only hacker culture but society at large.

As of 2021, the world's population was about 7.9 billion people, and 63% of them are internet users.[1] So approximately 4.97 billion people used the internet as of 2021. Satista estimates (*https://oreil.ly/Ogkhb*) that the collective amount of data on the internet hit 64 zettabytes in 2020, and global web traffic exceeded an estimated 1 zettabyte for the first time in 2015.[2] By 2025 it's expected to hit 175 zetabytes. That's some exponential web growth!

So how did the internet start? I'll summarize, since many of the players in this history have their own entries in this book.

---

1 International Telecommunication Union, "Measuring digital development: Facts and Figures 2022 (*https://oreil.ly/hyEc_*)."

2 Cisco, Annual Internet Report (*https://oreil.ly/LCDS3*), March 2020. Remember, the web is simply the most popular internet service, it's not the entire internet.

The 1950s and early 1960s were dominated by big, expensive vacuum-tube-powered computers, a massive logistical hassle, so only enterprises and institutions used them. Important conceptual work happened in the early 1960s, with Leonard Kleinrock at MIT (*https://oreil.ly/8BoFP*) writing on packet-switching theory and J. C. R. Licklider (also at MIT) outlining his "Galactic Network" concept. In 1965, as the first computers with transistors and integrated circuits were just starting to emerge, Lawrence Roberts connected two computers (*https://oreil.ly/uOT7u*) with a telephone line and acoustic modems and transferred a simple data packet between them. It was a miracle.

The modern internet wouldn't exist without its father, ARPAnet, launched by the US Defense Advanced Research Projects Agency (DARPA) in 1969. Kleinrock's and Licklider's work was integral to ARPAnet's invention. Through the 1970s, more and more institutions across the US connected their IBM computers (not PCs) and PDP minicomputers ("mini" meant fridge-sized) to ARPAnet.

By 1974, ARPAnet was widespread but unreliable, because its data-packet handling was a mess. Computer scientists Bob Kahn and Vint Cerf, tasked with finding a solution, invented TCP/IP, an internet protocol and data packet formatting suite. TCP/IP was very gradually implemented through January 1, 1983, when ARPAnet made it an official standard. Most experts consider that to be the internet's birthdate. (The internet is a Capricorn!)

In 1990, the last parts of ARPAnet that didn't use TCP/IP were taken out of service, and ARPAnet was decommissioned.

Aren't you happy to enter "oreilly.com" into your web browser's address bar rather than "104.86.226.29"? Domain names make using the web, email, and various other internet services more human-friendly by using memorable words rather than jumbles of hexadecimal numbers. For that, you can thank the Domain Name System (DNS), which Paul Mockapetris and Jon Postel (*https://oreil.ly/uOT7u*) invented in 1983. Tim Berners-Lee launched the World Wide Web in 1990 (*https://oreil.ly/xTy9_*), which also greatly popularized the internet and is perhaps the most commonly used internet service aside from email. Ever since, internet use by ordinary people has grown tremendously.

See also "ARPAnet" on page 17, "Berners-Lee, Tim" on page 33, "DARPA (Defense Advanced Research Projects Agency)" on page 72, "Hexadecimal numbering" on page 133, "IBM" on page 139, "Minicomputers" on page 176, "Massachusetts Institute of Technology (MIT)" on page 170, "Packet switching" on page 193, "TCP/IP (Transmission Control Protocol/Internet Protocol)" on page 239, "World Wide Web" on page 268, "Zettabyte Era" on page 279

Invisible Internet Project (I2P)

The Invisible Internet Project (*https://oreil.ly/gBEJ7*) (I2P), originally called the Invisible IRC Project, started in 2001 (*https://oreil.ly/_nlAM*) as a way to interface the Internet Relay Chat (IRC) protocol with Freenet for ultimate privacy. I2P developer Lance "oX90" James described it in (*https://oreil.ly/_nlAM*) 2002 as "Peer 2 Peer Internet. Using your peers to protect you."

I2P ultimately became a proxy network that's technologically similar to Tor. There is a whole part of the web that's only accessible through an I2P client, and those sites use the .i2p top-level domain. By 2003, development on the I2P and Tor proxy networks was well underway; one Bloomberg article heralded the emergence of "The Underground Internet" (*https://oreil.ly/71Y1t*).

If you explore the web part of the I2P network today, you'll see something very similar to the web part of the Tor network: some of it is the "dark web," and there are also I2P versions of innocuous news sites such as The Tor Times (*https://oreil.ly/On38T*).

Communicating online with the utmost of privacy is a major interest in hacker culture. Proxy networks like I2P and Tor anonymize users and servers through a series of proxy nodes, where each node's packets only have the IP address of the next node in the sequence. Only the exit nodes pointed at the user's machine and the server machine have the IP addresses for either destination. It's not impossible to track users on these proxy networks, but it's a lot more work than tracking them on the clearnet—the ordinary parts of the internet that most people use outside of the I2P and Tor networks.

See also "Dark Web/darknet" on page 71, "IRC (Internet Relay Chat)" on page 147, "Networking" on page 183, "Tor (The Onion Router)" on page 245

IRC (Internet Relay Chat)

Years before AOL Instant Messenger and ICQ (ask an elder Millennial or Gen Xer about those), there was Internet Relay Chat (*https://oreil.ly/Gjorc*) (IRC). Developed by Jarkko Oikarinen (*https://oreil.ly/hpcpb*) and launched in 1988 (*https://oreil.ly/HuPQs*), it even predates Tim Berners-Lee's World Wide Web—and it's still around today.[3]

Oikarinen administered a bulletin board system (BBS) at Finland's University of Oulu and wanted to extend its features with live chat. He used some code

---

3 See Daniel Stenberg's history of IRC (*https://oreil.ly/HuPQs*).

written by his friends Jyrki Kuoppala and Jukka Pihl. It was so nifty that he put it on the internet, rather than just the school's BBS.

In 1988, email and Usenet were popular. For chat, after 1985, you could use Quantum, which later became America Online (AOL) (*https://oreil.ly/oo_cO*) and which originally supported Commodore 64 computers. It was renamed America Online by 1991. CompuServe (*https://oreil.ly/oSem-*) and Prodigy (*https://oreil.ly/iahMY*) were also around in various forms when IRC debuted.

IRC quickly grew in popularity through the 1990s, and for much of the decade ordinary consumers mainly used AOL, CompuServe, and Prodigy. Until those platforms offered their customers web access in the mid-1990s, they were walled off from much of the general internet. But some consumers signed up for internet service providers that offered internet access, and many of them used IRC. It was also popular among hackers and in academia.

As Oikarinen wrote, "The IRC protocol is a text-based protocol, with the simplest client being any socket program capable of connecting to the server." You can use a wide range of clients to access IRC services. There are also several independent IRC networks, such as EFnet and DALnet. Each network has its own channels for different topics.

Go explore IRC and you'll find many niche communities full of hackers. 2600 magazine has its very own IRC network at irc.2600.net, and the channel for live participation during their Off The Hook radio show is #offthehook.

See also "Bulletin board systems (BBSes)" on page 37, "Internet" on page 145, "2600 (Twenty-Six Hundred): The Hacker Quarterly (magazine)" on page 250

10

J

Jack, Barnaby

Barnaby Michael Douglas Jack (1977–2013), born in New Zealand (*https://oreil.ly/ W59lw*), made a real splash in the cybersecurity world before his untimely death (*https://oreil.ly/sq6EJ*). Barnaby Jack was indeed his real name—and "jackpotting" was his game. Here's his story.

In my years researching financial cybercrime, I've learned that there are two ways to steal money from a bank. The first is to move the numbers around in the bank's computer system—digital means, like gaining access to a victim's online banking through a phishing attack, or by stealing their debit or credit card. The second is the old-fashioned way, by taking physical bills and coins. In Jack's innovative attack, which he called "jackpotting" (*https://oreil.ly/SxEHV*), no numbers are moved around in people's bank accounts. It simply removes the cash from the machine by exploiting vulnerabilities in ATMs that make them spit out all of the money they contain, like a slot-machine jackpot. A single ATM typically contains anywhere from $2,000 to $20,000 in cash, and many run modified versions of Windows.

Jack rose to relative fame at 2010's Black Hat conference in Las Vegas by publicly demonstrating his jackpotting attack on ATMs by two major manufacturers, Tranax Technologies and Triton Systems: "Every ATM I've looked at, I've found a game-over vulnerability that allows me to get cash from the machine." He put malware onto the Tranax ATM through its remote administration network connection, and on the Triton ATM with a USB stick. The Black Hat 2010 audience was wowed (*https://oreil.ly/bqAyf*).

In 2018, the first malicious jackpotting attacks to ATMs were reported (*https://oreil.ly/f1Sm4*). (What Jack did in 2010 was a proof-of-concept with ATMs he lawfully acquired, not a cyberattack.) Jackpotting has even inspired an episode of the TV crime drama *CSI: Cyber* (*https://oreil.ly/zKFkc*).

Jack went on to demonstrate security vulnerabilities (*https://oreil.ly/RsmLu*) in pacemakers and insulin pumps, eventually taking a job as the director of embedded device security (*https://oreil.ly/l1ncf*) at IOActive (which is also my employer as of this writing). However, Jack died at 35 of a drug overdose (*https://oreil.ly/dYXNw*). Rest in peace, Barnaby Jack.

See also "Cybersecurity" on page 68, "Exploit" on page 101, "Malware" on page 167, "Penetration testing" on page 196

Jackson, Mary

See "Hidden Figures (2017 film)" on page 134

Java

See "Programming" on page 204

JavaScript

See "Programming" on page 204

Jobs, Steve

Steven Paul Jobs (1955–2011) was born in San Francisco, adopted by the Jobs family, and raised in nearby Cupertino, California, in the heart of Silicon Valley. He first met Steve "Woz" Wozniak when he was 13 and Woz was 18. After a brief stint cultivating apples at a hippie commune in Oregon, Jobs returned to Silicon Valley in 1974, where he got a job at Atari. When the two met again, Woz was working for Hewlett-Packard. In 1973, Woz took a job at Atari, and he and Jobs began collaborating on *Breakout* (*https://oreil.ly/n8oKo*), a single-player version of *Pong*, Atari's first commercially successful video game.

When Steve Jobs and Steve "Woz" Wozniak started Apple Computer (*https://oreil.ly/-ngIb*) in 1976, they brought different strengths to what would eventually become one of the most profitable corporations on earth. Woz, the hacker wizard, designed the board that became Apple's first product, the Apple I, and designed the Apple II. Jobs was a hippie with big dreams who thought Woz's inventions would radically change the world, and he would hone his marketing instincts to design Apple's public image. Woz was science, Jobs was art.

In 1975, Woz and Jobs attended the first meetings of the Homebrew Computer Club and saw one of the earliest microcomputers marketed for home and hobbyist use, the Altair 8800. Inspired, Woz made a prototype for a similar computer, but his employer HP showed no interest. That's when Woz and Jobs started Apple Computer. Their first product, the Apple I hobbyist kit, was released in 1976. Jobs encouraged Woz to design a new computer that would be ready to use out of the box: the 1977 Apple II, Apple's big commercial breakthrough. It was such a successful platform that they produced Apple II computers until 1987 (*https://oreil.ly/llCyn*).

Controversially, Jobs preferred style over substance. While designing the Apple III's appearance (*https://oreil.ly/yxpvC*), he removed air vents and a fan that would've prevented the computer from overheating. Former Apple employee David Fradin (*https://oreil.ly/epNmY*) explains how Jobs interfered with the machine's potential for success:

Everyone at Apple had a different vision for the organization's future. And Steve Jobs didn't want any other product positioned in the market that might interfere with "his" Macintosh. Not only did he want the Apple II out of the marketplace—he failed to acknowledge that profits from the Apple III and Apple II computers were giving him the resources to develop, build, market, and sell the Macintosh.

Jobs visited Xerox PARC in 1979 and was amazed by the Xerox Alto prototype, with its mouse-driven graphical user interface (GUI). The Alto was the kind of computer that Jobs wanted Apple to make—and it did, with the Apple Macintosh. As far as consumers knew, it was the first mouse-controlled PC with a GUI operating system.

In 1985, Jobs found himself at odds with Apple CEO John Sculley. Apple's Board of Directors sided with Sculley, and Jobs was demoted to chairman, with no operational authority. Devastated, Jobs left to start NeXT Computer. The NeXT Cube, featuring the object-oriented NeXTSTEP operating system, launched in 1988, and Tim Berners-Lee used it to invent (*https://oreil.ly/EpPQR*) the World Wide Web in 1990. Jobs also bought the upstart computer-animation firm Pixar in 1986. After its 1989 short film, *Tin Toy*, won an Oscar, Pixar signed a deal with Disney that resulted in the 1995 smash hit *Toy Story*.

Apple was really struggling in 1996 (*https://oreil.ly/rBRKP*), though, and its new CEO—Gil Amelio, hired to rescue the company—bought NeXT for $400 million, reuniting Jobs with Apple. But Apple lost about $700 million in the first quarter of 1997, and with the help of Oracle founder Larry Ellison, Apple's board staged a coup and installed Jobs as CEO.

Jobs cancelled product lines that weren't selling well and launched 1998's candy-colored iMac, followed in 2001 by Mac OS X (which was based on NeXTSTEP and the BSD/UNIX kernel) and the iPod line of portable music players. Every major new product Apple released under Jobs's second period with Apple was a smash success—especially the iPhone, launched in 2007.

But just as Jobs reached his professional apex in 2003, he was diagnosed with cancer (*https://oreil.ly/sLkOk*). Initially, he rejected mainstream medical treatment in favor of alternative medicine, but his health continued to fail. Jobs resigned as CEO in 2011 and handed the reins to a handpicked successor, Tim Cook, before Jobs died on October 5, 2011.

See also "Apple" on page 13, "Atari" on page 22, "Berners-Lee, Tim" on page 33,"Graphical user interface (GUI)" on page 117, "Hewlett-Packard (HP)" on page 131, "Homebrew Computer Club" on page 136, "NeXT Computer" on page 184,

"Pirates of Silicon Valley (1999 film)" on page 202, "World Wide Web" on page 268, "Wozniak, Steve" on page 269, "Xerox" on page 273

Johnson, Katherine Coleman

See "Hidden Figures (2017 film)" on page 134

Joy, Bill

William "Bill" Joy (1954–) is a cofounder of Silicon Valley giant Sun Microsystems and an alumnus (*https://oreil.ly/nzsAf*) of the University of California at Berkeley's electronic engineering and computer science department. As a child, he loved ham radio, but his parents thought it was an antisocial hobby.

Among his major career accomplishments was working on the Berkeley Software Distribution (BSD) version of UNIXx in 1977, which laid groundwork for the BSD/UNIX kernel many popular operating systems use today. He did much of the work on his school's Digital Equipment Corporation (DEC) VAX minicomputers.

In 1978, he beat DEC itself to win a bid from DARPA to create software to connect DEC VAX computers to ARPAnet. In 1982 (*https://oreil.ly/ZiTcK*), he founded Sun Microsystems with Vinod Khosla, Andy Bechtolsheim, and Scott McNealy, with the goal of developing high-performance desktop computers for UNIX.

Joy worked on Sun's Network File System (NFS), popular with the enterprise market in the 1980s, and in the mid-1990s he helped to develop the strategy for Java. Java has since become a major programming language and the primary high-level programming language on Android devices. When I interviewed him, Joy expressed enthusiasm about that development: "I'm glad to see it! And iPhone and Apple OSes have a lot of BSD in them. I'm glad to have helped both!"

See also "Berkeley, University of California" on page 32, "DARPA (Defense Advanced Research Projects Agency)" on page 72, "Ham radio" on page 127, "Minicomputers" on page 176, "UNIX" on page 253

K

Kali Linux

Kali is a Linux-distribution operating system that's popular with hackers who work as penetration testers. Pentesting, as it's known, is all about simulating cyberattacks to find security vulnerabilities in computer systems. Defensive cybersecurity specialists then use that information to harden their systems' security.

Kali is open source and can be downloaded for free (*https://oreil.ly/vHwu2*). Originally Kali was designed for computers with x86/x86-64 architecture Intel or AMD CPUs. But now there are also versions of Kali that can be run on Android devices, Apple Silicon ARM64 devices (including newer MacBooks), and some other devices with ARM CPUs. All of those versions can be directly installed onto the machines or run as a live boot from a USB device, or there are also prebuilt images for virtualization in VMware and VirtualBox. There's also a Win-KeX interface version of Kali (*https://oreil.ly/zdXKB*) that can be run from Windows Subsystem for Linux.

Either way, you get a desktop computing environment—Xfce by default (*https://oreil.ly/CZFLh*) in most versions—with a wide variety of hacking scripts and applications preinstalled. Kali is a fork of Debian Linux, and applications designed for Debian are fully compatible. It includes tools for cracking WiFi, capturing packets, malware analysis, and many other fun purposes (*https://oreil.ly/BVktU*).[1]

See also "Debian" on page 76, "Linux" on page 161, "Penetration testing" on page 196

---

1 Many of these tools can also be used for engaging in cybercrime. But you're a good person, so you'd only use the tools on computers and networks that you have permission to hack on.

Key

There are keys on your keyboard, keys to your front door and mailbox, and I hear Florida has a lot of "Keys" too. But this entry is about encryption keys! An encryption key (*https://oreil.ly/PeLL-*) is a randomly generated string of bits used to turn plain text into ciphertext (*https://oreil.ly/QArcD*). Longer bit-length keys are generally harder to crack. The two basic types of encryption keys are symmetrical and asymmetrical (*https://oreil.ly/JFM5e*).

Symmetrical keys are used to encrypt data at rest, and symmetrical encryption algorithms work best for large amounts of data in storage. To massively simplify: symmetric keys mean that the decryption key is the encryption key in reverse. For example, if the encryption key is X × 6 + 4 – 7, the decryption key would be + 7 – 4 ÷ 6 = X. Revealing one key would reveal the other, so symmetric keys wouldn't be at all secure for granting public users internet access to data. They are used in closed systems as secret keys.

Asymmetrical keys are used in public-key cryptography, which is primarily for encrypting data in transit over the internet and other kinds of computer networks. I can't quite explain the math, but revealing the decryption key doesn't reveal the encryption key. For instance, the web pages you visit these days should all be sent to you through TLS (Transport Layer Security) encryption through the HTTPS protocol. In the background, your web browser uses the public key infrastructure (PKI) that the web server you're connecting to uses, and sends keys with the help of the Diffie-Hellman key exchange to keep them secure. TLS certificates assure the cryptographic authenticity of the web server. You don't generally see any of that work, although sometimes your web browser might warn you not to go to a webpage with a bad or expired TLS certificate.

Symmetric-key cryptography makes sure that anyone who physically steals your laptop and the solid-state drive in it will have trouble accessing your data without the password, and asymmetric-key cryptography is why you can shop online and be reasonably confident that cybercriminals won't discover your credit card number.

See also "Certificates (cryptography)" on page 45, "Cryptography" on page 63, "Diffie-Hellman key exchange" on page 84

Keyboard

Computer keyboards, unlike the musical kind of keyboard, have a typewriter-like interface that's rooted in the mechanical keyboards of the late 19th century. The earliest patent (*https://oreil.ly/QH03B*) for a typewriter-like typing machine dates all the way back to 1714, but the first practical mechanical typewriter was patented by Christopher Latham Sholes (*https://oreil.ly/MCnFA*) in 1868. Sholes and his partner James Densmore also invented the QWERTY letter configuration we're all familiar with. Early mechanical keyboards had physical limitations and couldn't handle someone typing 100 words per minute, so it's theorized (and probably true) that Sholes and Densmore designed the QWERTY configuration to slow typers down a little and avoid jamming the typewriter mechanisms.

See also "Hardware" on page 128

12

L

Lamarr, Hedy

Hedy Lamarr (1914–2000) was one of the most famous Hollywood movie stars of the 1930s and 1940s. Born in Austria, she played a few roles in Austrian and German films from 1930 to 1932. Her starring role in 1932's Czech erotic romance drama *Ecstasy (Ekstase)* caught the attention of MGM head Louis B. Mayer. Lamarr moved to Hollywood and starred in some of MGM's most notable films of the era, such as 1938's *Algiers*, 1941's *Ziegfeld Girl*, 1944's *The Conspirators*, and 1949's *Samson and Delilah*.

Despite being considered one of the most beautiful women in the world, she was often cynical of beauty standards and once said (*https://oreil.ly/ZOk4P*), "The brains of people are more interesting than the looks, I think."

What does any of this have to do with hacker culture? Plenty—you can thank Ms. Lamarr for WiFi technology.

Lamarr's inventor mindset began with disassembling music boxes as a young child. At the peak of Lamarr's filmmaking career, she dated eccentric, mega-wealthy businessman and pilot Howard Hughes, who encouraged her talents by giving her mechanical and electric equipment to work with in her film-set trailers.

When World War II broke out, Lamarr began designing seriously. Hughes asked her to help him develop faster airplanes for the US military, and she designed wings that combined elements of the natural aerodynamics of fish fins and the wings of fast birds. "You're a genius!" Hughes exclaimed.

To address the problem of Axis powers jamming US radio torpedo-control systems, Lamarr invented frequency hopping technology, which allows a radio transmitter and receiver to dynamically alter the radio frequency of their communications. Lamarr and her co-inventor George Antheil filed a patent for the technology in 1942, but the US Navy rejected it. They didn't start using frequency hopping technology until the 1960s.

Lamarr's patent was used in the invention of Code-Division Multiple Access (CDMA) cellular network radio as well as of global positioning systems (GPS), and was crucial to the development of WiFi and Bluetooth standards in the late 1990s.

Lamarr was a hacker before hackers were even called hackers! In 1997, she was awarded the Electronic Frontier Foundation Pioneer Award (*https://oreil.ly/ c5xIu*), and in 2014 she was posthumously inducted into the National Inventors Hall of Fame (*https://oreil.ly/TGDGk*).

See also "Electronics" on page 95, "Hacker" on page 121, "Ham radio" on page 127

Larsson, Stieg

See "Cyberpunk" on page 67, "Salander, Lisbeth" on page 219

Lawson, Jerry

Jerry Lawson (1940–2011) was a bright kid from New York City whose parents encouraged his curiosity as a hacker, even if the concept of being a hacker wasn't well established in the 1950s and '60s. He got into ham radio, and he repaired televisions as a teenager. In 1970, he moved to San Francisco to work as an engineer for Fairchild Semiconductor, which pioneered transistor and integrated circuit designs.

Lawson was one of only two Black members of the legendary Homebrew Computer Club, which also included Steve Jobs and Steve Wozniak. (The other Black member was Ron Jones.) In fact, Lawson interviewed Wozniak for a job at Fairchild and decided not to hire him.

Lawson led the development of the pioneering second-generation video game console Fairchild Channel F, which debuted in 1976. Lawson was instrumental in inventing the video game cartridge. The Atari 2600, which came out in 1977, commercially dominated the second generation of consoles, but it likely wouldn't have had swappable cartridges if not for Lawson's innovation. This also allowed for games to be produced after a console's release and for third-party developers to make games for a console.

Perhaps Lawson's most lasting contribution was the pause button! I can't imagine gaming without a pause button—what did players do when they had to go to the bathroom? But that was the reality of the first generation of video game consoles. Things gamers take for granted today, like the ability to *pause the damn game*, were innovations for which we should thank the late Jerry Lawson.

See also "Fairchild Semiconductor" on page 103, "Ham radio" on page 127, "Homebrew Computer Club" on page 136, "Jobs, Steve" on page 150, "Wozniak, Steve" on page 269

Levy, Steven

See "Hackers: Heroes of the Computer Revolution (2010 book)" on page 123, "WIRED magazine" on page 267

Linux

Linux is one of the most important operating systems ever developed, and it's as relevant now as ever. The Linux kernel is open source and is used in a wide range of CPUs and device types, from desktop operating systems to Android phones, from supercomputers (*https://oreil.ly/ZFeXT*) to many embedded systems.

You probably use Linux every day, even if you don't know it. Only a minority of consumers use Linux on their PCs—most use Microsoft Windows and Apple's macOS. But a lot of the web servers that deploy your web pages run Linux. The billions of Android devices currently in use have a Linux kernel. And Android is embedded (*https://oreil.ly/eavED*) in many other places, such as point-of-sale devices in retail stores and medical devices in hospitals.

Linux wouldn't exist if Linus Torvalds hadn't aspired to create his own version of MINIX as a student at the University of Helsinki.

MINIX (*https://oreil.ly/uLlzn*) is a UNIX-like operating system that was designed for the academic market in the 1980s by Vrije Universiteit Amsterdam computer science professor Andrew Tanenbaum. Torvalds encountered UNIX in school (*https://oreil.ly/Ugii2*) around 1990, and one of his coursebooks was Tanenbaum's *Operating Systems: Design and Implementation*, which set forth the principles and source code of MINIX.

In 1991, when Torvalds bought himself a PC with a 32-bit Intel 386 CPU (the hot new thing at the time), he realized it would be difficult to run MINIX 1.0, which was designed for 16-bit CPUs. Tanenbaum didn't allow developers to modify his code, but Torvalds was determined to develop a 32-bit MINIX. So he sought help on Usenet via this now-famous post (*https://oreil.ly/LcJl7*) on comp.os.minix:

> Hello everybody out there using minix -
>
> I'm doing a (free) operating system (just a hobby, won't be big and professional like gnu) for 386(486) AT clones. This has been brewing since april, and is starting to get ready. I'd like any feedback on things people like/dislike in minix, as my OS resembles it somewhat (same physical layout of the file-system (due to practical reasons) among other things).
>
> I've currently ported bash(1.08) and gcc(1.40), and things seem to work. This implies that I'll get something practical within a few months, and I'd like to know what features most people would want. Any suggestions are welcome, but I won't promise I'll implement them :-)
>
> Linus (torvalds@kruuna.helsinki.fi)
>
> PS. Yes - it's free of any minix code, and it has a multi-threaded fs. It is NOT protable [portable] (uses 386 task switching etc), and it probably never will support anything other than AT-harddisks, as that's all I have :-(.

"Just a hobby," he said! Not "big and professional like GNU," he said!

Let's pause for some super-technical nerd stuff. Monolithic kernels run user services and kernel services under the same address space. Microkernels run user services and kernel services in different address spaces. It's all about how memory and hardware directly interact with software. While Tanenbaum and GNU inventor Richard Stallman preferred microkernel architectures, Torvalds made Linux's kernel monolithic—touching off one of the fiercest online debates of the early 1990s.

Tanenbaum started it with a 1992 Usenet post titled "LINUX is obsolete" (*https://oreil.ly/LuhI9*). He argued that "among the people who actually design operating systems, the debate is essentially over. Microkernels have won." Tanenbaum concluded that MINIX was future-ready, whereas Linux was using a kernel system he considered outdated. The argument went on for weeks.

Linus Torvalds was the ultimate victor: his monolithic Linux kernel became a lot more popular than MINIX. As his post suggests, he didn't expect or intend for Linux to go big. The name itself was a placeholder; Torvalds wanted to call it "Freax," for "Free Unix." Ari Lemmke, who worked on Linux with Torvalds, convinced him to stick with "Linux." Today, Linux even has a mascot: Tux (*https://oreil.ly/744sb*) the penguin.

As for MINIX, it's still being developed, but very slowly. As of this writing, it's gone about nine years without a new stable version and six years without a new public beta. Tanenbaum eventually relented about letting others modify his code, releasing MINIX under the BSD license starting in 2000.

If you have an x86-64 PC (the vast majority of PCs these days), you may want to explore the popular desktop Linux distributions. Here is a sampling:

Debian

The first stable version of Debian (*https://oreil.ly/kxEL4*) was released in 1996. Vanilla Debian is still in development, but many of the most popular Linux distributions are based on it, like Ubuntu and Linux Mint. The two most popular Linux operating systems for cybersecurity penetration testing, Kali and Parrot, are also based on Debian, as are a wide range of other specialized distributions.

Red Hat Enterprise Linux

Red Hat Enterprise Linux (*https://oreil.ly/oIAgJ*) (RHEL) is its own massive branch of the Linux family tree. Fedora (*https://oreil.ly/FXIzN*), Torvalds' Linux distribution of choice, is based on RHEL.

Arch

Arch Linux (*https://oreil.ly/sevYS*) is another major Linux branch—but you could think of it as a chimera of all Linux branches, or of whichever Linux branches you'd like. It's sort of a "build your own operating system." Not for the faint of heart, but if you're a control-freak hacker, you'll fall in love with it.

Gentoo

Gentoo (*https://oreil.ly/kDBGW*) is another major Linux branch, in development since 2002. It's a different kind of "build your own operating system" and totally not for noobs.

That's just the tip of the Linux iceberg. There are hundreds of Linux distributions (at least). I highly recommend checking out DistroWatch.com (*https://oreil.ly/7FpvT*) if you need help choosing one.

See also "bash" on page 30, "Debian" on page 76, "Kali Linux" on page 155, "Red Hat" on page 213, "Stallman, Richard" on page 229, "UNIX" on page 253, "Torvalds, Linus" on page 246

Lovelace, Ada

Ada Lovelace (1815–1852), born Augusta Ada Byron (*https://oreil.ly/j3dVX*), was history's first computer programmer—and well ahead of her time.

Lady Byron was raised in London in fortunate circumstances, with a noble title and a famous father: the poet Lord Byron (*https://oreil.ly/QnwJP*). Her mother, Annabella Milbanke, had formal mathematical training and insisted that her daughter follow in her footsteps, despite the cultural norms of the time discouraging women from science and positions of authority. One of Lovelace's tutors was Augustus De Morgan, the first professor of mathematics at the University of London.

At a high-society party in 1833 (when she was 17), Lovelace met Charles Babbage (*https://oreil.ly/DIdUX*), a middle-aged widower and brilliant mathematician. Babbage mentioned his Difference Engine, a mechanical device to compile mathematical tables, and invited Lovelace to see it. It was a tower of numbered wheels (*https://oreil.ly/9DAGI*), powered by a handle connected to a series of gears, and perhaps the most advanced calculator machine of its time.

Babbage's next (but never completed) project was an Analytical Engine (*https://oreil.ly/FSTM8*): the first computer to use punch cards, albeit mechanical. Lovelace and Babbage kept in touch, and when Italian mathematician Luigi Federico Menabrea wrote a detailed French-language guide to the Analytical Engine in 1842, Lovelace published an English translation (*https://oreil.ly/lSA2V*). She added many of her own notes, including the first computer program, Note G (*https://oreil.ly/GK4Te*).

Lovelace died in 1852 (*https://oreil.ly/3cM5I*), when she was only 36 years old. A little over 120 years later, the US Department of Defense developed the Ada programming language (*https://oreil.ly/Pbrl_*) in her honor. It's still used by the military and the aviation, banking, and manufacturing industries today.

See also "Programming" on page 204

LulzSec

See "Hacktivism" on page 125

13

M

Macintosh

See "Apple" on page 13

macOS

See "Apple" on page 13

Malware

Malware, short for "malicious software" (*https://oreil.ly/DZvMl*), means any software that's designed to cause harm. Sometimes malware is classified according to how it spreads from computer to computer, such as through viruses and worms (*https://oreil.ly/GQJWo*). (Laypeople often erroneously call all malware "viruses.") These days, however, we primarily classify malware according to the harm it causes (*https://oreil.ly/m3oJw*).

Ransomware
    Ransomware maliciously encrypts data on infected computers, using a key that's only given to the computer's rightful owner if they pay a hefty ransom to the cyberattacker. In the past several years, enterprise ransomware has emerged that not only maliciously encrypts data, but also breaches data (*https://oreil.ly/P47wK*). This is likely because maliciously encrypted data can be restored from backups, but no amount of backups will help a company if its sensitive data gets breached!

Spyware
    Spyware spies on users, watching everything from keystrokes to passwords stored in web browsers to files on infected computers.

Rootkits

> Rootkits have "root" (administrative) access to a computer and can be used to give an attacker dangerous remote control.

Trojans

> Trojans require user interaction to execute, so they attract victims by appearing in the form of something a user might want, such as a media-playing application or a photo of a cute kitten attached to an email.

Some malware falls into multiple categories. For instance, ransomware that spreads through memory from computer to computer in a network can also be a worm.

See also "Cybersecurity" on page 68, "Ransomware" on page 211, "Spyware" on page 228, "Threat actor" on page 243, "Virus" on page 258, "Worm" on page 269

Manning, Chelsea

Chelsea Manning (1987–) is one of the most important hacktivists. She showed a natural talent for computers in her Oklahoma childhood and held a civilian computer-programming job in her teens. But because she didn't get along with her coworkers, she was fired. Her father kicked her out of their home, and she spent time living as a vagabond across the United States. She eventually moved to a relative's home in Maryland, then joined the US Army in 2007 and enrolled in the Fort Huachuca military intelligence school.

In 2009, Manning was deployed to a US Army base east of Baghdad, Iraq. Her role granted her access to lots of top-secret military data, including tons of evidence of alleged US war crimes, such as video of an American helicopter crew firing on Reuters journalists from the UK. As stated in the *United States v. Private First Class Chelsea Manning* (https://oreil.ly/8UmIk) court report:

> While working as an army intelligence analyst in Baghdad in 2010, Manning learned of violations of the U.S. Military's Rules of Engagement, as well as thousands of civilian deaths that were unreported and uninvestigated by the military. Deeply troubled by this information, Manning uploaded to WikiLeaks more than 700,000 classified documents regarding the wars in Iraq and Afghanistan, as well as a video, dubbed 'Collateral Murder,' taken from a military helicopter. The gunsight video shows soldiers in a US military helicopter shooting down suspected insurgents, who were in

fact civilians. The soldiers are heard congratulating each other on shooting the people, and even encouraging one another to shoot the wounded who are trying to crawl away, cheering when they get a kill.

That's some dark, disturbing content. Manning became a whistleblower, sharing the evidence with WikiLeaks, Julian Assange's online news platform.

Manning was first incarcerated in July 2010 and spent more than a thousand days in pretrial incarceration at a US Marine Corps facility in Quantico, Virginia, where she was tortured. She pled guilty to some of the more minor charges and was sentenced to a jaw-dropping 35 years in prison.

Soon after her sentencing in 2013, Manning, who was assigned male at birth, declared that she's female and that her name is Chelsea—a pretty courageous time to come out as a trans woman! The approximately four years of her formal prison sentence were torturous and full of human rights violations. She even went on hunger strike in 2016 in order to receive gender-affirming surgery. Could you imagine how horrific it is to not only spend years in prison, but also to be misgendered while doing so and surrounded by male inmates when you're a woman? I'm amazed that Manning survived that.

Near the end of his term in office, in 2017, President Barack Obama commuted Manning's sentence and released her from prison. However, she was re-incarcerated between 2019 and 2020 for courageously refusing to rat out Assange and WikiLeaks. She attempted suicide, unsuccessfully, after which a judge ruled that she was no longer required to testify and released her from prison.

In October 2022, Penguin Random House published her memoir, titled *README.txt*. Chelsea Manning is a living hero, and the powers that be are often brutally cruel to people who have a conscience.

See also "Assange, Julian" on page 18, "Hacktivism" on page 125, "WikiLeaks" on page 266

Massachusetts Institute of Technology (MIT)

Massachusetts Institute of Technology (MIT), founded in 1865 (*https://oreil.ly/EU1vo*) in Cambridge, Massachusetts, is one of North America's main centers of academic computer science and technology research. MIT has played (and still plays) an absolutely crucial role in the development of hacker culture. Its Tech Model Railroad Club, formed in the 1960s, is the origin of using the word "hacker" to mean someone who plays with technology.[1] As the Interesting Hacks To Fascinate People: MIT Gallery of Hacks (*https://oreil.ly/_REqi*) defines it:

> *A clever, benign, and "ethical" prank or practical joke, which is both challenging for the perpetrators and amusing to the MIT community (and sometimes even the rest of the world!). Note that this has nothing to do with computer (or phone) hacking (which we call "cracking").*

---

1 Steven Levy, *Hackers: Heroes of the Computer Revolution* (O'Reilly, 2010).

MIT has also played an integral role in the development of computer net-working technology and the internet. Most notably, MIT's Lawrence Roberts (*https://oreil.ly/XtgK-*) was one of the inventors of packet-switching technology for computer networks. He also helped to design ARPAnet, one of the earliest uses of packet switching and the precursor to the modern internet. His packet-switching design principles are still used for the internet today.

See also "ARPAnet" on page 17, "Hacker" on page 121, "Networking" on page 183, "Packet switching" on page 193, "Tech Model Railroad Club" on page 240

Meta

Facebook (*https://oreil.ly/iq_Eu*) was founded in 2004 by Harvard University students Mark Zuckerberg, Eduardo Saverin, Dustin Moskovitz, and Chris Hughes. Facebook's precursor was a sleazy website that Zuckerberg launched in 2003 called Facemash (*https://oreil.ly/Yg54f*). He used photos of his Harvard colleagues without their permission, and visitors were supposed to rate them on their presumed attractiveness. Harvard's administration shut Facemash down after a few days. Zuckerberg likely learned from that incident that it's better to profit from violating people's privacy when you can get them to *volunteer* to have their privacy violated.

Facebook launched in February 2004 as "Thefacebook." Initially, only users with a Harvard email address could join. Then it was opened up to colleges and universities across the United States and Canada, and in 2006, Facebook opened to anyone in the world (over age 13) with a verifiable email address of some kind. By the end of the year it had 12 million users. By August 2008, that was up to 100 million users, and by September 2009, 300 million. In 2022 (*https://oreil.ly/FVPyf*), Facebook had an average of 2.96 billion users.

Facebook has a long history of privacy abuses (*https://oreil.ly/HMRfy*). Here's a sampling:

- In 2006, when Facebook launched News Feed, users were unaccustomed to personal details from their profiles being shared with *all* of their friends and friends of friends. There was quite a lot of outrage, though now people are used to it.

- The following year, Facebook launched its Beacon feature, which let advertisers track users' purchases and notify their Facebook friends about those purchases. This too generated outrage.

- In July 2014, Facebook was caught engaging in a mood-manipulation experiment without user consent. The News Feed showed users either more negative or more positive stories and then gauged their reactions.

- In 2018, a Belgian court ordered Facebook to stop collecting private information about Belgian users through third-party cookies on external websites.

- This was overshadowed by the 2018 Cambridge Analytica scandal (*https://oreil.ly/ZREqB*), however, in which the consulting firm Cambridge Analytica stole the private data of 87 million Facebook users for use in Donald Trump's presidential campaign—and Facebook helped them do it.

In October 2021, Facebook announced (*https://oreil.ly/u2ypt*) that it would rename the corporation Meta, while keeping the name Facebook for the social media platform: "Meta's focus will be to bring the metaverse to life and help people connect, find communities and grow businesses. The metaverse will feel like a hybrid of today's online social experiences, sometimes expanded into three dimensions or projected into the physical world."

The "metaverse" was actually a poor-quality 3D online world, to be experienced through virtual-reality headsets: think *Second Life*, but uglier and in VR. Thankfully, the "metaverse" was a bust; Meta lost an estimated $24 billion (*https://oreil.ly/TxL_p*) in 2022.

See also "Augmented and virtual reality" on page 25, "Zuckerberg, Mark" on page 280

Metasploit Framework

The Metasploit Framework (*https://oreil.ly/mLN_K*) is a network-vulnerability scanner platform. It's frequently used in penetration testing (pentesting) and red-team engagements to test the security of a computer system by simulating cyberattacks. (Caution: doing this without the permission of the computer system's owner makes you a cyberattacker! And you could be breaking the law.)

A network-vulnerability scan isn't a pentest, and not all pentests are network-vulnerability scans. When used appropriately, network-vulnerability scanning is part of a pentest that includes other kinds of security testing.

Metasploit Framework is included in the two most popular pentesting operating systems, Kali Linux (*https://oreil.ly/Tqmjy*) and Parrot (*https://oreil.ly/zauZ7*). You can also install it (*https://oreil.ly/3FYim*) in Windows, macOS, and many popular Linux distributions (Debian, Ubuntu, CentOS, Red Hat, and Fedora.)

As noted in *Metasploit* by David Kennedy, Jim O'Gorman, Devon Kearns, and Mati Aharoni (No Starch Press), HD Moore developed the first version of Metasploit in 2003 using Perl, and it included 11 exploits. Rapid7 acquired Metasploit in 2009 and rapidly (pun intended) increased its exploit library and features. Now it has a huge collection of exploits and modules that target many of the most frequently used operating systems and applications, with members of the hacker community often developing their own exploit code to add to the library.

See also "Cybersecurity" on page 68, "Linux" on page 161, "Penetration testing" on page 196

Microcomputers

Until the mid-1970s, it was almost inconceivable to most people that a powerful multipurpose computer might one day fit on a desk, let alone belong in someone's home. Early computers were big enough to fill a room (like the IBM 701 (*https://oreil.ly/eH9wn*) in the 1950s), and even the minicomputers of the 1970s were the size of a refrigerator (such as the DEC PDP-11 (*https://oreil.ly/WNo5q*)).

Microcomputers (*https://oreil.ly/CLalj*) are one level smaller than minicomputers, and include (*https://oreil.ly/P5TP9*) all PCs and other sorts of computers about the size of a laptop or a desktop PC, and feature one or more integrated circuits or a CPU. For a long time, the term *microcomputer* was interchangeable with *personal computer*. The term is seldom used now that we have powerful computers small enough to fit in our pockets (smartphones) and on our wrists (smart watches).

The groundbreaking 1975 MITS Altair 8800, which inspired the Homebrew Computer Club and the founding of Apple Computers, is sometimes called the first microcomputer. But the *very* first microcomputer was probably the Q1 (*https://oreil.ly/4JMZs*), based on an Intel 8008, released in December 1972. It looked like an electronic typewriter and had a small, low-quality orange monochromatic plasma display built into it.

See also "Apple" on page 13, "CPU (Central processing unit)" on page 57, "Homebrew Computer Club" on page 136, "Minicomputers" on page 176, "Personal computers" on page 196

Microsoft

Microsoft is one of the biggest tech companies in history. It was founded in 1975 (*https://oreil.ly/E6WkJ*) (initially as Micro-Soft) by Bill Gates and Paul Allen; Gates was the face of the corporation and its CEO until 2000, when Steve Ballmer became CEO. It's best known for the Windows line of operating systems, the Xbox line of video game consoles, the Microsoft Office suite of productivity applications, and the Azure cloud platform. But that's just the tip of the iceberg.

Microsoft's very first product was Microsoft BASIC (*https://oreil.ly/hKQUP*), originally made for the legendary MITS Altair 8800 microcomputer, but then ported to lots of other personal computers of the 1970s and 1980s, including devices made by Atari and Commodore. BASIC lives on today as Visual Basic.

Microsoft had BASIC, but didn't yet have an operating system, so in 1981, Microsoft bought 86-DOS from Seattle Computer Products (*https://oreil.ly/dSGok*) for about $25,000—quite a bargain, since it would transform Microsoft into a billion-dollar and then trillion-dollar corporation! Gates worked out a deal to pre-install the operating system, then called PC-DOS 1.0, on IBM PC clones. The first version to use MS in its name was 1982's MS-DOS 1.25. MS-DOS also ran on the "IBM PC compatibles" made by companies like Dell, HP, and Compaq throughout the 1980s and 1990s.

Microsoft needed a graphical operating system, and the mouse-driven GUIs of the Xerox Alto (*https://oreil.ly/R2M9W*) and the first Apple Macintosh showed the way. Gates lured Xerox PARC alumni Charles Simonyi and Scott MacGregor (*https://oreil.ly/n6f1l*) to Microsoft in 1981 and began development on Windows 1.0. The pace was brutal. Gates expected soul-crushing crunch time from his workers. Team members so rarely left Microsoft headquarters that, according to legend, they would sometimes become delirious and conduct dangerous experiments in the cafeteria.

In 1992, Windows 3.1 made a huge commercial breakthrough in the graphical operating system market and was soon found in millions upon millions of homes and offices. The 1995 marketing campaign for Windows 95 was massive; Microsoft even licensed the Rolling Stones' classic song "Start Me Up."

The company's first operating system, PC-DOS (MS-DOS) 1.0, launched for the IBM PC in 1981.

Microsoft's first graphical operating system, Windows 1.0, launched in November 1985. All consumer Windows versions up until 2000's Windows Me (*https://oreil.ly/BfCjX*) ran as a layer on top of MS-DOS.

The first Xbox console launched in November 2001. Some people were skeptical that Microsoft would be successful in this endeavor, but time and multiple generations of Xbox consoles have proved the critics wrong.

In the late 1990s, Microsoft integrated Internet Explorer into Windows, taking full advantage of Windows' massive installation base to beat Netscape Navigator. Apple, Sun Microsystems, and Netscape were among the companies that wanted antitrust laws to slow Microsoft down (*https://oreil.ly/2bHSi*) in its quest for world domination, and they sued Microsoft under those laws in 1998. Microsoft lost the lawsuit in November 1999, but a few years later an appeals court ruled that Microsoft didn't have a monopoly. The company settled with the US Department of Justice in November 2001 and agreed to share some of its code with outside entities.

Microsoft's entry into cloud platforms, Microsoft Azure (*https://oreil.ly/-_cep*), launched in 2008. The Bing search engine launched in 2009 and for many years was less popular with users than its competitor at Google. But in 2023, interest in Bing grew (*https://oreil.ly/GYKlo*) when it integrated AI features from OpenAI.

Satya Nadella replaced Ballmer as CEO in 2014. Nadella's leadership has made Microsoft a company that's much friendlier with the open source community.

In the 2020s, Microsoft has made two major moves designed to help it further dominate the video game industry, announcing plans to acquire ZeniMax Media and Bethesda Softworks in 2020, and to acquire Activision Blizzard in 2022 (which still hasn't been completely approved (*https://oreil.ly/XbLXs*) as of this writing in April 2023).

See also "Activision" on page 2, "Artificial intelligence (AI)" on page 17, "Atari" on page 22, "Azure" on page 28, "Certificates (professional credentials)" on page 46, "ChatGPT" on page 47, "Commodore" on page 53, "DOS (Disk Operating System)" on page 86, "Gates, Bill" on page 109, "Git/GitHub" on page 113, "IBM" on page 139, "Personal computers" on page 196, "Pirates of Silicon Valley (1999 film)" on page 202, "Xerox" on page 273

Minicomputers

Minicomputers were prominent from roughly the mid-1960s to the beginning of the 1980s. They were called "mini" because they were merely the size of a refrigerator, rather than room-sized like the computers that preceded them. Home computing wasn't really a thing yet, but minicomputers (*https://oreil.ly/bDvzY*) made computing more affordable and accessible to institutions and businesses than ever before.

The earliest minicomputer (*https://oreil.ly/Mr2AN*) was DEC's PDP-8, which launched in 1965. Ken Olsen founded Digital Equipment Corporation (DEC) because his work at MIT showed him that hackers wanted more accessible and interactive computers. Minicomputers could generate output a lot quicker than the IBM punch-card computers that dominated the 1960s, which made it much easier for hackers to debug their programs. DEC, IBM, HP, and Honeywell were the most popular brands in the minicomputer market.

By the early 1980s, microcomputers (such as PCs) and dedicated server machines had made minicomputers obsolete. Still, the dawn of hacker culture at MIT's Tech Model Railroad Club in the 1960s was made possible by minicomputers!

See also "DEC (Digital Equipment Corporation)" on page 77, "IBM" on page 139, "Hewlett-Packard (HP)" on page 131, "Microcomputers" on page 173, "Massachusetts Institute of Technology (MIT)" on page 170, "Personal computers" on page 196, "Tech Model Railroad Club" on page 240

Mitnick, Kevin

Kevin David Mitnick (*https://oreil.ly/2bXfR*) (1963–2023), born in Van Nuys, California, was a legendary early hacker and the founder of Mitnick Security. According to his official biography (*https://oreil.ly/Xl-yG*), he grew up immersed in new phone and computer technology and got into phreaking (phone hacking) and computer hacking in his teens. Many of his most famous hacks were relatively low tech, involving dumpster diving and in-person and over-the-phone social engineering. Not all hackers are criminals, but Mitnick certainly was. Mitnick's life story also illustrates how some of the most spectacular hacks don't require a lot of computer programming skill—just the ability to fool human beings.

When Mitnick was 12, he found a clever way to ride Los Angeles buses for free (*https://oreil.ly/Cy3a1*). He found unused bus transfers in a dumpster next to the bus-company garage. Playing the role of "curious kid," he convinced a bus driver to tell him where to get the transfer-punching device. Once he memorized LA's bus schedules, he could create convincingly punched transfers—a hack that didn't involve computers.

Mitnick "became absorbed in everything about telephones," as he writes in the missing chapter of his book (*https://oreil.ly/o6oAe*) *The Art of Deception*. "After a while, I probably knew more about the phone system than any single employee." He even pranked a friend by hacking into the phone company's system and classifying his home phone as a pay phone.

In 1979, a friend dared him to penetrate "The Ark," Digital Equipment Corporation's (DEC's) software development network. Over the phone, Mitnick convinced a DEC employee to give him a username and password to access the system by claiming to be DEC developer Anton Chernoff. His exploits didn't always go well: Mitnick's first arrest (*https://oreil.ly/2bXfR*) was for hacking Pacific Bell's network in 1981.

Even more daring, in 1982 Mitnick hacked into a national security system: (*https://oreil.ly/3YI8i*) the North American Aerospace Defense Command (NORAD) network. The hack inspired 1983's *WarGames*, one of the very first Hollywood movies about computer hacking and cybercrime.

In 1995, Mitnick was arrested by the FBI (*https://oreil.ly/nKmth*) for breaking into the home computer of computational physicist Tsutomu Shimomura (*https://oreil.ly/2bXfR*). He was detained in a pretrial facility from 1995 to 1999. During that time, Mitnick's fans in the hacker community (*https://oreil.ly/b76r6*) ran a "Free Kevin" campaign to raise funds for his defense. He was sentenced to four years in prison (*https://oreil.ly/ss6WZ*), but credited for time served.

After his release, Mitnick coauthored a series of books about cybercrime and social engineering, including stories from his own life: 2002's *The Art of Deception*, 2005's *The Art of Intrusion*, 2011's *Ghost in the Wires*, and 2017's *The Art of Invisibility*. He also ran his own cybersecurity consulting firm, Mitnick Security (*https://oreil.ly/POa4C*). In July 2023, Mitnick died of cancer. At the time of his death, his wife Kimberley was pregnant with their child. Rest in peace.

See also "Cybersecurity" on page 68, "DEC (Digital Equipment Corporation)" on page 77, "Hacker" on page 121, "Phishing" on page 198, "Phreaking" on page 199, "WarGames (1983 film)" on page 263

Miyamoto, Shigeru

Shigeru Miyamoto (1952–) is probably the most famous game designer of all time, and creator of Mario (*https://oreil.ly/yd9C5*), the most iconic video game character of all time, as well as the *Legend of Zelda* franchise, *Star Fox*, and *Pikmin*.

Before working for Nintendo, Miyamoto studied industrial design (*https://oreil.ly/YKWiV*) at Kanazawa Municipal College of Industrial Arts in Japan, and was an aspiring manga artist. His first well-known "hack" for Nintendo was in 1979, when Taito's *Space Invaders* (*https://oreil.ly/V_-2l*) was the hot new craze in video games. Miyamoto converted the company's money-losing *Radar Scope* (*https://oreil.ly/2uoeD*) arcade-game machines into a new and profitable game: 1981's *Donkey Kong* (*https://oreil.ly/d42uo*).

In *Donkey Kong*, players control a little man named Jumpman. Jumpman became Mario in 1982's *Donkey Kong Jr.* (*https://oreil.ly/svXin*), and in 1983 Mario got his very own arcade game: *Mario Bros* (*https://oreil.ly/jAHoK*). In 1985, Nintendo released the first proper side-scrolling platformer video game, *Super Mario Bros.* (*https://oreil.ly/HJEnI*), for its Famicom and NES consoles. The rest is history.

Miyamoto might not call himself a hacker, but his work has brought the hacker spirit of inventiveness—hiding secrets in his games that inspire players to explore every nook and cranny— into popular culture, as well as inspiring the next generation of game designers.

In a keynote speech (*https://oreil.ly/OQeb9*) at 1999's Game Developers Conference, Miyamoto said, "My strength lies in [using] my pioneering spirit to make use of technology to create the best, interactive commodities possible, and use that interactivity to give users a game they can enjoy and play comfortably."

See also "Google Cloud Platform (GCP)" on page 117, "Nintendo" on page 185

MMO (Massively Multiplayer Online) games

Massively Multiplayer Online (*https://oreil.ly/zixol*) (MMO) video games are a type of roleplaying game played through a computer network with large numbers of human players. The precursor to MMOs were the Multi-User Dungeons (MUDs) (*https://oreil.ly/dwa6U*) of the 1970s, which were text-based, frequently inspired by Dungeons & Dragons, and often played through mainframe terminals or minicomputers.

World of Warcraft, an MMORPG launched in 2004 that is still running and expanding, pushed MMOs into popular culture. *Final Fantasy XIV* and *The Elder Scrolls Online* (*https://oreil.ly/aKwrB*) are two other widely popular MMORPGs.

Today, MMOs have evolved into "live service games" (*https://oreil.ly/sH3bI*), sometimes called GaaS (games as a service), such as *Fortnite* and *League of Legends*. MMOs frequently update their content, so they can go on for as long as the developer keeps running its servers and expanding its world, characters, and quest lines. Many a hacker has spent years playing a single MMO.

See also "Dungeons & Dragons (game franchise)" on page 90, "Minicomputers" on page 176, "Roleplaying games (RPGs)" on page 218

Moore's law

Renowned engineer Gordon Moore (*https://oreil.ly/Zpq5i*) spent much of his career on the cutting edge of semiconductor microprocessor development. A lot of the technological aspects of today's CPUs come from his work. He co-founded Fairchild Semiconductor in 1957 and was there through most of its 1960s glory days. In 1968, he co-founded Intel. *Moore's law* (*https://oreil.ly/4WKia*) was based on his prediction about the evolution of semiconductors, published in *Electronics* in 1965. Based on empirical data, Moore predicted that the number of transistors that could be put on a microchip would double each year. He later amended that period (*https://oreil.ly/dZmGp*) to every 18 months to 2 years.

Although consumers don't notice the effects of Moore's law in the smartphones and PCs that we use these days, it still holds true for advancements in the highest-tech CPUs for the enterprise and power computing markets.

See also "CPU (Central processing unit)" on page 57, "Fairchild Semiconductor" on page 103, "Intel" on page 144

Morse code

The telegraph, invented in the 1830s, was the earliest way to send electronic messages from one point to another. The earliest telegraph technology was invented concurrently by two teams: William Cooke and Charles Wheatstone in England, and Samuel Morse, Leonard Gale, and Alfred Vail in the United States.

Since telegraphs couldn't transmit voice or text, the technology needed a simple communication system. Morse and Vail invented the first version of Morse code around 1837. It was as simple as binary code, but with sequences of dots and dashes instead of ones and zeroes. Morse and Vail keyed certain sequences to letters and numbers to form a code. It was first used in a telegraph in 1844 and became widely used in the emerging railroad industry.

In telegraphy, Morse code was transmitted as sound, but its sequences can be adapted for communicating with many different kinds of technologies, even flashlight beams or smoke signals. The early radios of the 1890s couldn't transmit voice either, so they used Morse code over radio waves, calling it *radiotelegraphy*.

Most laypeople know the Morse code for "SOS," the international distress signal:

... --- ...

"SOS" doesn't stand for anything in particular; the letters were chosen because they're easy to transmit in Morse code.

Morse code is still commonly used in military training, as well as in the ham radio community.

Here's International Morse Code, if you want to start learning a fun new skill:

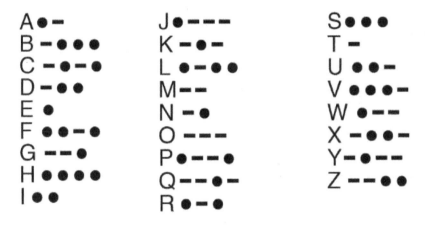

See also "Binary" on page 35, "Cryptography" on page 63, "Ham radio" on page 127

Mr. Robot (TV show)

Mr. Robot was a very popular TV show that aired on the USA Network from 2015 to 2019. Its protagonist Elliot Alderson (*https://oreil.ly/720Eo*), played by Rami Malek, is an "autistic-coded" cybersecurity engineer who is recruited by the mysterious "Mr. Robot" to join a hacktivist group called "fsociety." fsociety's nemesis is E Corp, a massive corporation that makes phones and devices and has a banking and consumer credit division that owns 70% of the global consumer-credit industry (very much like Samsung (*https://oreil.ly/xkP4_*) in South Korea).

The exploits portrayed in the show were much more realistic than those in the 1995 movie *Hackers*. One of my colleagues, threat intelligence researcher Cheryl Biswas, once told me that she believes the show carefully omitted certain details that would teach viewers how to conduct those cyber exploits successfully in real life to avoid responsibility for any real-world cyberwarfare or bank hacks. In particular, it depicted insider threats: when an employee or contractor cyberattacks their own employer. Internal attackers can be especially dangerous because of their inside knowledge and access to their attack target.

See also "Autistic" on page 26, "Exploit" on page 101, "Hackers (1995 film)" on page 122

MS-DOS (Microsoft Disk Operating System)

See "DOS (Disk Operating System)" on page 86

Multics

See "Timesharing" on page 243

14

N

Napster

See "Peer-to-peer (P2P) networks" on page 195

National Air and Space Administration (NASA)

See "Assange, Julian" on page 18, "Augmented and virtual reality" on page 25, "DARPA (Defense Advanced Research Projects Agency)" on page 72, "Fairchild Semiconductor" on page 103, "Hidden Figures (2017 film)" on page 134

National Security Agency (NSA)

See "Assange, Julian" on page 18, "Carr, Iris" on page 44, "Hellman, Martin" on page 128, "Snowden, Edward" on page 227, "WikiLeaks" on page 266

Networking

Computer networking is all about connecting multiple computers so they can share data with each other. The largest computer network in the world is the internet. There are also lots of much smaller computer networks.

In the early years of the Cold War (the late 1950s), a time when the most robust communications network was the telephone system, DARPA (then just ARPA) asked the RAND Corporation to help (*https://oreil.ly/KiLoN*) develop a communications network that could withstand nuclear warfare. Paul Baran led that project.

Meanwhile, at the National Physical Laboratory in England, Donald Davies was researching how to improve computer timesharing systems. The fixed bandwidth of existing telephone networks wouldn't cut it. In the mid-1960s, Baran and Davies concurrently invented the concept of packet switching. ARPAA chief scientist Lawrence Roberts collaborated (*https://oreil.ly/WTWou*) with Baran and Leonard Kleinrock of UCLA to create a distributed computer network based on it.

In October 1965 (*https://oreil.ly/OupP_*), Lawrence Roberts made the very first data transmission to another computer far away: from an MIT computer in Massachusetts to a Q32 computer in Santa Monica, California. Soon after, Kleinrock sent the very first transmission over a packet-switching network.

See also "DARPA (Defense Advanced Research Projects Agency)" on page 72, "Internet" on page 145, "Massachusetts Institute of Technology (MIT)" on page 170, "Packet switching" on page 193, "Peer-to-peer (P2P) networks" on page 195, "Ping" on page 200, "Timesharing" on page 243

NeXT Computer

Steve Jobs founded NeXT Computer in 1985 (*https://oreil.ly/SLCoP*), after he left Apple for a period.

In the early 1980s, Carnegie Mellon University's Raj Reddy compiled a set of ideal specifications for workstation computers that he called "3M" (*https://oreil.ly/RjEY5*): a megabyte of memory, a megapixel display, and a million instructions per second of processing power. Jobs founded NeXT Computer to fulfill those specifications and design the computer he'd always dreamed of.

NeXT's first product, the NeXT Cube (*https://oreil.ly/bloEE*) computer, was first shipped in December 1988 with a Motorola 68030 CPU and 4 to 16 megabytes of RAM (surpassing "3M"), priced for institutional buyers at a mere $6,500 (about $16,000 in 2023 dollars). It featured NeXT's own UNIX-based operating system, NeXTSTEP.

Tim Berners-Lee famously invented the World Wide Web on a NeXT computer, which he also used as the first web server. Still, NeXT Computer struggled. The market for expensive luxury computers was limited. In the mid-1990s, Apple purchased NeXT Computer and its operating system in-house, returning Jobs to Apple, this time as CEO. The first version of Mac OS X (*https://oreil.ly/_zJve*), launched in 2001, incorporated a lot of elements from NeXTSTEP, including its use of a UNIX kernel.

See also "Apple" on page 13, "Berners-Lee, Tim" on page 33, "Carnegie Mellon University" on page 43, "Jobs, Steve" on page 150, "UNIX" on page 253, "World Wide Web" on page 268

Nihon Falcom

Nihon Falcom is a Japanese game development studio that's incorporated the hacker spirit ever since its founding. In 1981, Masayuki Kato opened a store in Tokyo called Computerland Tachikawa. It was an authorized seller of Apple products, and Kato invited young hackers (*https://oreil.ly/v-Pk1*) to use the store as a hacker space for whatever computer programming they wanted to do. The name Falcom (*https://oreil.ly/47WsM*) was inspired by the *Millennium Falcon* ship from *Star Wars*, but used an "m" because it was all about computers. (*Nihon* is simply "Japan" in Japanese.)

Falcom published many games developed by the Computerland hackers. Its first breakthrough was 1984's *Dragon Slayer*, one of the earliest Japanese action RPGs. Along with the *Ys* RPG series, launched in 1987, Falcom's two biggest video game franchises continue to spawn new games.

Toshihiro Kondo (*https://oreil.ly/Jx2o0*), a fan of Falcom's *Legend of Heroes* series, created a fan site in 1996 that caught the attention of Falcom. The company hired him in 1998, and in 2007, he became president of Falcom, a position he still holds as of this writing. Kondo hacked his way to his dream job, and his genuine enthusiasm for Falcom's games makes every game feel like a labor of love. (I happen to be a *Legend of Heroes: Trails* series mega fan.)

See also "Roleplaying games (RPGs)" on page 218

Nintendo

Nintendo was founded in Kyoto, Japan (*https://oreil.ly/cjSdZ*), in 1889, just after the Meiji Restoration (*https://oreil.ly/vrfj_*) completely revolutionized the Land of the Rising Sun. Of course, this was long before electronic computers: Nintendo's first product was Hanafuda cards, used to play traditional Japanese games like Koi-Koi. Through the 20th century, Nintendo "hacked" itself through a wide range of products and services, from taxis to "love hotels" to fun mechanical and electronic toys. Many were invented by Gunpei Yokoi (*https://oreil.ly/2LWfV*), who would go on to lead development of the Game Boy.

Nintendo's first video game console was 1977's Color-TV Game 6 (*https://oreil.ly/f-9nq*), which played six different variations of Pong. Its Famicom console, released in 1983, took off in Japan—but the North American market was burned out by the Video Game Crash of 1983 (*https://oreil.ly/X8eLP*), crashing from $3.2 billion in 1982 to $100 million by 1985 (a 97% drop). American retailers were reluctant to sell video games, so Nintendo marketed the 1985 Nintendo Entertainment System (*https://oreil.ly/gneao*) (NES) as an "entertainment system" deliberately, bundling it with the R.O.B. toy robot accessory and the Zapper light gun. The NES single handedly rescued the North American and European game console markets.

Nintendo has used computer technology to deliver amazing fantasy worlds: *Super Mario Bros.*'s Mushroom Kingdom, *The Legend of Zelda*'s Hyrule, and the universe of Pokémon, the most profitable media franchise of all time (*https://oreil.ly/3CEdw*).

Today, even with heavy competition from Sony, Microsoft, gaming PCs, and smartphone gaming, the Nintendo Switch is going strong. I expect Nintendo's next console will also do very well.

See also "Miyamoto, Shigeru" on page 178, "Roleplaying games (RPGs)" on page 218

Nonfungible tokens (NFTs)

Nonfungible tokens (NFTs) aren't hacker culture, but many laypeople think they are—which is why this book addresses them. To explain why, and what they are, let's back up for just a moment.

A blockchain is a ledger of monetary transactions (or similar actions), logged into a "chain" that's implemented with cryptography. The first decentralized blockchain was invented by the anonymous person or collective known as Satoshi Nakamoto in 2008, and it soon formed the foundation of the very first cryptocurrency, Bitcoin. Most cryptocurrencies use blockchains to record buying, selling, and trades.

Each blockchain transaction is recorded as a "block," and each block has its own address—usually (but not always) a web URL of an image file, like website.com/imagefolder/imagefile.jpg.

Artist Kevin McCoy and tech entrepreneur Anil Dash invented the NFT during a 2014 hackathon. They called it Monegraph, short for "monetized graphics." As Dash later explained (*https://oreil.ly/4VevT*):

> *You couldn't store the actual digital artwork in a blockchain; because of technical limits, records in most blockchains are too small to hold an entire image. Many people suggested that rather than trying to shoehorn the whole artwork into the blockchain, one could just include the web address of an image, or perhaps a mathematical compression of the work, and use it to reference the artwork elsewhere.*

As Josh Constine summarized it in TechCrunch (*https://oreil.ly/TXuMV*):

People don't want to buy copies of art, they want the original.... Artists can visit the Monegraph site and sign in with Twitter. Then they submit the URL of a digital image they've created. In return they receive a blockchain key and value they can store in a NameCoin wallet, similar to how they would store bitcoin. This is their digital deed, a unique claim of ownership to the piece of art.

An NFT is a recording of the address of a digital entity in a blockchain block. The blockchain can prove that a transaction came from a specific cryptocurrency wallet. But it can't prove who owns an image hosted at a URL, nor can it prevent that image from being deleted from the web server. When a web-hosted image file is deleted from a server, the URL in the NFT will point to something that doesn't exist—equivalent to an HTTP 404 "file not found" error.

McCoy tried to market Monegraph for a few years, without much success. But NFTs emerged in 2020, each priced at the cryptocurrency equivalent of thousands, sometimes millions, of dollars. Dash regretted what happened (*https://oreil.ly/ZQLJ7*) to his invention:

This means that when someone buys an NFT, they're not buying the actual digital artwork; they're buying a link to it. And worse, they're buying a link that, in many cases, lives on the website of a new start-up that's likely to fail within a few years. Decades from now, how will anyone verify whether the linked artwork is the original?

There's a popular myth that buying an NFT grants you intellectual property rights over the image it links to. That's led to some hilarious incidents. For instance, in March 2021, someone paid the cryptocurrency equivalent of $2.9 million for an NFT of Twitter founder Jack Dorsey's first tweet. In April 2022, the buyer tried to sell it at an auction—and the top bid was for the equivalent of just $277.

NFT fans have often said that they want to revolutionize the internet as "Web3," which they envision as monetizing absolutely everything. This is the opposite of the hacker ethos that "knowledge should be free." Hacker culture is open source software. Hacker culture is pirating digital media and sharing its torrent files through search engines like the Pirate Bay. Hacker culture is when Aaron Swartz tried to breach the massive JSTOR database of publicly funded scientific research and make that knowledge free to the public.

Despite claims that NFTs would help digital artists make money from their work, in practice, NFTs have become a means for digital art thieves to make money from art they didn't create.

Since the great "crypto crash" of May 2022, the public has become a lot more cynical about NFTs. NFT prices are based on their perceived value, which as of this writing has plummeted.

See also "Cryptocurrency" on page 61, "Open source" on page 189, "Pirate Bay/Pirate Party" on page 202, "Swartz, Aaron" on page 235, "World Wide Web" on page 268

NVIDIA

NVIDIA is one of the most important computer hardware companies today. It was founded (*https://oreil.ly/piSoe*) in 1993 by Jensen Huang, Chris Malachowsky, and Curtis Priem. Their original vision was to produce 3D graphics hardware for gaming and media creation, but the company is now best known for its GeForce series of graphics cards and for its AI technology.

NVIDIA even claims to have invented the graphics processing unit (GPU) in 1999. NVIDIA's GPUs are used in at least half of all gaming PCs, as well as (*https://oreil.ly/rrBwI*) in Microsoft Xbox and Sony consoles. Its GPUs and other semiconductor technologies are also used in scientific research and AI development (not to mention lots of cryptomining (*https://oreil.ly/Mrti5*)).

See also "Artificial intelligence (AI)" on page 17, "Hardware" on page 128

15

O

OpenAI

See "Artificial intelligence (AI)" on page 17, "ChatGPT" on page 47

Open source

Open source licenses (*https://oreil.ly/1gaMT*) are the agreements that make free and open source software feasible. Open source licenses usually allow any entity developing software to use them as long as they follow certain rules, from one person developing simple PC games for fun to a big development studio developing and maintaining a complex and popular operating system. An open source license exists to say, "You may use this software code and make modifications to it without paying for it or directly asking for permission, but only under these terms."

There are lots of different open source licenses (*https://oreil.ly/ozKVU*); some of the most common are the GNU Public License, BSD License, MIT License, and Apache License. As noted in *Understanding Open Source and Free Software Licensing* by Andrew M. St. Laurent (O'Reilly), open source licenses differ, but their terms usually include at least some of the following:

- You must include a copy of the text of the open source license in your application or script's code (usually done using code commenting).

- You must not sell your software for any amount of money whatsoever. In the 1980s and 1990s, it was generally acceptable to pay for the materials cost of a floppy disk or optical disc, but not for the software itself. Now that open source software is distributed through the internet, no money should change hands. (Large corporations in the open source software business, like Red Hat, often sell customer support or other services but offer their actual software free of charge.)

- Other people and entities may use your code in other applications or make their own changes to your code as long as they abide by the license.

Richard "RMS" Stallman founded the GNU Public License system and the Free Software Foundation (*https://oreil.ly/xwCl5*), along with the GNU Project. RMS is often a controversial figure, but his legacy as one of the most influential figures in the history of hacker culture is consistently acknowledged. In the entry about him in this book, I'll go into more detail.

The GNU Public License (*https://oreil.ly/woPaA*) (GPL), founded by Stallman and maintained by the Free Software Foundation, is one of the most prominent "copyleft" open source licenses. That means that anyone who releases a modified open source program must also release the source code for that program under the same license. There is a political philosophy behind "copyleft"—the hacker ethos of "knowledge should be free!"

The Berkeley Software Distribution (BSD) License was one of the first licenses for open source software. It originated from BSD, a version of UNIX developed by Bill Joy in 1977. The last proper version of BSD was released in 1995, but BSD code has been used in many other operating systems ever since; you can find BSD code in Mac OS X/macOS, Windows XP, PlayStation 4, Nintendo Switch, and lots of other current operating systems and devices.

The MIT License (*https://oreil.ly/yCBs9*) was another early open source license and is likely the most popular today. It's a "permissive" license: you may use code from MIT-licensed software in commercial, proprietary software. Ruby on Rails, jQuery, and Node.js, software components used in a lot of commercial software, are released under the MIT License.

The Apache License (*https://oreil.ly/dF-Zq*) is another "permissive" license that permits using Apache-licensed code in proprietary commercial applications. The Free Software Foundation considers it the best "permissive" license.

See also "Apache/Apache License" on page 13, "GNU (software collection)" on page 114, "Joy, Bill" on page 153, "Nonfungible tokens (NFTs)" on page 186, "Shareware/freeware/abandonware" on page 223, "Stallman, Richard" on page 229, "UNIX" on page 253

Open Worldwide Application Security Project (OWASP)

The Open Worldwide Application Security Project (*https://oreil.ly/s6cpD*) (OWASP) is a nonprofit foundation devoted to web security, founded in 2001 by Mark Curphey (*https://oreil.ly/I9aDc*). Today, regular folks send more sensitive financial, medical, and authentication data through the web than ever before, so OWASP serves a vital need.

One of its best-known projects is the OWASP Top Ten (*https://oreil.ly/Wy9O-*), an important guide for web developers that outlines the ten most significant risks to website and web application cybersecurity. The list is updated every few years and includes OWASP's recommendations for mitigating these risks. Another is OWASP Zed Attack Proxy (*https://oreil.ly/8OtQ9*) (ZAP), a web vulnerability scanner that's similar to network vulnerability scanners like Metasploit and Nessus, but specifically for testing websites and web applications.

In July 2023, the ZAP application development project was transferred from OWASP to the Software Security Project (*https://oreil.ly/weFL-*) (SSP) (*https://oreil.ly/hJ_Ov*), a part of the Linux Foundation.

See also "Cybersecurity" on page 68, "Penetration testing" on page 196, "World Wide Web" on page 268

Operating systems

See "Android operating system" on page 11, "Apple" on page 13, "Debian" on page 76, "GNOME" on page 113, "Kali Linux" on page 155, "Linux" on page 161, "Microsoft" on page 174, "Red Hat" on page 213, "UNIX" on page 253, "Xfce" on page 274

Operational security

See "Cybersecurity" on page 68

16

P

Packet switching

All data transmitted over computer networks, whether through the internet or much smaller networks, is sent in the form of packets. It's a way of managing the bandwidth in our vast global telecommunications infrastructure. Paul Baran at the RAND Corporation for ARPA (now DARPA) and Donald Davies of the National Physical Laboratory in England invented packet switching separately in the early and mid-1960s, and the concept of network packets soon followed.

ARPAnet, the precursor to the modern internet, launched in 1969. The various academic institutions, government entities, and big tech companies that joined it used a wide range of packet-switching standards, many of which were technologically incompatible. To address this problem, Vint Cerf and Bob Kahn invented TCP/IP (*https://oreil.ly/Qs5O_*) in the mid-1970s.

TCP/IP packets have components that interface with four of the seven layers of the *open systems interconnection (OSI) model* (*https://oreil.ly/itzyN*)—application layer, transport layer, network layer, and data link layer. There are a wide range of TCP/IP ports which use different-looking packets. Most TCP/IP packets (*https://oreil.ly/eaQJ3*) contain a header, payload, and trailer. The header contains the sender and recipient's IP addresses, an indicator of the protocol (such as HTTPS, SMTP, or FTP), and the packet's number in its sequence. The payload is the content itself, such as the audio and video data in the YouTube videos you watch, or the digital file of an ebook. Finally, the trailer declares the end of the packet and corrects any errors.

The birthdate of the internet is considered to be January 1, 1983 (*https://oreil.ly/IMD3e*), when ARPA enforced the policy that all packet switching must use the TCP/IP standard.

See also "ARPAnet" on page 17, "DARPA (Defense Advanced Research Projects Agency)" on page 72, "Internet" on page 145, "Networking" on page 183, "TCP/IP (Transmission Control Protocol/Internet Protocol)" on page 239

Page, Larry

Larry Page (*https://oreil.ly/OoRIV*) (1973–), cofounder of Google with Sergey Brin, grew up in East Lansing, Michigan, where his father was a computer-science professor at Michigan State University.

Page and Brin met as Stanford students in 1995, and they were still students when they founded Google in 1998. Page was Google's first CEO (*https://oreil.ly/38Q5u*) from then until until 2001. Because he was in his late twenties, many in the industry considered him an inexperienced kid with some middle-aged business advisors. Page handed the CEO position to "grown-up" Eric Schmidt in 2001, but resumed the CEO role in 2011—older and presumably wiser. When Page and Brin founded their holding company Alphabet Inc. in 2015, Page became CEO there. He retired from that position in 2019 and has since lived in New Zealand as a reclusive billionaire, spending much of his time funding flying-car and space-exploration startups.

See also "Alphabet Inc." on page 8, "Google" on page 114, "Silicon Valley" on page 224, "Stanford University" on page 230

PEBKAC

Sometimes technical problems aren't problems in the technology itself, but in how the user is using it. This is a scenario IT support people (*https://oreil.ly/rUEqm*) call "problem exists between keyboard and chair," or PEBKAC (*https://oreil.ly/YMMiU*).

For example, I started my computing career as a remote tech support agent in the 2000s. I mostly dealt with malware infections, but sometimes I'd encounter scenarios like this:

> *Customer: Windows keeps telling me my password is wrong! It's not letting me in! My computer is lying to me! My password really is "John-Smith1979"!*
>
> *Me: Please, never ever tell anyone your password. Now tell me, is the caps lock on your keyboard on?*
>
> *Customer: I don't know what that is. Anyway, Windows is lying to me! I'm gonna make an angry phone call to Bill Gates!*

However, user experience (UX) designers, who perhaps are kinder, often argue that in such situations, the best thing to do is improve the user interface so users are less likely to make mistakes or misunderstand what's happening.

Peer-to-peer (P2P) networks

In a peer-to-peer (*https://oreil.ly/BaA9P*) (P2P) network, files are shared between users and endpoints, without a server as an intermediary.

Napster made music piracy and P2P networks popular when it launched (*https://oreil.ly/tc6If*) in 1999. The record industry was motivated to shut Napster down, and succeeded with a 2001 (*https://oreil.ly/hj1nP*) court injunction. Although Napster was a P2P network, it had a centralized index server that helped users connect to the other users who had the files they wanted. But P2P networks are legal; it's the piracy they're sometimes used for that's illegal.

An example of a popular P2P network today is BitTorrent. A lot of files are shared through BitTorrent lawfully, such as open source software and public domain media, but it's also often used for piracy.

See also "Networking" on page 183, "Piracy" on page 200

Penetration testing

Penetration testing, or "pentesting" for short, is the craft of executing simulated cyberattacks to test the security of a computer system. (Some people call it ethical hacking, but that's a bit controversial.) Laypeople sometimes confuse pentesting with cyberattacking or vulnerability auditing. Unlike cyberattacking, pentesting is done with the consent of the hacked system's owner. And unlike vulnerability assessment (which is a scan based on known vulnerabilities without simulating an attack), pentesting simulates cyberattacks to find vulnerabilities.

All computer systems can benefit from proper vulnerability scanning and auditing. But only computer systems with mature security in place benefit from pentesting.

If you want to do consensual hacking for a living, there are a lot of great online platforms to learn and practice, like TryHackMe, Pentester Academy, and my former employer, Hack The Box. These platforms serve an important need by giving hackers a lawful environment in which to simulate cyberattacks. Experience on those platforms is usually a bonus for job hunters as well.

If you want to learn more, here are two books I've written on the subject:

- Phillip L. Wylie and Kim Crawley, *The Pentester BluePrint: Starting a Career as an Ethical Hacker* (John Wiley & Sons, 2020).

- Kim Crawley, *8 Steps to Better Security: A Simple Cyber Resilience Guide for Business* (John Wiley & Sons, 2021).

See also "Cybersecurity" on page 68, ""Ethical" hacking" on page 100

PGP

See "Pretty Good Privacy (PGP)" on page 203

Personal computers

When the MITS Altair 8800 (*https://oreil.ly/RlOOb*) became available for sale in early 1975, it kicked off a lot of very important events in the history of hacker culture. It was the first device Microsoft commercially developed software for:

the Microsoft version of the BASIC programming language. It inspired the launch of the Homebrew Computer Club in Menlo Park, California. Furthermore, it inspired Homebrew Computer Club member Steve Wozniak to develop his prototype for the Apple I, which was the first product sold by Apple Computer...which was co-founded with fellow Homebrew Computer Club member Steve Jobs.

All that happened because the Altair 8800 was the first microcomputer to make lots of hackers believe home computing is possible, even though it wasn't the first microcomputer chronologically. That honor goes to 1972's Q1 (*https:// oreil.ly/F8TOn*).

The Altair 8800 was simply a box with a lot of switches and LED lights. It didn't come with any user-friendly monitor, keyboard, or mouse peripherals. Only some peripherals were compatible, and those would have to be acquired and added by the user. So I wouldn't really consider it to be a PC, although the Altair 8800 helped to spur on PC development.

Conceptually, the grandfather of the PC was the "Mother of All Demos" (*https://oreil.ly/MD17B*), the development of which was led by Douglas Engelbart. It was made at the Stanford Research Institute with DARPA (Defense Advanced Research Projects Agency) funding, and shown publicly in December 1968. It had a graphical user interface, hypertext links, the first mouse, a keyboard, and limited network connectivity, although it wasn't too usable beyond being a really impressive prototype. So the father of the PC was 1973's Xerox Alto (*https://oreil.ly/Bh_uN*). The Alto was at many offices at Xerox PARC, but never commercially sold. It was definitely based on the Mother of All Demos, but made to be an actually fully usable computer. Steve Jobs and some of the Apple team got to see the Alto in 1979, and it influenced the development of the 1984 Apple Macintosh. Microsoft was also influenced by the Alto, which resulted in the first version of Windows in 1985.

The first PC to be called a PC was 1981's IBM PC (*https://oreil.ly/RzNTa*). Although the first IBM PC didn't have a graphical operating system, it had PC-DOS, which was later renamed MS-DOS. It was Microsoft's first commercially successful operating system. When Windows debuted in 1985, it was made for IBM PCs and "IBM PC compatibles" from companies like Compaq, Dell, and HP. The IBM PC standard was designed to be made with "off-the-shelf" components that were compatible with Intel x86 CPUs. IBM famously allowed Microsoft to sell PC-DOS/MS-DOS to other manufacturers as per their contract. But IBM thought they could prevent successful IBM PC copycats by locking down their proprietary BIOS. Compaq found a hack around that restriction, and released their first Compaq Portable IBM PC clone in November 1982. All with BIOS that Compaq had Phoenix Technologies help develop (*https://oreil.ly/BVx8K*). And the rest was history.

I remember the phrase "IBM PC compatible" being commonly used all the way up until about the launch of Windows 95 in 1995. Now in people's minds, PC is synonymous with "Microsoft Windows computer." For instance, PC gaming generally refers to gaming on Windows PCs with Microsoft DirectX graphics. I'm using such a gaming PC right now. Although for the longest time, my work PC was my Kubuntu Linux self-built desktop. And for most of 2021, I used a MacBook Pro that Hack The Box gave me. As someone with lots of familiarity with all three of the most common microcomputer operating system platforms, I think any microcomputer made for consumers is a PC. So there!

See also "Apple" on page 13, "DARPA (Defense Advanced Research Projects Agency)" on page 72,"Graphical user interface (GUI)" on page 117, "Homebrew Computer Club" on page 136, "IBM" on page 139, "Jobs, Steve" on page 150, "Microcomputers" on page 173, "Microsoft" on page 174, "Wozniak, Steve" on page 269, "Xerox" on page 273

Phishing

Phishing (*https://oreil.ly/ehTBQ*) is a destructive cyberattack technique and the most common kind of social engineering exploit.

Just about any medium can be used for phishing: text messages, emails, web pages, social media posts, phone calls. In a phishing attack, a threat actor uses one of those mediums to pretend to be an entity you trust, such as a bank, an online service (such as Netflix or Facebook), a utility company, or even an individual like a friend, a family member, your doctor, or your boss.

Phishing (*https://oreil.ly/GuRb_*) attacks vary greatly, but generally the threat actor wants some sort of sensitive information or computer access from you. Here's a typical example. An attacker pretending to be your cellphone provider sends you a text that says, "You need to pay your phone bill now. Click this link." If you click on the link, a website that looks identical to your cellphone provider's real website presents a form and asks you to enter your username and password. If you do, the attacker can use your account to impersonate you or fraudulently charge transactions to your credit card.

Certain Dark Web markets and forums sell phishing kits, which contain the web page files and images attackers need to effectively impersonate a specific company or government agency.

See also "Cybersecurity" on page 68, "Dark Web/darknet" on page 71, "Exploit" on page 101, "Jack, Barnaby" on page 149, "Mitnick, Kevin" on page 177

Phreaking

Many of the most famous hackers in history got their start with *phreaking*, or phone hacking.

Joe Engressia (*https://oreil.ly/Y1e_l*), age eight, made a fascinating discovery in 1957. Engressia was blind, and he also had perfect pitch. He enjoyed phoning numbers that played pre-recorded messages. One day, while listening to a call, he began whistling, and the call abruptly ended. So Engressia started to experiment. Eventually he learned that phone companies used a 2,600 hertz tone to take control of a trunk line, and realized that his whistle must have been precisely 2,600 Hz. He realized this could be exploited to make free long-distance calls. (It won't work with modern phone systems.)

Years later, Engressia taught his 2,600 Hz hack to John Draper, who found that a toy whistle (*https://oreil.ly/QDnee*) distributed in boxes of Cap'n Crunch cereal reliably produced a 2,600 Hz tone—earning him the nickname "Captain Crunch."

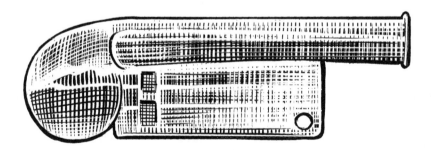

Before Steve Wozniak and Steve Jobs founded Apple Computer, they sold devices called Blue Boxes that were inspired by Draper's hack. Jobs told an interviewer (*https://oreil.ly/Y1e_l*) that, as young teens, "our first project together was, we built these little blue boxes to make free telephone calls."

Kevin Mitnick, too, was a phreaker as a child (*https://oreil.ly/9fZuI*) in the 1970s. Mitnick said, "I set a goal for myself: I'm going to try to compromise every large phone company in America and gain access to their switches. Once you have switch access, you have full control of the phone company."

See also "Captain Crunch (John Draper)" on page 41, "Cybersecurity" on page 68, "Exploit" on page 101, "Jobs, Steve" on page 150, "Mitnick, Kevin" on page 177, "2600 (Twenty-Six Hundred): The Hacker Quarterly (magazine)" on page 250, "Wardriving" on page 263, "Wozniak, Steve" on page 269

Ping

The `ping` command is a handy tool that tests whether or not a network connection works (*https://oreil.ly/bkoe9*). Virtually all network-capable operating systems use it. If there's some sort of working network connection available, `ping` will also tell you how well it works, providing Time-to-Live (how long the packet is allowed to exist in the network), bytes received, packet loss, round-trip times, and how long the response took to receive.

In most operating systems (including Windows), try opening your terminal and typing `ping` and then an IP address at the command line. In my tech support days, we often used an IP address belonging to Google: 8.8.8.8. It's a great way to test if network packets are being sent from your computer effectively, because Google's network is pretty reliable!

See also "Networking" on page 183, "Packet switching" on page 193

Piracy

Traditional piracy is robbery or theft on the high seas or in the air, in international waters or airspace. In hacker culture, piracy is all about "stealing" data that doesn't lawfully belong to you or distributing data that doesn't belong to you in an unlawful way (*https://oreil.ly/TmQxD*).

A lot of digital media is protected by intellectual property law: commercial music, television and movies, proprietary software and video games, and books like the one you're reading right now. I think it's great that O'Reilly Media ebooks don't have DRM—but technically speaking, as long as O'Reilly Media sells this book for money, downloading or uploading it on BitTorrent or other peer-to-peer networks constitutes piracy.

In my opinion, intellectual property law is a "necessary evil" as long as capitalism exists. I personally care about being paid for my work because living my life costs money. But even if I didn't need to earn a living, I would write simply because I enjoy it and I want to get my ideas out into the world.

There are definitely problems with intellectual property law, including that it tends to gate keep art and information for commercial ends. For instance, one of the many problems that piracy is actually helping to solve is video game preservation (*https://oreil.ly/FX5H9*). Big video game corporations such as Nintendo and Sony aren't very good at preserving their entire game libraries. Lots of smaller, more obscure (but often delightful) games could be lost altogether if not for hackers pirating them.

See also "DRM (Digital Rights Management)" on page 89, "Hacker" on page 121, "Nintendo" on page 185, "Peer-to-peer (P2P) networks" on page 195, "Pirate Bay/Pirate Party" on page 202

Pirate Bay/Pirate Party

The Pirate Bay is the quintessential peer-to-peer networks search engine, founded in 2003 by Fredrik Neij, Gottfrid Svartholm Warg, and Peter Sunde through Piratbyrån (*https://oreil.ly/oN1bs*), an anti-copyright group from Sweden. No other online piracy platform has such a strong brand. Movies, music, ebooks, video games, and software applications—if a piece of media is being shared through BitTorrent networks, you'll likely find it on the Pirate Bay.

In most of the world, distributing proprietary media without authorization is piracy and thus illegal. But the Pirate Bay founders believe that pirating media is a noble calling, in line with the hacker ethos that knowledge should be free.

BitTorrent is a peer-to-peer (P2P) protocol, which means users host the media they're sharing. None of the Pirate Bay's servers directly host pirated media. Rather, torrent search sites host links with information about how to find the files hosted on other people's computers. It's about abiding by the letter of the law, not its spirit. The site also moves its servers around to different parts of the world. The hacker ingenuity of these strategies has made the Pirate Bay resilient.

Still, the Pirate Bay's founders have been criminally charged and imprisoned several times. The site went offline in December 2014 and came back online in January 2015. It continues to thrive years later, with millions of users every day. Pirate Parties have formed around the world (*https://oreil.ly/sWf-D*) to advocate for anti-copyright policy, digital rights, and hacker freedom, and in many countries they are officially recognized as electoral parties.

See also "DRM (Digital Rights Management)" on page 89, "Hacktivism" on page 125, "Nintendo" on page 185, "Peer-to-peer (P2P) networks" on page 195, "Piracy" on page 200

Pirates of Silicon Valley (1999 film)

The legends of Apple and Microsoft and their founders, especially Steve Jobs and Bill Gates, are intertwined with the history of personal computing. Jobs and Gates were "frenemies" years before they became billionaires. That relationship is at the core of *Pirates of Silicon Valley*, a 1999 made-for-TV movie directed by Martyn Burke, which features one of Hollywood's first fictional depictions of Jobs and Gates. It follows their careers from the University of California, Berkeley, in the early 1970s to the late 1990s, when Jobs returned to Apple.

Jobs didn't appreciate the film, but admitted that Noah Wyle played him very well—and even had Wyle join him to play a prank on the audience at Macworld

1999 (*https://oreil.ly/gceM8*). Bill Gates found Michael Anthony Hall's portrayal of him (*https://oreil.ly/lCkPM*) "reasonably accurate." And Steve Wozniak, played by Joseph Slotnick, enjoyed the film.

Coming as it did in 1999, following the massive commercial successes of Windows 3.1 and Windows 95, the film portrays Microsoft and Gates as the victors of the battle. Apple struggled in the 1990s without Steve Jobs at the helm, but the iMac, iPod, and iPhone changed that. Had *Pirates of Silicon Valley* been made in the 2000s or 2010s, the film might have ended on a different note.

See also "Berkeley, University of California" on page 32, "Gates, Bill" on page 109, "Google" on page 114, "Jobs, Steve" on page 150, "Microsoft" on page 174, "Silicon Valley" on page 224

Pizza

See Crunch time

Pretty Good Privacy (PGP)

Pretty Good Privacy (*https://oreil.ly/k-WLu*) (PGP) is an encryption program that was introduced in 1991. It is mainly used to encrypt emails and verify signatures in open source software-development communities and on the Dark Web (though your mileage may vary).

Using and distributing PGP encryption technology is now considered perfectly lawful, but it was once controversial. The US government subjected PGP's inventor, Phil Zimmermann (*https://oreil.ly/tKCff*), to a three-year criminal investigation in the 1990s, arguing that his work in sharing PGP with the world was a violation of US export restrictions for cryptographic software.

PGP encrypts data using a combination of cryptographic functions: hashing, data compression, symmetric-key cryptography, and public-key cryptography. In public-key cryptography, a public key is generated and sent to any user who requests one to encrypt data. That user specifies who is authorized to decrypt that data, and a private key is sent to them.

Here's an example of a public key:

```
-----BEGIN PGP PUBLIC KEY BLOCK-----

Version: BCPG v1.58

mIoEWiOMeQEEAImCEQUnSQ54ee+mnkANsjyvZm2QsC1sGIBEp-
myJbh2xWuluJ/KV
```

TIUSqbkLOEq4COIlzGofhur-
uUWBM2+ANazq5jkxLrYmHX4AwA2Q6jvd3xE8B1uVj

qToTEKyZtmBwesEswUxb+vOwVLdWKXpcySXtIQhoKWAUVzG7e5uEa-
wyXABEBAAGo

BWFuaXNoNoiJwEEAECAAYFAlojjH-
kACgkQmCS94uDDx9lHewP/UtsSk3lyj5GnHyoT

HZMz+sUFpFlan7agqHf6pV2Pgdb9OMC-
VauMwl9bjPY9HSHQg/a3gTQ5qNq9txiI2

4Fso2Q3AR6XcVk2wQxS6prJ9imPiinpXarCwZkEgWLXWLuQL-
HoxRWHf9olUqeW7P

kwQlJ1K9Ib85pCTvxi6DN7QwQv8=
=Qteg
-----END PGP PUBLIC KEY BLOCK-----

You can use mobile PGP apps like OpenKeychain (*https://oreil.ly/_kmD7*), or this PGP web app from 8gwifi.org (*https://oreil.ly/DF6-C*) to generate your own PGP public and private keys. Give your friends the public key and ask them to use it to send you encrypted emails. To do that, they should just copy all the text from `-----BEGIN PGP MESSAGE-----` to `-----END PGP MESSAGE-----` and paste it in the body of an email to you. You keep the private key, and only you will be able to decrypt it.

This fun secret-message technology for hackers is free of charge thanks to the OpenPGP project (*https://oreil.ly/WuKvf*). They've been keeping PGP technology free—both "free as in free lunch" and "free as in freely shared"—since 1997.

See also "Cryptography" on page 63, "Cybersecurity" on page 68, "Diffie-Hellman key exchange" on page 84, "Hacktivism" on page 125, "Key" on page 156

Programming

Computer programming (*https://oreil.ly/u4Zwd*) means giving a computer instructions in code to execute (*https://oreil.ly/Xr9im*). It's something that most hackers do, at least sometimes.

The first programmer (*https://oreil.ly/aqTXo*) was Ada Lovelace, a woman who lived and died in the 19th century. There are thousands of computer programming languages. They range from very low-level machine code and assembly languages, which speak directly to computers, to more human-readable high-level programming languages, such as Java and C. All electronic computers work with machine code, and many can also work with high-level code if they have some sort of operating system.

Programs written in high-level code always need some sort of compiler to create machine code that can be directly processed by a CPU. The creator of the very first compiler (*https://oreil.ly/DU2OU*) was also a woman, Admiral Grace Hopper. She designed the A-0 compiler for the UNIVAC I computer in 1952.

See also "Assembly" on page 20, "Hopper, Grace" on page 137, "Integrated development environment (IDE)" on page 143, "Lovelace, Ada" on page 164, "Syntax" on page 236

Proprietary software

Proprietary, or *closed source* (*https://oreil.ly/QPx_h*), software is the opposite of open source software. The most important distinction between proprietary software and open source software is the former has closed source code, and you're not allowed to use any of that code unless the entity that owns the rights to it gives you explicit permission.

Open source software, by contrast, makes its code publicly available, and you can use open source code in other programs free of charge, as long as you comply with the open source license it was published with. Proprietary software is often only lawfully used if it's been paid for. (Some proprietary software is free, often called *freeware;* other proprietary software may be free, but offer in-app purchases.)

Some proprietary software contains open source code components—*including macOS* (*https://oreil.ly/XAOsP*). Some open source licenses permit code to be used in proprietary software under certain conditions, while others completely forbid this practice.

See also "Open source" on page 189, "Shareware/freeware/abandonware" on page 223

Proxy networks

See "Invisible Internet Project (I2P)" on page 147, "Tor (The Onion Router)" on page 245

Python

See "Programming" on page 204

17

Q

Quantum computing

Quantum computing is where quantum mechanics and computing meet. *Quantum* means really, really tiny things—the tiniest things, atomic and subatomic particles. Physicists tell me that the physics of these really tiny things are strange: the laws of physics that apply when you drop a tennis ball down a flight of stairs don't exactly apply to these really, really tiny things. The study of how they work is called *quantum mechanics*.

The data our computers process is all binary. Even when you use higher-level computer programming languages with human-readable words, it all eventually gets converted to 1s and 0s in our CPUs. A "1" or "0" is called a bit. That's how the electronic signals in our computers behave.

Quantum computers (*https://oreil.ly/1UFzx*) are designed to leverage the properties of quantum mechanics. So, instead of using bits, they use *qubits*, or quantum bits. Because of the weirdness of quantum mechanics, a qubit can be "1," "0," or both "1" and "0" simultaneously. It's mind-blowing! And when a unit of computer data can be 1 and 0 simultaneously, it greatly increases how much math a computer can do at any given time.

Quantum computers have been in research and development ever since physicist Richard Feynman proposed the concept (*https://oreil.ly/9jPEt*) in 1982. In 2017, IBM launched the first properly working quantum computers: the IBM Q (*https://oreil.ly/6nnTG*) project. Microsoft also has a quantum computing service, Azure Quantum (*https://oreil.ly/7GbVI*). As of 2023, quantum computing is still experimental and accessible only for enterprise and institutional purposes (kind of like computers in general were in the 1950s and 1960s).

Quantum networking (*https://oreil.ly/z6g3e*) is the transmission of qubits through computer networks. There aren't any publicly accessible quantum networks (*https://oreil.ly/_a_Qe*) as of this writing, but there have been some successful experiments. For instance, in 2020, a Chinese experiment (*https://oreil.ly/JHDno*) transmitted "entangled quantum memories" over a 50-kilometer fiber cable. When usable quantum networks are built, they'll use fiber-optic cable to transmit qubits with pulses of light. Other telecommunications cable materials don't work for qubits.

Quantum cryptography is digital cryptography done by quantum computers. It's so much more advanced than the binary cryptography we use today. Conversely, quantum computers can crack binary cryptography so easily that it renders ordinary binary cryptography pointless. That's why the US National Institute of Standards and Technology has been assessing quantum-safe cryptography standards (*https://oreil.ly/S1rQp*).We'll soon need reliable post-quantum cryptography to secure our binary computers, in a world where threat actors can use quantum computers.

See also "Binary" on page 35, "CPU (Central processing unit)" on page 57, "Cryptography" on page 63, "IBM" on page 139

18

R

Radio

See "Akihabara, Tokyo" on page 6, "Baer, Ralph" on page 29, "Captain Crunch (John Draper)" on page 41, "Carr, Iris" on page 44, "Electronics" on page 95, "Ham radio" on page 127, "Hewlett-Packard (HP)" on page 131, "Lamarr, Hedy" on page 159, "Morse code" on page 180, "RadioShack" on page 209, "Tokyo Denki University" on page 245, "2600 (Twenty-Six Hundred): The Hacker Quarterly (magazine)" on page 250

RadioShack

RadioShack (originally spelled Radio Shack) was a hacker's dream retailer. Founded in 1921 by brothers Theodore and Milton Deutschmann, the chain sold mostly radio equipment. When it faced financial difficulties in the early 1960s, the Tandy corporation purchased the company and expanded its offerings, even adding a store electronics brand. Radio Shack flourished. In 1977, the chain launched its very own personal computer, the TRS-80 (TRS stood for "Tandy Radio Shack"). It sold quite well for a few years.

RadioShack had about 8,000 stores worldwide at its 1999 peak. Like many hackers of my generation, I have fond childhood memories of shopping at Radio Shack in the 1980s and 1990s. I was awed by all the amateur radio equipment, antennas, televisions, remote-controlled toy cars and helicopters, digital clocks, personal computers and calculators, and other home electronics and electrical equipment. When I wanted to learn how to make simple electronics using a lemon as a battery, my late father took me to Radio Shack for a kit. These kits, for which Radio Shack was well known, were basically decorated circuit boards under cardboard that came with a collection of wires that could be connected between the kit's resistors and other electronic circuit components, and a guidebook to various projects you could make with it, like a very simple FM radio receiver. Of course, if you wanted to make professional-quality electronics, Radio Shack sold those components as well.

By the late 1990s, however, Radio Shack was struggling again. They rebranded as "RadioShack" and focused on the emerging cellphone market. Business didn't improve, however, and in 2017 the company declared bankruptcy. In 2020, Retail Ecommerce Ventures (which also owned Pier 1 Imports and Linens 'n Things) bought RadioShack and closed most of its brick-and-mortar stores. Today the brand is mainly being used to sell a cryptocurrency platform called RadioShack DeFi.

See also "Cryptocurrency" on page 61, "Electronics" on page 95, "Ham radio" on page 127, "Hardware" on page 128

Ramachandran, Vivek

Vivek Ramachandran (1983–) has contributed immensely to our understanding of network security and penetration testing (*https://oreil.ly/kofRg*). In 2004, he graduated with a BA in electronics and communications degree from the Indian Institute of Technology, Guwahati, one of India's top technical schools.

Ramachandran played a crucial role in the development of the 802.1x protocol and port security in Cisco's 6500 Catalyst line of switches. He has many other impressive technological accomplishments: he cracked WEP (wired equivalent privacy) cloaking, conceptualized backdoors for enterprise WiFi, and in 2006 won a major cybersecurity hacking competition, the Microsoft Security Shootout.

In 2007, Ramachandran discovered the Cafe Latte attack, a cyberattack that circumvents firewall protection to bring down a system's defenses, clearing the way for man-in-the-middle attacks on WEP-encrypted WiFi. As Ramachandran told *Computerworld* (*https://oreil.ly/-q8BE*) magazine, "Until now, the conventional belief was that in order to crack WEP, the attacker had to show up at the parking lot. With the discovery of our attack, every employee of an organization is the target of an attack."

Over the years, Ramachandran has conducted extensive research on ARP spoofing (ARP is how IP addresses are associated with MAC addresses that identify networking hardware), distributed denial-of-service attacks, and anomaly-based intrusion-detection systems. He also invented Chellam (*https://oreil.ly/fhwpE*), the world's first WiFi firewall.

In 2007, Ramachandran founded SecurityTube (*https://oreil.ly/TiRMo*), an "information security training portal that disseminates knowledge online," and in 2011, he founded Pentester Academy (*https://oreil.ly/O-NC5*), an online pentesting educational platform that's a major rival to Hack The Box. Ramachandran is one of the most influential minds in network security history.

See also "Cybersecurity" on page 68, "Indian Institute of Engineering Science and Technology (IIEST); Indian Institutes of Technology (IIT)" on page 141, "Networking" on page 183, "Penetration testing" on page 196

Ransomware

Ransomware is malware that encrypts the data on an infected computer (*https://oreil.ly/G3gpo*) without giving the computer's rightful owner access to the decryption key. A note appears on the infected computer demanding a ransom be paid to the cyberattacker for the target to get their data back.

The first known ransomware attack (*https://oreil.ly/YJcJy*), in 1989, waited until the user had powered their Windows computer on 90 times (which I assume would take a few months), then replaced the AUTOEXEC.BAT file and maliciously encrypted the data on the hard drive.

Before the advent of cryptocurrency in 2009, ransomware typically demanded payment to a credit card number or by wire transfer, both of which are easy for law enforcement to trace. Cryptocurrency is difficult (but not impossible) to trace, so it is now the currency of choice for ransomware.

In recent years, ransomware attacks have targeted businesses and institutions a lot more than ordinary people. It makes sense: the former can pay much larger ransoms. Most enterprise ransomware also still maliciously encrypts data, but now threatens to breach it (*https://oreil.ly/KY8s3*), too. Enterprises are much better at keeping robust data backups than they used to be, so "we will expose your sensitive data" is a more effective threat.

See also "Cryptocurrency" on page 61, "Cryptography" on page 63, "Cybersecurity" on page 68, "Exploit" on page 101, "Malware" on page 167

Raspberry Pi

A Raspberry Pi (*https://oreil.ly/8xoCL*) is a small computer based on an ARM CPU (*https://oreil.ly/9x9NA*) and a smartphone-sized motherboard. There are various models, all with WiFi support and USB ports. Some models have Ethernet ports (*https://oreil.ly/eboVl*). Raspberry Pis vary a bit in what kind of ARM CPU they have, how much RAM they have, and their input/output device support.

Usually the user has to provide their own display and input peripherals, but the official Raspberry Pi store now sells some kits (*https://oreil.ly/macgo*) that come with a mouse and keyboard.

These devices are very popular among hackers. You can use one to do many of the things you'd do with a PC, like surf the web, play games, or write a manuscript for a publisher that's eagerly anticipating it. But there are many more use cases (*https://oreil.ly/JaaRv*) for a Raspberry Pi: you could build a media streaming center, augment your TV, build a weather station (*https://oreil.ly/AuoDR*) or an FM radio station, or run your own virtual private network (VPN) server (*https://www.pivpn.io*).

I used one to make a video game emulation device with the RetroPie operating system (*https://retropie.org.uk*).

See also "ARM (Advanced RISC Machines)" on page 16, "CPU (Central processing unit)" on page 57, "Hardware" on page 128

README files

README files are a source of basic information for users (*https://oreil.ly/MOdF4*) about a piece of software, with a long legacy. A README is typically a simple text file with a name like "readme.txt." The DOS games I played in the early 1990s came with README files, which usually included basic troubleshooting instructions, information about graphics and keyboard input settings, and a brief history of the game as a technical project.

If you use GitHub, you'll likely encounter README files frequently (*https://oreil.ly/ZYYYz*). They often contain a version history, general information about the purpose of the software and how to use it, how to get involved in the software's future development, some troubleshooting information, and how to contact the developer for help.

See also "Git/GitHub" on page 113

Reddit

Reddit (*https://oreil.ly/iLib5*), a web-based forum host with a wide range of categories similar to the earlier Usenet, emerged in June 2005 (*https://oreil.ly/7Lk6h*), co-founded by Steve Huffman and Alexis Ohanian with Y Combinator funding.

Reddit is supposed to sound kind of like "read it," and the founders aspired to make it the "front page of the Internet." In the early months, they even made lots of fake accounts and posts to make Reddit look more popular. But Reddit became genuinely popular quite quickly. Magazine giant Condé Nast bought the site for US$20 million in 2006, when it averaged 500,000 users per day (though Reddit became independent from Condé Nast in 2011).

Any user with an account in good standing can create their own forum, or *subreddit*. There are basic rules to follow that are supposed to forbid harassment and cybercrime. Subreddit moderators can create their own additional rules; one of the rules of one of my favorite subreddits, /r/ZeroCovidCommunity, forbids users from posting comments that minimize the seriousness of COVID-19.

Subreddits for nerdy interests are especially popular, but there are subreddits for almost every personal interest, political affiliation, and cultural community imaginable.

There's also a completely unaffiliated Reddit equivalent on the Dark Web called the Dread forums.

See also "Dread forums" on page 88, "Internet" on page 145, "Usenet" on page 255

Red Hat

Bob Young ran a catalogue-based computer supply business. Marc Ewing was a hacker who developed one of the earliest versions of Usenet. They both believed in the potential of open source operating systems and were determined to compete against proprietary tech giants (a radical idea at the time). When they met at a tech conference in 1993 (*https://oreil.ly/yuVmm*), what happened next was kind of like "I make buns, you make hot dogs, let's get into the hot dog business!" Young and Ewing founded Red Hat Software in 1995 based on their Linux distribution, Red Hat Linux.

Ewing was really early in the realm of Linux distribution development; the project started in 1991 and Version 1.0 (*https://oreil.ly/vn3Il*) was released in 1994. Selling open source software directly would violate the letter and the spirit of open source license agreements, so Red Hat has always been free to download, install, and use. The company's monetization model is based on companies and institutions paying for support, and it has been a smash success.

Red Hat usage gradually grew in the business market through the 1990s. The company became publicly traded in 1999 (*https://oreil.ly/7d1Rv*), and became the first billion-dollar open source software company in 2012.

Red Hat launched a spin-off, Fedora, in September 2003. It's a Linux distribution based on most of Red Hat's core code and features, designed to be accessible to ordinary home users. IBM bought Red Hat for $34 billion in 2019, and today it is one of the most popular operating systems in the enterprise market.

See also "IBM" on page 139, "Linux" on page 161, "Open source" on page 189, "Usenet" on page 255

Ritchie, Dennis

Dennis Ritchie (1941–2011) was born (https://oreil.ly/IRcIq) in Bronxville, New York, the son of a Bell Labs researcher.

Ritchie got his doctorate in physics and applied mathematics from Harvard in 1967—the same year he started his own Bell Labs career. His earliest work there was on the Multics operating system, a timesharing system being jointly developed by AT&T (the owner of Bell Labs), MIT's Project MAC, and General Electric. Effective timesharing systems were important because no one had a personal computer back then. Ritchie also helped to port the BCPL programming language to Multics.

By 1969, the Multics project was abandoned. Ritchie was eager for his next project, and his colleague Ken Thompson wanted to develop a new operating system for the Labs' DEC PDP-7 minicomputer. Thompson developed the very first version of UNIX, which took Multics as inspiration. In 1971, the team ported UNIX to the PDP-11, and that required a higher-level programming language. Ritchie used the language B, which was derived from BCPL. In the process, he realized that B could be greatly improved. So he developed C (https://oreil.ly/fUHSW) in 1972, and the following year, he and Thompson rewrote UNIX in C.

C had a tremendous effect on how operating systems are developed. For instance, Windows 11 is predominantly written in C, C++, and C#, and Android in Java. The C family of languages now includes C++ and Java. In 1983, Ritchie and Thompson received a Turing Award (https://oreil.ly/rp556) for their work on C and UNIX.

See also "Bell Labs" on page 31, "Massachusetts Institute of Technology (MIT)" on page 170, "Programming" on page 204, "Thompson, Ken" on page 242, "Turing, Alan" on page 248, "UNIX" on page 253

Rivest, Ron

Ron Rivest (1947–), born in Schenectady, New York, is a professor at MIT's Computer Science and Artificial Intelligence Laboratory (https://oreil.ly/5oftW). He is also a cryptographer, famous for his work on the development of public-key cryptography, the technology that makes it possible to encrypt data in transit through the internet and other computer networks. If you've used the web, you've used public-key cryptography (indirectly).

Rivest began his career with a BA in mathematics from Yale in 1969 and a PhD in computer science from Stanford in 1973: the perfect foundation for a cryptographer. He joined MIT's Department of Electrical Engineering and Computer Science in 1974, where he met Leonard Adleman and Adi Shamir. The three developed Rivest-Shamir-Adleman (RSA) cryptography, the cryptographic algorithm that public-key cryptography uses. In 2002, Rivest, Shamir, and Adleman received a Turing Award (*https://oreil.ly/gQVIM*) for their work.

See also "Adleman, Leonard" on page 3, "Cryptography" on page 63, "Diffie-Hellman key exchange" on page 84, "Key" on page 156, "Rivest-Shamir-Adleman (RSA) cryptography" on page 215, "Shamir, Adi" on page 223, "Turing, Alan" on page 248, "World Wide Web" on page 268

Rivest-Shamir-Adleman (RSA) cryptography

When Whitfield Diffie and Martin Hellman published their paper "New Directions in Cryptography" (*https://oreil.ly/2aLqe*) in 1976, it laid a foundation that Ron Rivest, Adi Shamir, and Leonard Adleman could build upon.

Public-key cryptography is necessary for encrypting computer network transmitted data, especially if it's publicly accessible, like the internet. Public-key cryptography uses asymmetric keys, which means the public encryption key doesn't reveal the private decryption key. Because users on public networks need to receive the private decryption key so that they can read the data, the key exchange process needs to be protected. With a lot of complicated math, that's what the Diffie-Hellman key exchange does.

In 1977, Rivest, Shamir, and Adleman published an algorithm for public-key cryptography named for the three of them (RSA). The RSA algorithm (*https://oreil.ly/wwhQ-*) is used to generate a *cipher*: a secret code to scramble and unscramble data that needs to be kept secret when it travels through a network. The Diffie-Hellman key exchange is used to protect the keys that are being sent to encrypt and decrypt the RSA-encrypted data.

Back in the 1990s, only some internet-transmitted data was encrypted, such as credit card data for online purchases. Thanks to Diffie-Hellman and RSA, though, today we send encrypted data through the internet every day. The common wisdom is that as much internet traffic should be encrypted as possible, even if its contents are completely innocuous.

Diffie, Hellman, Rivest, Shamir, and Adleman figured out a lot of compli-cated math. But they weren't the first people to come up with the key exchange or the encryption algorithm. British Government Communications Headquarters (GCHQ) mathematician Clifford Cocks came up with *(https://oreil.ly/7fHpA)* a similar cryptography system in 1973. It wasn't practical for computer technology at the time, since it would have been very expensive to deploy. His cryptography idea *(https://oreil.ly/Z5HG3)* remained classified until 1997, so it wasn't available to Rivest, Shamir, and Adleman as they came up with their algorithm; they've well earned the RSA in the algorithm's name.

See also "Adleman, Leonard" on page 3, "Cryptography" on page 63, "Diffie, Whitfield" on page 83, "Diffie-Hellman key exchange" on page 84, "Hellman, Martin" on page 128, "Key" on page 156, "Rivest, Ron" on page 214, "Shamir, Adi" on page 223, "Turing, Alan" on page 248, "World Wide Web" on page 268

Robotics

Robots have existed in fiction since at least the 19th century, if not even earlier *(https://oreil.ly/hP262)* (some see the animated clay Golem from the Talmud as a sort of robot). Rosie, from the futuristic 1960s cartoon *The Jetsons*, performed a variety of household chores for the animated Space Age family with personality and sass. In the 21st century so far, real household robots are more common-place than ever, like the Roomba automatic vacuum (launched in 2002) and a wide variety of children's toys. Honda retired its walking robot, Asimo, in 2022 after 20 years *(https://oreil.ly/Haovt)* and is now working on a new model.

Other applications of robotics are less friendly: Boston Dynamics, which spun off of MIT in 1992 *(https://oreil.ly/eeg9C)* and is now owned by Google par-ent company Alphabet, has been producing impressive yet creepy headless robot dogs for the military and law enforcement market since 2005. In October 2022, the company said their robots wouldn't be used for violence against civilians, but take that with a grain of salt: just a month later, the San Francisco Police Department *(https://oreil.ly/EJZ-N)* proposed giving police robots the right to use deadly force.

You'll hear the word "bot" a lot in the context of computing. A *bot* is a script or software application that performs automated tasks, but doesn't really have a physical form (unlike a robot). Bots are programmed to perform a variety of automated tasks *(https://oreil.ly/1_WKy)*. If their programmer gives them the ability, they can converse and sometimes even pass a Turing test!

Some common bots include web crawler bots, which index web pages into search engines like Google; chat bots on corporate websites; and moderation bots for online discussion platforms such as Reddit.

Bots can also be harmful. Any sort of harmful software is malware. Bots can scrape email addresses and flood us with spam email, or crawl computer networks and spread other kinds of malware, such as ransomware. They can automate cyber exploits, such as credential stuffing attacks.[1]

A *botnet* is a network of bots, usually malicious. Cyberattackers use zombie malware to make your endpoint, server, or networking device a part of a botnet without your knowledge. Then they use command-and-control servers to execute commands to the bots in their botnet, often to attack or infiltrate other systems.

What is a botnet?

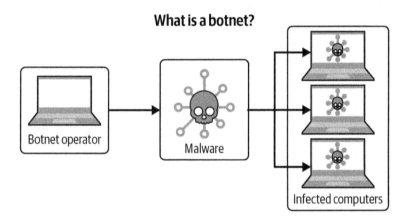

There are thousands of botnets on the internet (at least). One of the most infamous is the Mirai botnet (*https://oreil.ly/jLZIH*), which has existed since 2016. It exploits vulnerabilities in routers and Internet of Things devices to install zombie malware and conduct distributed denial-of-service (DDoS) attacks. Your phone or PC might be a part of a botnet! Mobile antivirus software can sometimes detect the zombie malware that's used in botnets.

See also "Alphabet Inc." on page 8, "Carnegie Mellon University" on page 43, "Cybersecurity" on page 68, "Exploit" on page 101, "Malware" on page 167,

---

1 A *credential stuffing* attack is when a threat actor gets one of your account passwords and tries it with your other online accounts. This kind of attack is the main reason I recommend using a unique password for each account you open, plus a password manager.

"Massachusetts Institute of Technology (MIT)" on page 170, "Ransomware" on page 211, "Turing, Alan" on page 248, "Virus" on page 258

Roleplaying games (RPGs)

Roleplaying games (RPGs) are strategy games in which players each assume the role of a fictional character of their invention (or a pre-created character, often available in today's RPGs.) Many hackers over the years have shown passion for RPGs of all kinds, bringing tabletop games onto computers and developing their own tabletop and computer RPGs.

Dungeons & Dragons (1974) is generally considered the first proper RPG (*https://oreil.ly/hcDGR*), though the lines are murky. *D&D* was largely inspired by fantasy fiction, particularly the works of J. R. R. Tolkien, as well as by wargaming, which has existed for possibly hundreds of years. *Dungeon & Dragons* popularized a lot of the concepts that are now standard in RPGs, such as hit or health points (HP), magic or mana points (MP), characters moving through levels and improving their stats as they go, and character classes (such as mage, warrior, or cleric).

Gary Whisenhunt and Ray Wood (*https://oreil.ly/5tZ_f*) developed what's probably the first computer game RPG, *dnd*, pretty much a direct simulation of tabletop *Dungeons & Dragons*. Both use text and players' imaginations to visualize characters and scenes.

Japanese gamers developed their own RPG style in the 1980s, initially inspired by *Wizardry*, one of the earliest computer RPGs to become popular. When *Wizardry* was translated into Japanese in 1981, it was a surprise hit in Japan and inspired many Japanese game developers. Yuji Horii (*https://oreil.ly/wV6ZQ*) was one of them. He led the development of *Dragon Quest* (1986) and the ensuing series, which in turn inspired Hironobu Sakaguchi (*https://oreil.ly/9XefN*) to develop the *Final Fantasy* (*https://oreil.ly/CYa8q*) series (1987). These two series defined the Japanese RPG style.[2]

See also "Akihabara, Tokyo" on page 6, "Dungeons & Dragons (game franchise)" on page 90, "Miyamoto, Shigeru" on page 178, "MMO (Massively Multiplayer Online) games" on page 179, "Nintendo" on page 185

---

2 Horii-sensei and Sakaguchi-sensei, I am eternally grateful for your work!

19

S

Sakura, Futaba

Futaba Sakura is a fictional character who debuted in the video RPG *Persona 5*, a spin-off from the popular *Shin Megami Tensei* series by Atlus.

Futaba is a teenage girl (*https://oreil.ly/nSoaD*) and an introverted, autistic-coded (*https://oreil.ly/eUu-J*) hacker who is ostracized in school for her neurological quirks. After her mother dies under mysterious circumstances, Futaba blames herself for her mother's death, which profoundly harms her mental health. However, Futaba becomes a brilliant hacker, developing software and founding Medjed, a fictional hacktivist group. She and her friends, the Phantom Thieves, rely on her l33t hacker skills to navigate the Metaverse (*https://oreil.ly/tiMlq*) (a parallel world made from people's dark emotions, not Mark Zuckerberg's failed business venture).

Futaba has been an inspiration to many people in the hacker community. For instance, a hacker made a Discord bot that simulates her. Its source code is available on GitHub (*https://oreil.ly/bQlHs*).

See also "Atlus" on page 24, "Autistic" on page 26, "Meta" on page 171, "Roleplaying games (RPGs)" on page 218

Salander, Lisbeth

Lisbeth Salander is a fictional character in Swedish novelist Stieg Larsson's Millennium series of books and films (*https://oreil.ly/ oz5EO*),[1] best known in the English-speaking world for the title of its first installment, *The Girl with the Dragon Tattoo* (originally *Män som hatar kvinnor*). Salander, a goth hacker chick,

---

1 Larsson wrote three books in the series before his death, and the more recent three installments were written by David Lagercrantz.

is "The Girl" referred to in the books' titles. Salander, a survivor of extreme abuse, uses her hacker skills and tough-as-nails personality to help protagonist Mikael Blomkvist with his journalistic and criminal investigative work.

In one of Salander's most amazing hacks, she transfers millions of dollars from one bank account to another. Cybersecurity expert Kevin Poulsen (*https://oreil.ly/aTmSi*) describes Salander's cybercrimes throughout the book and movie series as having realistic outcomes, but argues that the way she conducts them is "completely nonsensical as a technical matter."

See also "Cyberpunk" on page 67, "Cybersecurity" on page 68

SCADA (Supervisory control and data acquisition)

Supervisory control and data acquisition (*https://oreil.ly/Ogrl-*) (SCADA) is a type of computer system often found in industrial facilities that needs a particular combination of specialized hardware and software.

SCADA is used to automate industrial production processes (*https://oreil.ly/jx8il*), log events and record production metrics, and control industrial mechanisms, such as valves, motors, sensors, and pumps. SCADAs consist of many programmable logic controllers and/or remote terminal units, which are microcomputers that directly interface with various factory components.

Cyberattacks on industrial plants and utility company facilities target SCADAs with unfortunate frequency. The most notorious cyberattack on a SCADA (*https://oreil.ly/TRTVo*) was the Stuxnet worm, discovered in 2010, which targeted the Natanz nuclear facility in Iran.

See also "Malware" on page 167, "Microcomputers" on page 173, "Stuxnet" on page 232, "Worm" on page 269

Schneier, Bruce

Bruce Schneier (*https://oreil.ly/5S70S*) (1963–) describes himself as an "internationally renowned security technologist," while *The Economist* describes him as a "security guru." He is also a cryptographer; a board member of the Electronic Frontier Foundation, Access Now, and the Tor Project; a fellow at the Berkman Klein Center for Internet and Society at Harvard University; a lecturer in public policy at the Harvard Kennedy School; and chief of security architecture at Inrupt, Inc. He has authored several books and is a frequent guest expert on television and other news media. His blog, *Schneier on Security* (*https://oreil.ly/44G99*), is essential reading for everyone in cybersecurity. Oh, and of course, he's a hacker.

Schneier is a passionate advocate for cryptography and digital privacy rights. He's especially known for speaking up when law enforcement agencies argue, as they often do, that tech companies should build "backdoors" (deliberately designed means of bypassing security, especially in encryption) into their technology products to facilitate criminal investigations. Schneier argues that backdoors are dangerous, regardless of intent. In my writing, I've repeatedly cited one particular Schneier quote (*https://oreil.ly/W3ul1*): "If a backdoor exists, then anyone can exploit it. All it takes is knowledge of the backdoor and the capability to exploit it. And while it might temporarily be a secret, it's a fragile secret. Backdoors are how everyone attacks computer systems."

See also "Cryptography" on page 63, "Cybersecurity" on page 68, "Exploit" on page 101, "Hacktivism" on page 125, "Spyware" on page 228, "Tor (The Onion Router)" on page 245

Script kiddie

"Script kiddie" (*https://oreil.ly/zMKfa*) is a derogatory term among hackers for an apparently unskilled cybercriminal or computer hacker. The term refers (*https://oreil.ly/uDveM*) to simply executing malicious scripts that skilled hackers created, rather than writing your own. It's kind of like making musical recordings mainly from samples of other people's musical recordings.

With the advent of the Dark Web, script kiddies have become more destructive than ever. Its markets and forums are convenient places to acquire ransomware, exploit kits, remote-access Trojans, and sensitive breached data.

See also "Dark Web/darknet" on page 71, "Exploit" on page 101, "Malware" on page 167, "Ransomware" on page 211

Search engines

See "DEC (Digital Equipment Corporation)" on page 77, "Deep Web" on page 78, "Google" on page 114, "Microsoft" on page 174, "Pirate Bay/Pirate Party" on page 202, "Yahoo!" on page 277

Sega

Nintendo has an entry in this book. So as a kid of the 1990s, I absolutely must give Sega its own entry as well. Sega has shown great hacker ingenuity in the various forms the company has taken over the years. It was founded (*https://oreil.ly/-SoNX*) in Hawaii in 1940 as Standard Games and made coin-operated games, such as pinball machines. Its main clients were American military bases, some of which were in Japan. In 1952, Sega became a Japanese company and was renamed Service Games (abbreviated as Sega).

Sega's big arcade hit of 1966 was *Periscope*, an electro-mechanical submarine shooting simulation with some impressive mechanical innovations.

In the 1980s, as computer technology finally became accessible to ordinary consumers, Sega's hits were computer arcade games, such as 1982's *Zaxxon* and 1986's *Out Run*. While Sega (*https://oreil.ly/jHSgL*) was doing well in arcades, Atari and Nintendo demonstrated the commercial potential of home video game consoles. Sega released its first home console, the SG-1000, in 1983 (the same year Nintendo released Famicom, the original version of the NES). It sold fairly well in Japan, Australia, and eventually Taiwan, but it was definitely overshadowed by Nintendo.

Sega released the SG-1000's successor, the Sega Master System, in Japan in 1985. The following year it launched the Master System in the US, just as Nintendo's NES also became widely available there. The Nintendo-Sega rivalry was truly on! The console eventually amassed an impressive game library.

Sega released a 16-bit console, the Sega Genesis, in 1988 (ahead of Nintendo this time). Its sales were just OK at first. Sega realized that to beat Nintendo, it would need a mascot—one even cooler than Mario. So its Japanese and US teams collaborated to develop an "extreme" character: Sonic the Hedgehog, a blazing-fast blue rodent who could demonstrate the proprietary blast processing of the Genesis. Sonic was a smash hit from the moment his first game launched in 1991, and he's still popular today.

For a while, the Genesis even outsold the Super Nintendo. But Sega stumbled a bit with the Sega CD and the Sega Saturn. The Sega Dreamcast, released in 1998, was supposed to rescue the company from its money-losing mid-1990s consoles. The Dreamcast is a technologically impressive console. It now has a niche fan base (*https://oreil.ly/TPsvK*) developing their own games for it without any commercial support—truly a part of hacker culture!

As innovative as the Dreamcast was, it couldn't keep Sega in the console business. The company dropped console development in 2001 and became primarily a software developer—though it is still in the arcade game business, and its Club Sega arcades are still popular in Japan. Today, Sega games are released for PCs and a variety of consoles, including the Sony PlayStation, Microsoft Xbox, and even Nintendo consoles.

See also "Atari" on page 22, "Nintendo" on page 185

Semiconductors

See "CPU (Central processing unit)" on page 57, "Electronics" on page 95, "Fairchild Semiconductor" on page 103, "Intel" on page 144, "Moore's law" on page 180

Shamir, Adi

Adi Shamir (*https://oreil.ly/7knAZ*) (1952–) is a renowned cryptographer from Tel Aviv, Israel. He got his bachelor's degree in mathematics from Tel Aviv University in 1973 and his doctorate in computer science from the Weizmann Institute in 1977. In 1978 he joined the faculty of MIT, where he met Ron Rivest and Leonard Adleman: Shamir is the S in RSA cryptography!

In 2002, Shamir, Rivest, and Adleman received a Turing Award (*https://oreil.ly/6FkpY*) for their work in developing RSA cryptography.

See also "Adleman, Leonard" on page 3, "Cryptography" on page 63, "Diffie-Hellman key exchange" on page 84, "Key" on page 156, "Massachusetts Institute of Technology (MIT)" on page 170, "Rivest, Ron" on page 214, "Rivest-Shamir-Adleman (RSA) cryptography" on page 215, "Turing, Alan" on page 248, "World Wide Web" on page 268

Shareware/freeware/abandonware

Shareware and abandonware are two different types of *freeware*, a term that encompasses all proprietary software that's lawfully free of charge to use. The other major type of freeware is proprietary software that companies release for free from the get-go, such as the Zoom client or Microsoft's Internet Explorer browser.

Freeware (*https://oreil.ly/EiTV2*) shouldn't be confused with open source software, though open source advocates like Richard Stallman and the Free Software Foundation refer to it as "free software." (So freeware isn't "free software"—don't get it twisted!) Open source software is also lawfully free of charge, but the source code is open to anyone and the code can be used in any way that doesn't violate its license.[2]

Shareware (*https://oreil.ly/e--fw*) was a popular software promotional model in the 1990s. For example, Apogee released several PC games that way, such as *Commander Keen*, *Crystal Caves*, and *Secret Agent*. The first game in the series was

---

2 Pirated software isn't freeware because if you're enjoying it for free, you're not doing so legally!

released free of charge or at a very low cost (to cover the expense of the floppy disk and a small profit for retailers). The idea was that if you really liked the first game, you'd purchase the other games in the series.

Abandonware (*https://oreil.ly/ZvGE6*) is formerly proprietary software that became freeware because the owner allowed its rights to expire or decided to stop supporting it commercially. There are a lot of DOS games from the 1980s and 1990s in this category.

See also "DOS (Disk Operating System)" on page 86, "Floppy disk" on page 105, "Open source" on page 189, "Proprietary software" on page 205, "Stallman, Richard" on page 229

Signal (messaging app)

Signal is a secure messaging app (*https://oreil.ly/j2QZO*) that features end-to-end encryption through its own open source Signal Protocol. There are native apps (*https://oreil.ly/iL_ae*) for iPhone, iPad, Android, Windows, macOS, and Linux.

Signal users can be identified by phone number, although the app doesn't use any phone or SMS protocols by default. It has a solid reputation for protecting user privacy and is very popular in the hacker community (*https://oreil.ly/z4bz8*). I'm an avid user of Signal.

Signal was created by security researcher Moxie Marlinspike and roboticist Stuart Anderson, who founded Whisper Systems in 2010 (*https://oreil.ly/kDSsx*). Signal was first released with that name in 2015. It has its own internet protocol and is open source licensed under the GNU Affero General Public License.

See also "Cybersecurity" on page 68, "Open source" on page 189

Silicon Valley

Silicon Valley (*https://oreil.ly/GyakR*) is a region in the San Francisco Bay area of California and is the global capital of the computer technology industry.[3] William Hewlett and David Packard kicked off its development in 1938, when they started Hewlett-Packard in a garage not far from Stanford University. The Homebrew Computer Club is an example of Silicon Valley's importance to hacker culture.[4]

Today, Silicon Valley is a massive economy unto itself and is home to the headquarters of many major tech companies. It's centered in Palo Alto and at

---

3 At least in terms of corporate residency; most semiconductor and electronic circuitry manufacturing is done in Asia these days, particularly Taiwan and Malaysia.

4 Malcolm Harris, *Palo Alto: A History of California, Capitalism, and the World* (Hachette UK, 2023).

Stanford University, and includes towns and cities like Cupertino (Apple), Menlo Park (Meta/Facebook), Santa Clara (Intel), Mountain View (Google), and San Jose (Samsung).

While many bright minds and important inventions come from Silicon Valley, I strongly dislike the recent trend of tech bros "inventing" apps that are just a worse version of something that has existed for decades (such as taxis or juicers). Perhaps some future innovators will "disrupt" the systems of capitalism and venture capital, too.

See also "Apple" on page 13, "Google" on page 114, "Hewlett-Packard (HP)" on page 131, "Homebrew Computer Club" on page 136, "Intel" on page 144, "Meta" on page 171, "Pirates of Silicon Valley (1999 film)" on page 202, "Stanford University" on page 230

Silk Road

Silk Road was a pioneering darknet market created by Ross "Dread Pirate Roberts" Ulbricht (1984–), an infamous Texas-born libertarian hacker who is currently serving a life sentence in prison.

Darknet markets operate on the Dark Web and work sort of like eBay, but for illegal things, like illicit drugs, malware, cyberattack services, sensitive data gained by cyberattack (especially credit card data), firearms, stolen accounts for paid online services (unlawful access to lawful pornography is especially popular), phishing kits, and "fullz" (data that's used to commit identity fraud against individuals and companies).

The very first darknet market was The Farmer's Market (*https://oreil.ly/ xWooe*), a clearnet site that moved to the encrypted Tor network in 2010. The Farmer's Market took easily traceable PayPal as a payment method and was shut down by law enforcement in 2012. After Bitcoin, the first cryptocurrency, emerged in 2009, it became a useful means for buying and selling illegal goods and services on darknet markets. Cryptocurrency transactions are much more difficult to trace than transactions via credit cards, wire transfer, or payment platforms like PayPal or Stripe.

Ulbricht launched Silk Road in January 2011 (*https://oreil.ly/ioimE*), using the handle "Dread Pirate Roberts." It was the first darknet market to originate from the Tor network and to allow only Bitcoin transactions. The site made money by taking a percentage of the vendors' sale revenue and used a reputation rating system to allow users to decide whether to do business with one another.

Ulbricht made the mistake of using Silk Road to sell his own drugs, and then writing a digital journal entry (*https://oreil.ly/ihMYs*) about it.

Ulbricht's sloppiness with his online identity led IRS investigator Gary Alford (*https://oreil.ly/mYwY5*) to identify him as the man behind "Dread Pirate Roberts." In October 2013, federal agents caught Ulbricht at a public library in San Francisco and confiscated his laptop while it was logged in and running. This allowed FBI agents to extract evidence such as Ulbrich's browser history and documents without needing to acquire his password or crack his operating system's encryption. In 2015, Ulbricht was found guilty of multiple drug trafficking charges (*https://oreil.ly/3l3CN*) and sentenced to life in prison (*https://oreil.ly/JJMAc*).

In December 2021, Ulbricht sold multiple pieces of his visual art as an NFT for about $6 million. There are some real suckers out there!

See also "Cryptocurrency" on page 61, "Dark Web/darknet" on page 71, "Malware" on page 167, "Nonfungible tokens (NFTs)" on page 186, "Phishing" on page 198, "Tor (The Onion Router)" on page 245

Smartphone

Smartphones, as you likely know, are pocket-sized general-purpose computers with cellular phone functionality. If desktop and laptop PCs are microcomputers, does that make smartphones, tablets, and smartwatches (all of which use the same sort of CPUs and software but in different form factors) nanocomputers? Wikipedia editors consider that to be a possibility (*https://oreil.ly/9HPBX*).

Since about 2010 or so, the smartphone market has been completely dominated by Apple's iPhone and iOS, and by various manufacturers' Android phones. Cellular phones have been around since 1973 (*https://oreil.ly/SogcY*). In the 1980s they were very expensive, were supported by unreliable radio telephone networks, and were the size of a brick! A smartphone is a cellphone that can be used as a general-purpose computer.

The first smartphone, believe it or not, wasn't the iPhone: it was IBM's Simon Personal Communicator (*https://oreil.ly/Ts8a3*), released in 1994. It wasn't a smash success commercially, but it was definitely a sign of things to come.

Almost all adults and many children and teenagers own a smartphone these days, and many people have a smartphone but no PC (*https://oreil.ly/iQbf4*). Like a lot of people, I seldom use my phone to do phone things. "The scenery in the garden was beautiful, so I took out my phone to take photos" is a perfectly normal sentence in 2023, but it would have sounded absolutely absurd in the 1990s.

See also "Android operating system" on page 11, "Apple" on page 13, "IBM" on page 139, "Hardware" on page 128, "Microcomputers" on page 173, "Personal computers" on page 196

Snowden, Edward

Edward Snowden (*https://oreil.ly/WkbtM*) (1983–) is one of hacker culture's most celebrated heroes, and for good reason. He was born in North Carolina, but Snowden's family moved to Maryland when he was a kid—not far from the Fort Meade headquarters of the National Security Agency (NSA). His mother worked for a federal court as a chief deputy clerk, and his father was a Coast Guard officer. Snowden was a hacker from childhood and taught himself to be a competent computer programmer. He dropped out of high school in the late 1990s and eventually got his GED, then refined his computer skills at Anne Arundel Community College. He joined the US Army reserve for a few months in 2004, then was discharged. A year later, he worked as a security guard at the University of Maryland's Center for Advanced Study of Language, which is affiliated with the NSA.

It seems like Snowden was (*https://oreil.ly/Ibxcq*) destined to do cybersecurity work for the NSA, even though he didn't have a computer science degree. But the Central Intelligence Agency (CIA) got him first, recruiting him in 2006 on the strength of his aptitude with computers. The CIA gave him a security clearance in 2007 and sent him to Geneva, Switzerland, to work as a network security technician. (A *security clearance* gives an individual access to some information that's classified by an intelligence agency.)

In 2009, however, Snowden fell under suspicion that he was trying to illicitly access classified files. So he went to work for the private sector, first at Dell and then at Booz Allen Hamilton, a private-sector entity that's as deep into the US military-industrial complex as Raytheon. Through both companies, he was working on subcontracted projects for the NSA. Snowden began gathering intel on the NSA's intel gathering. One of his discoveries was the PRISM surveillance program (*https://oreil.ly/4dJ8U*), which surveils billions of ordinary people worldwide through the internet with the help of tech companies (*https://oreil.ly/wyc1Z*) like Microsoft, Yahoo!, Google, Facebook, Paltalk, YouTube, AOL, Skype, and Apple. Assume that PRISM (or something like it) is still spying on you!

Once Snowden gathered enough evidence, he took medical leave from his job. On May 20, 2013, he flew to Hong Kong, where he met with a journalist from the UK's *Guardian* newspaper and presented his evidence. On June 6, both the *Guardian* and the *Washington Post* published Snowden's revelations about PRISM, complete with evidence. From his Hong Kong hotel suite, Snowden said (*https://oreil.ly/NeXK5*): "I'm willing to sacrifice [my former life] because I can't in good conscience allow the US government to destroy privacy, internet freedom and basic liberties for people around the world with this massive surveillance machine they're secretly building."

Soon, he was on the run. He eventually found refuge in Russia, which doesn't have an extradition treaty with the US (*https://oreil.ly/LLUgW*) and thus didn't have to deport Snowden back to the US if they didn't want to. He's been staying in Russia ever since. If he were to leave, he'd face criminal trial in the US and could well end up the way Julian Assange has—tortured in prison with no foreseeable release. Russian president Vladimir Putin granted Snowden Russian citizenship in 2022.

Snowden's NSA revelations rocked the US and international mainstream media for several months. In August 2013, President Barack Obama announced a panel to review US surveillance policies, though (in my opinion) nothing substantial came out of it.

The 2014 documentary *Citizenfour* tells Snowden's story, including footage of him speaking to journalists in Hong Kong. The Hollywood film *Snowden* (*https://oreil.ly/YHrHw*), starring Joseph Gordon-Levitt, was released in 2016, and Snowden published a memoir, *Permanent Record*, in 2019.

As I write this, a decade after Snowden's PRISM revelations, the disturbing truth about our collective lack of digital privacy is seldom discussed anymore.

See also "Apple" on page 13, "Assange, Julian" on page 18, "Cybersecurity" on page 68, "Google" on page 114, "Hacktivism" on page 125, "Meta" on page 171, "Microsoft" on page 174, "Spyware" on page 228, "Yahoo!" on page 277

Social media

See "Meta" on page 171, "Zuckerberg, Mark" on page 280

Spyware

Spyware is a category of malware that spies on its targets. In the CIA triad of cybersecurity, it targets confidentiality. Spyware is alarmingly common and its victims range from multibillion-dollar corporations (through corporate espionage) to governments (through cyberwarfare) to ordinary people on their smartphones, using what seem to be legitimate commercial applications. Notoriously, in the 1990s, the media software RealPlayer was caught (*https://oreil.ly/-KjWS*) covertly gathering data on users' listening habits and locations!

Spyware can do a variety of malicious things (*https://oreil.ly/M3a45*). It can open backdoors (*https://oreil.ly/Vd-Q_*) into your computer that other attackers can use to spy on your data. It can log your keystrokes and send the data to cybercriminals. It can monitor and steal your online activity and even sensitive financial data. There's even a type of spyware called *stalkerware* (*https://oreil.ly/GvBFH*). It's marketed for monitoring children and employees, but abusers often use it as a tool in domestic violence.

See also "CIA triad (confidentiality, integrity, availability)" on page 49, "Cybersecurity" on page 68, "Exploit" on page 101, "Malware" on page 167

Stallman, Richard

Richard Stallman (1953–), also known as RMS and as "St. IGNUcius (*https://oreil.ly/BpnMX*)" in the Church of Emacs, is one of the most eccentric and controversial figures in hacker culture. In *Hackers: Heroes of the Computer Revolution*, Steven Levy calls Stallman "The Last of the Hackers," adding that "he vowed to defend the principles of hackerism to the bitter end. Remained at MIT until there was no one to eat Chinese food with."

Stallman studied physics at Harvard in the early 1970s and worked on artificial intelligence at MIT, where he also developed the application he's best known for: the Emacs text editor.

In 1983, Stallman launched the GNU Project to develop an open source version of UNIX. Stallman believes very strongly that proprietary software violates people's freedoms. He's also adamant about preferring the term *free software* over *open source*. That distinction may sound trivial, but it's a hot topic among many hackers. Stallman (*https://oreil.ly/LYPUH*) writes:

> The terms "free software" and "open source" stand for almost the same range of programs. However, they say deeply different things about those programs, based on different values. The free software movement campaigns for freedom for the users of computing; it is a movement for freedom and justice. By contrast, the open source idea values mainly practical advantage and does not campaign for principles. This is why we do not agree with open source, and do not use that term.

The GNU Public License (*https://oreil.ly/cVZUI*) (GPL) is probably the most influential product of the GNU Project. Other notable GNU Public Licence published applications (*https://oreil.ly/n7aP8*) include MySQL, WordPress, Git, and the Linux kernel.

You could spend literal years reading all of Stallman's opinions on every topic imaginable from stallman.org (*https://oreil.ly/pfZIg*).

Stallman founded the Free Software Foundation (FSF) in 1985 and ran it until 2019, when he resigned under criticism about his public statements regarding sexual harassment and assault, as well as about allegations related to a donation that child trafficker Jeffrey Epstein made to MIT. Stallman returned to the FSF's Board of Directors in 2021.

See also "Artificial intelligence (AI)" on page 17, "bash" on page 30, "The Cathedral and the Bazaar (1999 book)" on page 44, "Emacs" on page 97, "Git/GitHub" on page 113, "Hackers: Heroes of the Computer Revolution (2010 book)" on page 123, "Linux" on page 161, "Massachusetts Institute of Technology (MIT)" on page 170, "Open source" on page 189, "Proprietary software" on page 205, "Shareware/freeware/abandonware" on page 223

Stanford University

Stanford University was founded (*https://oreil.ly/Fmb_G*) in Stanford, California, in 1885 and is the academic center of Silicon Valley. Stanford engineering graduates (*https://oreil.ly/gJa1C*) William Hewlett and David Packard founded Hewlett-Packard in 1939. The HP Garage (*https://oreil.ly/XjqQk*) is very close to Stanford's campus and was dedicated as "the Birthplace of Silicon Valley" on HP's 50th anniversary in 1989.[5]

Stanford's computer science department (*https://oreil.ly/aaJO3*) was founded in 1965. Some of its other notable hacker alumni (*https://oreil.ly/eEGFo*) include:

Sergey Brin and Larry Page
    Google founders

Jawed Karim, Chad Hurley, and Steve Chen
    YouTube founders

Jerry Yang and David Filo
    Yahoo! founders

---

5 Malcolm Harris, *Palo Alto: A History of California, Capitalism, and the World* (Hachette UK, 2023).

Sandy Lerner and Len Bosack
Cisco founders

Martin Hellman and Whitfield Diffie
Diffie-Hellman key exchange inventors who worked as a research programmer at Stanford Artificial Intelligence Laboratory

Aaron Swartz
Hacktivist

See also "Diffie, Whitfield" on page 83, "Diffie-Hellman key exchange" on page 84, "Google" on page 114, "Hellman, Martin" on page 128, "Hewlett-Packard (HP)" on page 131, "Page, Larry" on page 194, "Silicon Valley" on page 224, "Swartz, Aaron" on page 235, "Yahoo!" on page 277

Startups

See "Google" on page 114, "Hewlett-Packard (HP)" on page 131, "Silicon Valley" on page 224, "Y Combinator" on page 278

Steam

Steam is a PC gaming platform developed and run by the game studio Valve, launched in 2003. As of 2021 (*https://oreil.ly/IbrXJ*), Steam had 120 million monthly active users and more than 50,000 games, making Valve one of many scrappy little 1990s PC game-development startups that went on to innovate in ways that have transformed popular culture.

Valve was founded by former Microsoft developers Gabe "Gaben" Newell and Mike Harrington (*https://oreil.ly/JCoP-*) in 1996. In 1998, Valve released *Half-Life*, a first-person shooter made with the Quake engine that revolutionized the genre, scoring a 96 on Metacritic (*https://oreil.ly/yEAcl*). *Half-Life 2* was released in 2004. To play it, you had to install a client for Valve's brand-new gaming service, Steam. Perhaps some gamers grumbled, used to installing PC games from CDs and DVDs.

At first, Steam only published Valve games: it was mainly a way for Valve to control game distribution and the multiplayer gaming backend. Valve wanted to control the delivery of its products, so that rival game studio Sierra couldn't let people play their games for free at internet cafés (Valve sued Sierra (*https://oreil.ly/UX8cF*) over this in 2002). Valve also wanted a more reliable way to deploy game patches and maintain online gaming servers.

Half-Life 2 became the first Steam-exclusive game in November 2004. You could buy a physical copy of *Half-Life 2* at a retail store, but installing it from disc still required users to install the Steam client to be installed. That was a clever way to teach PC gamers the new habit of simply launching the Steam client and buying a game as a digital download.

As consumer network connectivity greatly improved, Steam became something even bigger than any of Valve's games. Valve slowed its own game development and began publishing third-party games on Steam in 2005. Thousands of third-party titles have been released there since, and Steam's success (alongside that of Xbox Live in 2002 and PlayStation Network (*https://oreil.ly/5mE6j*) in 2006) turned online game retailing into a much bigger business.

Valve's first entry into the hardware market was the Steam Machine (*https://oreil.ly/G6Rkb*) platform, sold from 2015 to 2018. It wasn't successful, but it paved the way for 2022's Steam Deck, a handheld console running SteamOS with the ability to play Steam PC games. Steam Deck has been well received by gamers and the industry (*https://oreil.ly/s8r5W*). It's deliberately designed to be hackable: you can install alternative operating systems on it without jailbreaking, so people have been using Steam Decks (*https://oreil.ly/-zzca*) for everything from emulating video game consoles to creating digital music to ham radio.

Stuxnet

The Stuxnet worm was perhaps the first malware to cause profound physical damage to its target. It's been described as the first digital weapon.[6] When it was first detected in late June 2009, it perplexed and intrigued the cybersecurity community.

Stuxnet's target was the Natanz uranium enrichment facility in Iran, and it succeeded in its goal of making the facility's centrifuges burn out. Natanz's SCADA wasn't connected to the internet, so attackers had to sneak the malware in via USB drives. The worm targeted specialized Microsoft Windows systems with Siemens Step 7 software connected to programmable logic controllers.

Because Stuxnet's makers obfuscated its binary code using code packing, an advanced cyberwarfare technique, it's widely alleged that the worm was created by American and Israeli cyberwarfare units (*https://oreil.ly/aNSry*), including the

---

6 Kim Zetter, *Countdown to Zero Day: Stuxnet and the Launch of the World's First Digital Weapon* (Penguin, 2014).

National Security Agency and the Central Intelligence Agency (and I for one believe it).

My friend Luther "Chip" Harris, a prominent cyberattack investigator who worked for the US Department of Defense for 14 years, explained in an interview:

> Stuxnet, as it came to be known, was unlike any other virus or worm that came before. Rather than simply hijacking targeted computers or stealing information from them, it escaped the digital realm to wreak physical destruction on equipment the computers controlled. It is the world's first cyber weapon that was created and used against Iran's nuclear program. It's the first operational technology virus that was explicitly created for counter-espionage against a specific country for the sole purpose of stopping the production of nuclear material against another country.

In the years since, Stuxnet has spawned several other kinds of advanced SCADA malware, including 2011's Duqu, 2012's Flame, 2013's Havex, 2016's Industroyer, and 2017's Triton.

See also "Binary" on page 35, "Cybersecurity" on page 68, "Malware" on page 167, "SCADA (Supervisory control and data acquisition)" on page 220, "Virus" on page 258, "Worm" on page 269, "Zero day" on page 279

Sun Microsystems

See "DARPA (Defense Advanced Research Projects Agency)" on page 72, "DEC (Digital Equipment Corporation)" on page 77, "Google" on page 114, "Joy, Bill" on page 153, "Microsoft" on page 174

Supercomputers

Supercomputers are the most powerful and rarest class of computers, used primarily for scientific research (*https://oreil.ly/etoyI*). Wanna buy a supercomputer? You'd better be ready to spend 5 to 7 million dollars—not to mention the electric bill! Supercomputers, for this reason, are generally for big institutions and are usually custom designed. However, a few low-end supercomputers go for merely $10,000-$20,000 (*https://oreil.ly/lvLGZ*).

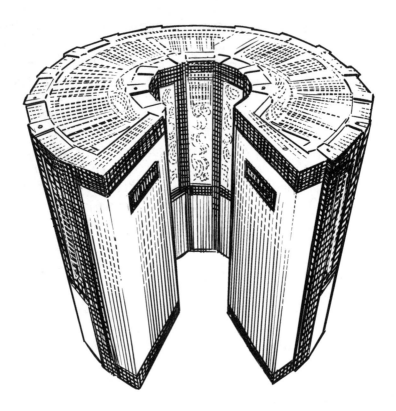

Seymour Cray and Cray Computers built the first supercomputer, Cray-1, in 1976. It ran at 160 megaflops. Supercomputers have become exponentially more powerful in the years since, running multiple CPUs and processing massive amounts of data. Their power is measured in floating-point operations per second (FLOPS). According to IBM (*https://oreil.ly/1OIzL*), the fastest supercomputers as of 2023 are:

- Fugaku (Japan): 442 petaflops
- Summit (Oak Ridge National Laboratory, Tennessee): 148.8 petaflops
- Sierra (Lawrence Livermore National Laboratory, California): 94.6 petaflops

See also "CPU (Central processing unit)" on page 57, "Cray, Seymour" on page 58, "IBM" on page 139, "Zettabyte Era" on page 279

Swartz, Aaron

Aaron Swartz (1986–2013) was a revolutionary hacker who lived a very short but eventful life.

Swartz got into computers as a very young child and learned all he could. At 12 years old, in 1999, he created and coded *The Info Network*, a user-generated encyclopedia that won the ArsDigita Prize. For context, Wikipedia didn't launch until 2001; Swartz was ahead of his time. In 2005 he studied at Stanford University for a year, but left early.

In 2000, Swartz was part of developing version 1.0 of RSS (Really Simple Syndication), a webfeed news-aggregator technology that's still in use today. He was involved in creating both Reddit and the Creative Commons content licensing. Other important innovations in which Swartz also played an integral role include the Markdown web development language, DeadDrop technology (which lets sources send sensitive documents to journalists anonymously), and the Tor2web HTTP proxy for the Tor Network.

These projects were all products of Swartz's love not only for computers, but also for the free exchange of information. That's the hacker ethos: "knowledge should be free." His passion for the cause of "knowledge should be free" would eventually lead to his death.

By 2010, Swartz was a research fellow at Harvard University, which granted him an account on JSTOR, a huge database of scientific research, as well as access to the resources of the Massachusetts Institute of Technology (MIT). Much of the research hosted through JSTOR is taxpayer-funded; the researchers don't make money from it. Academic institutions pay fees to access JSTOR, but those fees are high enough to be prohibitive to most individuals.

Swartz wanted the whole world to have free access to the knowledge locked inside JSTOR, so he started to use his physical access to MIT to hack JSTOR's library. Swartz's data breaches continued for about six months, until he was arrested by MIT Police and a Secret Service agent. A federal grand jury indicted him for unlawfully obtaining information from a protected computer, recklessly damaging a protected computer, wire fraud, and computer fraud. In 2012, nine more felony counts were added. Swartz was potentially facing a fine of $1 million and 50 years in prison—longer than most sentences for first-degree murder (*https://oreil.ly/67yIn*)!

The pressure was overwhelming, and on January 11, 2013, Swartz died by suicide. Tim Berners-Lee gave a eulogy at his funeral. Swartz was only 26 years old.

See also "Berners-Lee, Tim" on page 33, "Hacker" on page 121, "Hacktivism" on page 125, "Massachusetts Institute of Technology (MIT)" on page 170, "Open source" on page 189, "Reddit" on page 212, "Stanford University" on page 230, "Tor (The Onion Router)" on page 245, "Wikipedia" on page 267

Syntax

In prose writing, *syntax* is "the arrangement of words in sentences, clauses, and phrases, and the study of the formation of sentences and the relationship of their component parts" (*https://oreil.ly/r7BnK*). As a writer, I know I'm writing with a syntax, but I construct it subconsciously until my editor tells me I've goofed.

Syntax has also been crucial in computer programming (*https://oreil.ly/hcNLb*) from its very beginning. Syntax varies widely across programming languages, and even between different versions of the same language.

Here is a "Hello World" script in Python 2:

```
print 'Hello world'
```

And here's a "Hello World" script in Python 3:

```
print('Hello World')
```

I learned about Python syntax the hard way: I once wrote a 200-line Python script with tabs in its whitespace instead of spaces. When my script wouldn't execute, I had the tedious job of replacing all those tabs with four spaces each. And Python is supposed to be among the easiest of the high-level programming languages to learn!

See also "Hello World" on page 130, "Integrated development environment (IDE)" on page 143, "Programming" on page 204

20

T

TCP/IP (Transmission Control Protocol/Internet Protocol)

The Transmission Control Protocol (TCP) is featured in the internet protocol suite. All packets sent through computer networks use TCP or UDP (User Datagram Protocol). UDP is a simpler protocol which lacks the upper layer protocol indications for message delivery that TCP uses. Most of the packets that are sent to and from your phone or PC through the internet are TCP packets—sections of data that are transmitted across computer networks of all kinds.

In TCP, ACK is a command used to establish a connection between an endpoint (such as your phone or PC) and a server. This is called the "three-way handshake."

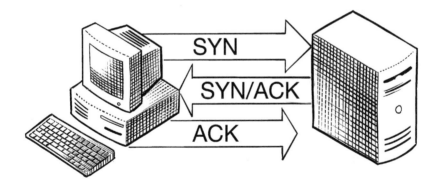

Here's how the three-way handshake (*https://oreil.ly/qICHV*) works. First, a client (the endpoint) sends a SYN command to a server. If the server processes the SYN command successfully, it'll send the client a packet with the SYN-ACK command. If that's successful, the client sends the server a packet with ACK. SYN is for establishing a data sequence, and ACK means "acknowledged!"

When the client is ready to close a connection to a server, it sends the server a packet with FIN. The server responds with ACK. Then the server sends a packet with SYN, and the client responds to the server with ACK. You guessed it, FIN means "finish."

Every time your phone or PC successfully downloads web pages from the internet in your web browser, there are TCP packets with SYN, SYN-ACK, ACK, and FIN being sent between your endpoint and web servers as you go from website to website. TCP packets are also used for most other internet services, such as email. TCP packets are also used in other kinds of computer networks; the internet is just the largest and most popular. There's all this nifty packet activity going back and forth all the time, and you can only see it happening if you use packet analysis software like Wireshark.

Because UDP lacks upper layer protocol indicators, UDP doesn't use the SYN, SYN-ACK, ACK, or FIN signals.

The hacker space is full of nerd humor that features TCP/IP. Here's an example:

> Do you want to hear a joke about TCP/IP?
>
> Yes, I'd like to hear a joke about TCP/IP.
>
> Are you ready to hear a joke about TCP/IP?
>
> I am ready to hear a joke about TCP/IP.
>
> Here is a joke about TCP/IP.
>
> Did you receive the joke about TCP/IP?
>
> I have received the joke about TCP/IP.

See also "ARPAnet" on page 17, "Internet" on page 145, "Networking" on page 183, "Packet switching" on page 193

Tech Model Railroad Club

MIT's Tech Model Railroad Club was launched in 1946 by MIT students who loved model railroads (*https://oreil.ly/rCDGN*), and still exists today. In the 1950s and 1960s, however, the club also became a place to tinker with electronic circuitry and eventually early computers, like the IBM 704 (which cost MIT millions of dollars) and DEC PDP-1. Today the club is widely considered to be the birthplace of hacker culture (*https://oreil.ly/zmmuh*).[1]

The Tech Model Railroad Club is also credited with coining the technological senses of the terms *hack* and *hacker*, which it defines on its website as:

> Someone who applies ingenuity to create a clever result, called a "hack". The essence of a "hack" is that it is done quickly, and is usually inelegant. It accomplishes the desired goal without changing the design of the system it is embedded in. Despite often being at odds with the design of the larger system, a hack is generally quite clever and effective.

The writers take pains to separate this from any connotations of cybercrime, noting that cyberattackers "are certainly not true hackers, as they do not understand the hacker ethic."

Peter Samson was one of the club's most important members in the invention of hacker culture. That was largely due to his position in the club's Signals and Power Subcommittee, and his masterful ability to create new programs with machine code. He joined the club in the fall of 1958. Other club members who were integral to the earliest days of hacker culture include Alan Kotok and Bob Saunders. Kotok helped to create one of the earliest chess programs in 1959, while Saunders helped to create *Spacewar!* in 1961.

See also "Atari" on page 22, "DEC (Digital Equipment Corporation)" on page 77, "Hacker" on page 121, "IBM" on page 139, "Massachusetts Institute of Technology (MIT)" on page 170, "Programming" on page 204

Telephones

See "Apple" on page 13, "Bell Labs" on page 31, "Bulletin board systems (BBSes)" on page 37, "Captain Crunch (John Draper)" on page 41, "DEF CON" on page 80, "Internet" on page 145, "Mitnick, Kevin" on page 177, "Morse code" on page 180, "Networking" on page 183, "Phishing" on page 198, "Phreaking" on page 199, "Smartphone" on page 226, "2600 (Twenty-Six Hundred): The Hacker Quarterly (magazine)" on page 250, "Wardriving" on page 263, "Wozniak, Steve" on page 269

---

1 Levy, Steven. *Hackers: Heroes of the Computer Revolution* (O'Reilly Media, 2010).

Texas Instruments

A lot of people think of Texas Instruments (*https://oreil.ly/dQ-Z3*) as simply a calculator company. While calculators are an important product line, Texas Instruments (TI) has also played a crucial role in the development of computer technology as a whole (much like Xerox).

John Clarence Karcher and Eugene McDermott founded the company in 1930 (*https://oreil.ly/2bfWe*) to provide seismographic data for the oil industry (which, in the US, is centered in Texas). It was incorporated as Geophysical Service Inc. (GSI) in 1938 and was renamed Coronado Corporation in 1939, with GSI becoming a subsidiary. During World War II, the US Navy became GSI's top customer, buying electronic detection equipment. GSI diversified its electronic products after the war and rebranded as Texas Instruments (*https://oreil.ly/7x_be*) in 1951.

In 1958, Texas Instruments researcher Jack Kilby invented the integrated circuit independently, but simultaneously with Fairchild Semiconductor's Robert Noyce (who would go on to found Intel). An *integrated circuit* is a little piece of technology that contains a lot of different transistors for computation purposes. It's the technological foundation of the CPU. The US military uses TI's integrated circuits in ballistic-missile guidance systems. Not until 1972 was it used in the first pocket calculator: the TI Datamath.

TI's other major invention, in 1982, was the single-chip digital signal processor, which is used in a wide variety of devices, from modems to car brakes to telecommunications infrastructure. TI sold its military equipment division to Raytheon in 1997 and is now focused on semiconductors and calculators.

See also "CPU (Central processing unit)" on page 57, "Electronics" on page 95, "Fairchild Semiconductor" on page 103, "Hardware" on page 128, "Xerox" on page 273

Thompson, Ken

Ken Thompson (1943–) is best known as the co-developer of Unix and the B and C programming languages. He studied electrical engineering and computer science at the University of California, Berkeley, and joined Bell Labs in the late 1960s, where he worked on the Multics timesharing operating system project.

In 1969, influenced by Multics, Thompson and fellow Bell Labs researcher Dennis Ritchie developed UNIX. They originally designed it to run on the DEC PDP-7 minicomputer, but to port it to different computers, they needed to use a high-level programming language (*https://oreil.ly/_Dhq7*). FORTRAN didn't work;

BCPL from the Multics project didn't satisfy them either. So Thompson developed the B programming language, based on BCPL. Ritchie helped to develop the C programming language from B, and then Thompson rewrote the UNIX kernel in C.

Today, UNIX is the foundation of a wide range of operating systems, including most of the non-Windows operating systems in wide use, like macOS and Android, as well as hundreds of different UNIX and Linux distributions. C is still widely used, and has also evolved into several of the most-used programming languages in operating system development: C++ (pronounced "C plus plus"), C# (pronounced "C sharp"), Objective C, and Java.

Ken Thompson is largely responsible (*https://oreil.ly/a8ayb*) for how we enjoy operating systems and software application development today. For their innovations, Thompson and Ritchie jointly received a Turing Award (*https://oreil.ly/dGKuC*) in 1983.

See also "Bell Labs" on page 31, "Berkeley, University of California" on page 32, "Linux" on page 161, "Programming" on page 204, "Ritchie, Dennis" on page 214, "Timesharing" on page 243, "Turing, Alan" on page 248, "UNIX" on page 253

Threat actor

Over the course of my career, I have deliberately avoided calling cybercriminals hackers. Hackers are morally neutral or positive. In the early days of my work, I would usually call cybercriminals cyberattackers. In recent years, I've used the terms *cybercriminal* and *threat actor* more often. Threat actor sounds so friggin' cool. It's the kind of language used by prestigious cybersecurity research firms. It's someone who acts to create threats. In the context of cybersecurity, those threats are *cyber threats*: threats to the security of our computers and computer data.

The National Institute of Standards and Technology (NIST) defines a threat actor as "the instigators of risks with the capability to do harm" (*https://oreil.ly/Daxrd*). Badass!

See also "Cybersecurity" on page 68, "Hacker" on page 121

Timesharing

Timesharing was the earliest kind of truly interactive electronic computing. The first electronic computers in the 1940s and 1950s were massive room-sized machines that required rare technical expertise to operate. The transition between computers like ENIAC and today's personal computing ecosystem was largely defined by mainframe computers, minicomputers, and timesharing.

In the 1960s, computers became powerful enough to manage multiple programs at a time, but they were way too big and expensive to be used by only one person. So the academic, enterprise, and government institutions that used computers in the 1960s and 1970s needed timesharing systems that allotted periods of computer time to one person, then another. You know how you can now set up multiple accounts on Windows, Mac, and Linux PCs? The technological origins of user accounts and user access permissions lie in timesharing systems.

Stanford computer scientist John McCarthy was one of the first people to conceptualize timesharing (*https://oreil.ly/oz1Gs*). In a 1959 memorandum (*https://oreil.ly/s-d6E*) about MIT receiving a transistorized IBM 709, he proposed "an operating system for it that will substantially reduce the time required to get a problem solved on the machine." And in 1960, MIT computer pioneer J. C. R. Licklider wrote a paper (*https://oreil.ly/IZD2O*) envisioning a more interactive style of computing. The batch-processing model of the 1950s involved putting a bunch of punch cards into a huge computer, waiting an hour or more, then getting output in a bunch of newly punched cards. Licklider wrote:

> *Man-computer symbiosis is an expected development in cooperative interaction between men [as in humans, Licklider's language reflected the sexism of his time] and electronic computers. It will involve very close coupling between the human and the electronic members of the partnership. The main aims are 1) to let computers facilitate formulative thinking as they now facilitate the solution of formulated problems, and 2) to enable men and computers to cooperate in making decisions and controlling complex situations without inflexible dependence on predetermined programs.*

The earliest working timesharing system was the Compatible Time-Sharing System (CTSS), built by Fernando Corbato and Robert Jano at MIT, for the same IBM 709 computer McCarthy mentioned in his memorandum. However, the most important system was Multics, a timesharing operating system developed in the late 1960s by Ken Thompson and Dennis Ritchie, with initial help from Corbato. Thompson and Ritchie went on to develop UNIX.

See also "ENIAC (Electronic Numerical Integrator and Computer)" on page 98, "IBM" on page 139, "Massachusetts Institute of Technology (MIT)" on page

170, "Minicomputers" on page 176, "Ritchie, Dennis" on page 214, "Thompson, Ken" on page 242, "UNIX" on page 253

Tokyo Denki University

Tokyo Denki University, in Tokyo's Kanda district, is perhaps the most important technical school in Japan. It was founded as Denki School by engineers Seiichi Hirota and Shinkichi Ogimoto (*https://oreil.ly/ymgtu*).

First, a little historical context. The Meiji Restoration (*https://oreil.ly/liDlg*), which began in 1868, ended the era of the shogunate. It forced tremendous modernization and opened Japan up to the rest of the world, especially the United States and United Kingdom. Denki School was founded in 1907, near the end of the Meiji Era, to teach brilliant young Japanese people about mechanical engineering and electric technology.

The school conducted its first experimental radio broadcasts in 1924, just before the 1926 founding of Japan's national broadcaster, NHK. The school was renamed Tokyo Denki University in 1949, just after the end of World War II.

One of Tokyo Denki University's most notable hacker alumni (*https://oreil.ly/ V7YPq*) is Tomohiro Nishikado, creator of *Space Invaders*, the most popular arcade game of the late 1970s and early 1980s. Another is Hisashi Koinuma (*https://oreil.ly/oRgjU*), who produced many well-loved modern games, including the *Samurai Warriors* series, *Nioh*, and *Atelier Ryza 2*, and is now the chief operating officer of Koei Tecmo.

See also "Akihabara, Tokyo" on page 6

Tor (The Onion Router)

The Onion Router (*https://oreil.ly/3eOXT*), usually known as Tor, is an anonymizing proxy network used by an average of 2.6 million client devices (*https://oreil.ly/ 87jTb*) every day.

The genesis of Tor came at the US Naval Research Lab in 1995, when David Goldschlag, Mike Reed, and Paul Syverson had an idea: what if they could provide internet users some privacy by giving them a way to make their IP addresses untraceable?

In the early 2000s, Syverson and MIT graduate Roger Dingledine started work on Tor. The Tor network was initially deployed in 2002, and the Tor Project became a nonprofit organization in 2006. Using Tor makes it very difficult—but not impossible—for law enforcement and threat actors to trace your online activity.

Here's how onion routing works. Your client machine (usually a PC or mobile device) connects to the proxy network, where a series of network nodes routes your traffic to and from the destination server. The entry node knows your IP address, and the exit node knows the IP address of the server. But each of the nodes in between only knows the IP addresses of the nodes on either side of it, sending information to it and receiving from it. This makes it very difficult to track users. However, with a great deal of effort, law enforcement can sometimes identify users through data at the exit node or relay (*https://oreil.ly/sGyOm*).

One of the most common ways to use Tor is to install the Tor Browser (*https://oreil.ly/wjo9W*) on your PC or phone. The Tor Browser is a fork of Firefox that automatically connects to the Tor network. Websites that can only be accessed through the Tor network use the top-level domain *.onion*. But the Tor Browser can also route all web traffic through Tor, including the clearnet sites you visit every day.

Tor is important for protecting people like investigative journalists and political activists, but can also make it safer to conduct illegal activity. The Dark Web is the part of the web that's only accessible through the Tor and Invisible Internet Project (I2P) proxy networks; it contains both legal and illegal content. (In a similar vein, you can use a lighter to light candles and campfires, but you can also use it to commit arson.)

See also "Dark Web/darknet" on page 71, "Invisible Internet Project (I2P)" on page 147, "Networking" on page 183

Torvalds, Linus

Linus Torvalds (*https://oreil.ly/CVjMq*) (1969–) was born in Helsinki, Finland. At age 10, he started to learn computer programming (*https://oreil.ly/PlXaU*) on his grandfather's Commodore VIC-20. He went on to study computer science at the University of Helsinki, where he learned the C programming language and more about operating systems.

By 1991, Torvalds had a PC that ran MS-DOS, but he preferred the UNIX-based operating systems on his school's computers. He resolved to create his own version of UNIX to run on his PC, and started developing Linux. (He initially called it "Freax," dismissing the name "Linux" as too egotistical, but his colleague Ari Lemmke (*https://oreil.ly/wUNso*) renamed the FTP server folder "Linux" and that was that.) In 1991, Torvalds announced his OS project on Usenet and started to find many collaborators around the world. Linux kernel 1.0 was released in 1994.

Another one of Torvalds' notable accomplishments is leading the development of Git (*https://oreil.ly/My3U-*) in 2005, originally with the goal of improving Linux development. Check out Linus Torvalds's GitHub profile (*https://oreil.ly/VCKav*) if you'd like to explore some legendary living artifacts of hacker culture.

See also "DOS (Disk Operating System)" on page 86, "Git/GitHub" on page 113, "Linux" on page 161, "Programming" on page 204, "UNIX" on page 253, "Usenet" on page 255

Tramiel, Jack

See "Amiga" on page 10, "Atari" on page 22, "Commodore" on page 53

Transistor

See "Fairchild Semiconductor" on page 103, "Texas Instruments" on page 242

Tribe of Hackers

Tribe of Hackers is a series of books written by Marcus J. Carey and Jennifer Jin and published by Wiley Tech. Each book features interviews with many of the top minds in the cybersecurity industry. (Full disclosure: I was interviewed in the first book in the series, and I count the authors as friends.) The interview questions, which are the same for each interviewee, range widely, covering topics like cybersecurity, mythbusting, career advice, and hacker culture.

The series includes:

- *Tribe of Hackers: Cybersecurity Advice from the Best Hackers in the World* (2019)

- *Tribe of Hackers Red Team: Tribal Knowledge from the Best in Offensive Cybersecurity* (2019)

- *Tribe of Hackers Security Leaders: Tribal Knowledge from the Best in Cybersecurity Leadership* (2020)

- *Tribe of Hackers Blue Team: Tribal Knowledge from the Best in Defensive Cybersecurity* (2020)

See also "Cybersecurity" on page 68

Turing, Alan

Alan Turing (1912–1954) is considered the father of modern computing. He was incredibly brilliant, but he was killed by homophobia and ableism. Turing's family lived in the Paddington area of London. His father was a civil servant, so his parents could afford him the best schooling, but Turing struggled in school. His teacher (*https://oreil.ly/GE-D9*) called his writing "the worst I have ever seen." However, he went on to study mathematics at Cambridge.

Turing bridged the gap between mathematics and what would soon become electronic computing. He wrote a 1936 paper (*https://oreil.ly/V4c-T*) that became the basis of his Universal Turing Machine (*https://oreil.ly/GE-D9*) concept. Turing went on to obtain his PhD (*https://oreil.ly/WwfGa*) in mathematical logic from Princeton in 1938. That summer, he returned to England and enrolled in the Government Code and Cypher School.

When Britain declared war on Nazi Germany in September 1939, the UK and Polish governments were working to crack Enigma. It was an electromechanical cryptography machine captured from the Germans, who used it to encrypt their radio communications. Turing was assigned to work on that project at the UK's cryptography headquarters at Bletchley Park, Buckinghamshire. By 1942, Turing's cryptanalysis team was cracking more than 39,000 intercepted messages a month.

Some other German messages were encrypted in binary 1s and 0s by a machine the researchers at Bletchley Park called Tunny. That's the computational foundation of our modern electronic computers. Turing learned how to decipher Tunny messages by hand, but the process was too slow, so the Bletchley Park team developed Colossus (*https://oreil.ly/2P4MV*), the very first programmable electronic computer. It was ready for operation by December 1943, two years before the US deployed ENIAC. For decades, ENIAC was credited as the first programmable electronic computer, because the existence of Colossus was classified until 1974.

After the war, Turing was recruited to the National Physical Laboratory to work on his Automatic Computing Engine (ACE), the first all-purpose electronic stored-program digital computer. Turing's colleagues had difficulty engineering his initial ACE design and instead built a smaller computer, the Pilot Model ACE, in 1950.

Turing conceptualized the "Imitation Game" (*https://oreil.ly/ArZDO*) (subject of a 2014 film by the same name) in 1950. This work is the origin of the *Turing test*, now a key concept in artificial intelligence. The test evaluates an AI by whether or not it can fool a human into thinking that it has human intelligence. (Turing, however, considered the question of whether or not machines could think to be "too meaningless" to consider.)

One bit of Turing's legacy that's often overlooked is his contribution to the field of biology. His childhood fascination with daisies led him to write a groundbreaking 1952 work on *morphogenesis* (*https://oreil.ly/DQJaG*), a new area of mathematical biology.

Alan Turing was a gay man at a time when homosexuality was illegal, and modern researchers believe he was probably autistic (*https://oreil.ly/zdoZ7*), too. In March 1952, Turing was criminally convicted of "gross indecency" and sentenced to 12 months of hormone "therapy." He died by suicide (*https://oreil.ly/207Px*) in 1954.

See also "Artificial intelligence (AI)" on page 17, "Autistic" on page 26, "Cryptography" on page 63, "ENIAC (Electronic Numerical Integrator and Computer)" on page 98

2600 (Twenty-Six Hundred): The Hacker Quarterly (magazine)

2600 magazine is perhaps the longest-running, most legendary publication in the history of hacker culture. Its first issue was published in January 1984, which would turn out to be the most important month in the history of hacker culture: it's when Jack Tramiel founded the Atari Corporation, the groundbreaking "1984" Super Bowl commercial introduced the Apple Macintosh to the world, the Commodore Amiga team presented their working prototype at the Consumer Electronics Show, and...I was born!

2600 magazine has been published four times per year ever since it debuted. Its articles typically cover clever hacks and exploits of phone, electronic, and computer systems, often in great technical detail, as well as the state of hackers and hacking.[2]

---

2 Full disclosure: I have written two articles on hacker culture for *2600*.

Eric "Emmanuel Goldstein" Corley and David Ruderman founded 2600. Goldstein is still its editor and also hosts a radio program, *Off The Hook* (*https:// oreil.ly/alI76*).

I had the honor of interviewing Mr. Goldstein for this book. He credits the magazine's longevity to:

> *A combination of determination and refusal to accept what the naysayers always tell you. Two years after* **2600** *started, we were being told that hacking was dead and it just wasn't like it used to be.... We also try out new things as much as possible. We embraced the digital method of putting out a zine as well as the traditional methods. I think the mistake most of us make is embracing one thing over another, instead of trying to see how you might make many different approaches work to your—and everyone's—benefit.*

Goldstein's pen name was inspired by a character in George Orwell's *1984*. He says the idea came to him while speaking to a reporter:

> *The day after the FBI had raided WUSB and a friend's house. It was all because of something I had done—hacking into all sorts of machines on a nationwide network protected by a one-character password. The FBI hadn't yet figured out it was me and I was actually trying to help them along so others wouldn't be targeted. But I wasn't yet comfortable having my real name exposed to the media, so I told the reporter, "You can call me Emmanuel Goldstein."*

Goldstein says that hacking is as much a mindset as an activity: "I try to remind people of this when they assume that you have to be a particular type of person in order to be a hacker or that it's something that you can just learn by taking classes. You can develop skills in that way but the hacker mentality is something that evolves throughout your life." He adds, "It's something that's within you and it either comes out or it doesn't, based on how you live your life and what you get exposed to.... I'm not technical, nor am I a programmer. But I love to experiment and think of new applications for all sorts of technology."

Goldstein is optimistic about the future of hacker culture:

> *The hacker spirit will remain fairly constant and hopefully will be appreciated more by the mainstream. I think we've seen that to a degree with the embracing of hacker ideals, like open platforms, the right to*

repair, freedom of speech, etc. But there are also negative trends, such as increased surveillance, harsh penalties for compromising insecure systems, and an overall lack of trust.

Connecting with the mainstream is crucial in getting them to value hackers rather than fear them. It's already this way in movies and TV shows—the hacker is nearly always the hero, because they think outside the box and embrace individuality. Most people get that.

But if we become inaccessible, mysterious, and ominous, then we're in danger of being defined by those who imagine themselves to be in charge—and they will always see hackers as a threat to that power. Which we are. Of course, the technology itself will change, get faster, do more. But our spirit won't. We'll always be trying to defeat security and expose the stuff that isn't right. There will be a lot to explore.

See also "Captain Crunch (John Draper)" on page 41, "Hacker" on page 121, "Phreaking" on page 199

Twitter

See "Meta" on page 171, "Nonfungible tokens (NFTs)" on page 186, "Zuckerberg, Mark" on page 280

21

U

UNIX

UNIX is the most influential operating system ever. UNIX's core design, including how it manages the kernel and a multiuser environment, is the foundation for a wide range of popular operating systems (*https://oreil.ly/Gxarc*), from FreeBSD and macOS to Android and many hundreds of other Linux-based operating systems. Even recent versions of Microsoft Windows (*https://oreil.ly/BQtn8*), the only major operating system that does not have a UNIX-derived kernel, have built-in support for Linux applications and operating systems. And, of course, Linux is derived from UNIX.

UNIX was born (*https://oreil.ly/lVOxw*) at Bell Labs in 1969, from a project led by Ken Thompson and Dennis Ritchie. It was initially an improved timesharing system for the DEC PDP-7 minicomputer. In the 1970s, Ritchie and Thompson helped to develop the C programming language (*https://oreil.ly/KaZkx*) so that UNIX could be ported to other types of computers. This initiative was so successful that UNIX spawned an amazing variety of operating systems, open source and proprietary, for almost every kind of computer you can think of.

See also "Bell Labs" on page 31, "DEC (Digital Equipment Corporation)" on page 77, "Linux" on page 161, "Microsoft" on page 174, "Minicomputers" on page 176, "Open source" on page 189, "Programming" on page 204, "Proprietary software" on page 205, "Ritchie, Dennis" on page 214, "Thompson, Ken" on page 242, "Timesharing" on page 243, "Torvalds, Linus" on page 246

Unreal Engine

If you play video games made in the 21st century, you've probably played some games created with Unreal Engine.

I first encountered Epic Games in the 1990s, when they were known as Epic MegaGames and led by Tim Sweeney; I begged the adults in my life to buy me a *Jill of the Jungle* (*https://oreil.ly/ZzLWf*) floppy disk at the mall. Sweeney founded Epic MegaGames (*https://oreil.ly/b4-Sl*) in 1991; it was a tiny company, but the name, Sweeney told *Gamasutra* (*https://oreil.ly/XEFJu*), was "kind of a scam to make it look like we were a big company." The company has been Epic Games since 1999.

The 1998 first-person shooter game *Unreal* (*https://oreil.ly/zav64*) was Epic's big commercial breakthrough. As popular as *Unreal* was at the time, its real legacy is the groundbreaking game engine Epic created to build it. Unreal Engine is now used for hundreds of games (*https://oreil.ly/pvaJB*). While writing this book, I've played *Harvestella* (*https://oreil.ly/55fx_*), a Japanese RPG with farming-simulation game mechanics, and *Crisis Core* (*https://oreil.ly/bVGsO*): *Final Fantasy VII Reunion*, an action RPG. Both were produced with Unreal Engine 4.

Sweeney built his first game engine for the very first Epic game, *ZZT*, made when the company was briefly known as Potomac Computer Systems. *ZZT* featured simple ASCII art and, as Sweeney explains (*https://oreil.ly/PPjQv*), "served as a conceptual blueprint for Unreal: a game engine with a high-productivity, what-you-see-is-what-you-get tools pipeline, bundled with a programming language aimed at simplifying gameplay logic."

That programming language is UnrealScript (*https://oreil.ly/-ekZq*), an object-oriented scripting language. Just for fun, here's Hello World! in UnrealScript (*https://oreil.ly/qqIEq*):[1]

```
class HelloWorld extends Mutator;

function PostBeginPlay()
{
  Super.PostBeginPlay(); // Run the super class function
  Log("Hello World");    // Write our log message
}
```

Unreal Engine 5's stable version (*https://oreil.ly/b_mMV*) has been available to developers since April 2022. Perhaps by the time this book is published, we'll already be playing games made with it.

See also "Hello World" on page 130, "Programming" on page 204, "Roleplaying games (RPGs)" on page 218

---

1 Actually running this code in Unreal Engine is a bit more complicated: you have to compile the *.uc* file and create a package interface file.

Usenet

Usenet was the early internet's equivalent of Reddit today, though it technically predates the official birth of the internet (January 1, 1983) (*https://oreil.ly/b_Xj1*). It was launched by Duke University graduate students Tom Truscott and Jim Ellis (*https://oreil.ly/oo1V9*) in 1980 on an ARPAnet server as a way to deploy internet forums. Like Reddit, users can start their own forums on any topic; unlike Reddit, Usenet has its own internet protocol, Network News Transfer Protocol (NNTP). There were client applications dedicated to reading and posting on Usenet. Group names have this syntax: comp.os.linux.misc, alt.folklore.computers. Usenet still exists, and so do those particular groups (*https://oreil.ly/d-AcV*)! However, Usenet's popularity has plummeted. Duke University shut down its Usenet server in 2010 due to "low usage and rising costs" (*https://oreil.ly/G9WRq*).

Some pivotal moments in the history of hacker culture occurred on Usenet. In August 1991, Tim Berners-Lee announced the very first web software (*https://oreil.ly/y3YpC*) on alt.hypertext; Linux Torvalds announced his Linux project (*https://oreil.ly/8JzcY*) on comp.os.minix.

What caused Usenet's downfall? In the late 1990s, a cyber threat actor called HipCrime (*https://oreil.ly/CyKlt*) exploited its poor security implementation and used custom software (*https://oreil.ly/XK134*) to flood Usenet groups with spam posts in the earliest web-distributed spambot attack. But spam continued to flourish even after HipCrime's demise. Server storage problems and the rise of Reddit likely also contributed.

See also "ARPAnet" on page 17, "Berners-Lee, Tim" on page 33, "Bulletin board systems (BBSes)" on page 37, "Linux" on page 161, "Reddit" on page 212, "Threat actor" on page 243, "Torvalds, Linus" on page 246, "World Wide Web" on page 268

22

V

Valve

See "Steam" on page 231

Vaughan, Dorothy

See "Hidden Figures (2017 film)" on page 134

Version control

See "Git/GitHub" on page 113

vi

One of the fiercest debates in the hacker community has been the text-editor wars: Emacs or vi? It's like Coke versus Pepsi, but much more passionate. Why do nerds fight over whose text-editor preference is superior? First, let's look into the history of vi.

vi was originally created by Bill Joy (*https://oreil.ly/Jou3Z*) in 1976. Joy also developed an editor called ex (*https://oreil.ly/BlCoP*). Later, he would go on to found Sun Microsystems and create Java (*https://oreil.ly/PikFE*), one of today's most important application development languages.

Joy created vi as the *visual* mode of ex—a friendlier face for a relatively archaic application. Those of us who got into computing after the 1980s may wonder what "visual mode" means. Most versions of vi have a fully text-based user interface, but even that does have a visual component! Even though it's all text, you'll see that you're running an application, and the lines are numbered for handy reference.

As open source software, vi has been forked many times. A particularly popular fork is Vim—for "visual improved" (*https://oreil.ly/qfvAm*). Hackers who prefer vi (or Vim) to Emacs tout it for being flexible, customizable, portable, and lightweight.

Tim O'Reilly, who founded the company that publishes this book, used to use a version of Emacs until the Emacs profile he was using disappeared. He tried vi and was hooked. He wrote in 1999 (*https://oreil.ly/GqwVJ*) that he found it "remarkably easy to use and tremendously powerful. Like a lot of things about UNIX, it only *seems* difficult. After a small barrier to entry, it is orders of magnitude more powerful and easy to use than commercial word processors."

If you're just getting into programming, I recommend trying multiple text editors. O'Reilly Media publishes a number of guides to using vi and Emacs that can help you in your journey.[1]

See also "Emacs" on page 97, "Joy, Bill" on page 153, "Open source" on page 189, "UNIX" on page 253

Video games

See "Activision" on page 2, "Atari" on page 22, "Augmented and virtual reality" on page 25, "Commodore" on page 53, "Consumer Electronics Show (CES)" on page 57, "DOOM (video game)" on page 85, "Electronic Arts" on page 93, "Electronic Entertainment Expo (E3)" on page 94, "Google Cloud Platform (GCP)" on page 117, "Lawson, Jerry" on page 160, "Miyamoto, Shigeru" on page 178, "MMO (Massively Multiplayer Online) games" on page 179, "Nihon Falcom" on page 185, "Nintendo" on page 185, "Roleplaying games (RPGs)" on page 218, "Sega" on page 221, "Steam" on page 231, "Unreal Engine" on page 253, "Watch_Dogs (video game series)" on page 264

Virtual reality (VR)

See "Augmented and virtual reality" on page 25

Virus

Laypeople often refer to all malware as "viruses," but in cybersecurity, the term *virus* (*https://oreil.ly/zez8g*) describes how malware is transmitted. Computer viruses self-replicate by inserting their code into other programs. Viruses can target operating system files, application files, documents, media—all kinds of data. It's

---

1 For instance: Arnold Robbins and Elbert Hannah, *Learning the vi and Vim Editors*, 8th ed. (O'Reilly); Debra Cameron, James Elliott, Marc Loy, Eric Raymond, and Bill Rosenblatt, *Learning GNU Emacs*, 3rd ed. (O'Reilly); Daniel J. Barrett, *Efficient Linux at the Command Line* (O'Reilly).

even possible for a virus to simply insert itself into a process running in memory without changing any of the files in your data storage (called a *fileless malware* (*https://oreil.ly/S9inG*) *attack*). There have probably been millions of different computer viruses over the past few decades!

The word *worm* (*https://oreil.ly/KaTow*) is used to describe a different way that malware can be transmitted: by self-replicating without inserting its code into programs. Because *virus* describes how malware is transmitted, it's sometimes combined with a word describing the kind of harm that malware does: so it's possible for malware to be a ransomware virus, a spyware virus, or a cryptomining virus. But it's not possible for one piece of malware to be both a virus and a worm.

Mathematician John von Neumann first conceptualized computer viruses in the 1940s. His ideas were published in his 1966 report, "Theory of Self-Reproducing Automata" (*https://oreil.ly/8Tw2s*).

The earliest actual computer virus on record is Creeper (*https://oreil.ly/cbPRv*), developed by BBN Technologies' Bob Thomas in 1971. Creeper was a working proof-of-concept, perhaps made to test Neumann's theories. It was distributed through ARPAnet, the precursor to the modern internet. Creeper was written in PDP-10 assembly language, and targeted the TENEX operating system. If it successfully infected a machine, it would print the message "I'M THE CREEPER. CATCH ME IF YOU CAN!"

There's a long history of hackers creating malware as an innocent prank, like 2001's Anna Kournikova virus (*https://oreil.ly/v6SNI*). Kournikova was a famous tennis player; at the time, she was at the top of her career and was widely seen as a sex symbol, appearing in magazines like *Maxim* (*https://oreil.ly/uoRTz*). Her name was thus a popular search-engine term. Dutch student Jan de Wit created a virus that sent targets an email that claimed to contain a picture of Kournikova. What it really contained was a file that, if executed, ran a program that accessed the victim's email contacts and sent the same email to those contacts. (Don't open email attachments from unfamiliar senders!)

Other viruses and other malware aren't so innocent and can cause tremendous real-world harm. Hostile governments use spyware for espionage. Ransomware often targets hospitals, hijacking their systems until a ransom is paid. This can kill people by limiting hospital workers' access to critical data and distracting them from their lifesaving work (*https://oreil.ly/b2Klr*).

VX Underground (*https://oreil.ly/Uoj_5*) is a website where hackers share malware samples and information. It's a treasure trove for hackers and cybersecurity. It features a whole section (*https://oreil.ly/F7C4g*) on attacks to utility company SCADAs, including lots of documents on the infamous and perplexing Stuxnet attack. There's a huge collection of malware analysis documentation (*https://oreil.ly/SWUSo*) as well. The site emerged in 2019 and became much better known around 2021 (*https://oreil.ly/4xrSO*). VX Underground's creator, "smelly_vx," says they were inspired (*https://oreil.ly/4xrSO*) by a similar malware-sharing platform they visited as a teenager, VX Heavens, which was shut down by Ukrainian police in 2012.

Another site, VirusTotal (*https://oreil.ly/humDz*), offers a huge complimentary collection of antimalware intelligence, gathered through the cooperation of multiple antivirus vendors. You can even submit malware samples for analysis from their homepage. (Unlike VX Underground, VirusTotal won't actually distribute malware samples to users for independent research.)

I think there's room in this world for both VX Underground and VirusTotal to exist. Their services overlap a bit, but the former site has more of the spirit of hacker culture and is more susceptible to suspicion from law enforcement. Darknet markets have shown us that even if VX Underground is shut down, researchers and threat actors alike will find their malware samples *somewhere*.

See also "ARPAnet" on page 17, "Assembly" on page 20, "Cybersecurity" on page 68, "Dark Web/darknet" on page 71, "Exploit" on page 101, "Malware" on page 167, "Ransomware" on page 211, "SCADA (Supervisory control and data acquisition)" on page 220, "Spyware" on page 228, "Stuxnet" on page 232, "Threat actor" on page 243, "Worm" on page 269

VisiCalc

VisiCalc was the very first consumer spreadsheet program, and it was quite revolutionary for its time.[2] Dan Bricklin and Bob Frankston (*https://oreil.ly/prblP*) developed the first version for the Apple II computer in 1979. Before VisiCalc, spreadsheets were mainly analog. You'd make them with a pen and paper or perhaps on a chalkboard. If you needed to add all of the cells in one column, you'd have to do the math manually. VisiCalc is credited for popularizing personal computers in the early days. Businesses wanted and needed a digital solution, so VisiCalc became the Apple II's "killer app," giving it an edge over the competition.

---

2 The first electronic spreadsheet system (*https://oreil.ly/IdOXH*) was 1969's LANPAR, but it required a lot of technical expertise and was only used by large corporations.

Today we consider Microsoft Excel and similar programs to be completely ordinary. But without VisiCalc, the Apple II might never have taken off—and today's tech world would be very different.

See also "Apple" on page 13, "Microsoft" on page 174, "Personal computers" on page 196

23

W

Wardialing

See "Wardriving" on page 263

Wardriving

Wardriving and *wardialing* (*https://oreil.ly/8xoiI*) are great examples of cool-sounding hacking terminology. Both are derived from the 1983 film *WarGames*. Wardialing is a kind of phreaking activity where you use an automatic dialer to mass-call as many phone numbers as possible that have the same area code and exchange (for instance, one could wardial all the numbers that start with 416-555). If computers with modems are connected to any of those numbers, the hacking program tries to connect to them.

Wardriving (*https://oreil.ly/6A8DW*) is when you travel around an area with a WiFi-capable device like a smartphone or laptop in your car, looking for publicly accessible, unencrypted WiFi networks. If a wardriver had malicious intentions, they could cyber exploit the wireless access point and any devices that were connected to it. Whereas a pentester who wardrives would report the unencrypted WiFi and what it may entail as a possible security vulnerability. (Despite the name, pedestrians can wardrive, too!) I once met a hacker who put a great big antenna on the roof of his van so he could wardrive around the city.

See also "Penetration testing" on page 196, "Phreaking" on page 199, "WarGames (1983 film)" on page 263

WarGames (1983 film)

"Shall we play a game?"

WarGames (*https://oreil.ly/wnN-B*) is perhaps the first proper Hollywood movie about computer hackers. In it, Matthew Broderick plays David Lightman, a teenage hacker with a PC who connects to networks to look for games to play. One day, he connects to the Pentagon's computer system and finds a game called "Global Thermonuclear War." But it's not just a game: it triggers the US nuclear arsenal at the height of the Cold War. FBI agents eventually arrest David and take him to North American Aerospace Defense Command (NORAD) for questioning. The movie ends with a dramatic scene where David and an AI researcher confuse a computer by making it play tic-tac-toe against itself.

WarGames debuted at the Cannes Film Festival in May 1983, just months after what's now considered to be the birth of the internet: January 1, 1983 (*https://oreil.ly/tCojw*). That's the day ARPAnet made TCP/IP its communications protocol standard, opening its network to the world and eventually resulting in the internet we know today.

See also "ARPAnet" on page 17, "Artificial intelligence (AI)" on page 17, "Internet" on page 145, "TCP/IP (Transmission Control Protocol/Internet Protocol)" on page 239, "Wardriving" on page 263

Watch_Dogs (video game series)

Watch_Dogs (*https://oreil.ly/MJYwO*) is an Ubisoft video game series about hackers fighting against authority in the present day and near future. Its first game, simply titled *Watch_Dogs*, was released in 2014.

In the fictional year 2012 of the games, Chicago is the first city to deploy a dystopian computer network called Central Operating System (ctOS) to which everyone's computing devices connect. Players control hacker characters who use ctOS to do Hollywood hacks like stealing money from bank accounts, unlocking doors, controlling transportation infrastructure, stopping other people's devices from working, and so on. In the first game, the player character hopes to avenge his niece's murder while also fighting the evil powers-that-be that operate ctOS.

Watch_Dogs 2 (2016) introduces a hacktivist group called DedSec that is determined to protect the public from being harmed by ctOS. And 2020's *Watch Dogs: Legion* includes another hacktivist group, called Zero Day, in a near-future police-state version of London for a violent cyberpunk battle.

See also "Cyberpunk" on page 67, "Hacktivism" on page 125, "Roleplaying games (RPGs)" on page 218, "Zero day" on page 279

Waterloo, University of

The University of Waterloo (*https://oreil.ly/mQNO6*), in Ontario, Canada, with its Cheriton School of Computer Science (*https://oreil.ly/plxwX*), is one of the most important (if not *the* most important) computer science schools in Canada.

Many Canadian tech companies have come out of Waterloo, but the most notable is BlackBerry (formerly Research In Motion, or RIM). Today, BlackBerry's Advanced Technology Development Labs has a partnership (*https://oreil.ly/LRJW9*) with the University of Waterloo.

Whiteboard interviews

In a *whiteboard interview* (*https://oreil.ly/DDpvR*), a potential employer asks a job candidate to solve a programming task by writing on a whiteboard with a marker. Whiteboard interviews are unfortunately common in hiring processes for computer programmers and software engineers. Programmers dread them, and for good reason, in my opinion. One problem is that programmers rarely do their work with zero assistance. A lot of their work is looking stuff up! They often refer to manuals, documentation, and sites such as StackOverflow. Sometimes they even adapt other people's open source code. A lot of the work that programmers actually do in real life involves looking stuff up.

The other problem with whiteboard interviews is that they're better at measuring a candidate's ability to endure psychological stress than their programming ability, according to researchers, who compare them to (*https://oreil.ly/Oghda*) "the Trier Social Stress Test, a procedure used for decades by psychologists [as] the best known 'gold standard' procedure for the sole purpose of reliably inducing stress."

The same research team noted that such interviews can also be sexist: "We also observed that no women successfully solved the problem in the public setting, whereas all women solved it correctly in the private setting."

Like crunch time, I'd love to see whiteboard interviews disappear from the tech industry.

See also "Crunch time" on page 60, "Programming" on page 204

Whitehat hackers

See "Cybersecurity" on page 68, ""Ethical" hacking" on page 100, "Hacker" on page 121, "Hacking Is Not a Crime" on page 124, "Penetration testing" on page 196

WiFi

See "Hak5" on page 126, "Kali Linux" on page 155, "Lamarr, Hedy" on page 159, "Ramachandran, Vivek" on page 210, "Wardriving" on page 263

WikiLeaks

WikiLeaks is a website that's used to disclose sensitive or classified documents, usually by whistleblowers seeking to expose the harmful actions of powerful institutions (like governments and corporations) to news media. A *wiki* (*https://oreil.ly/bC4fI*) is an online collaboration method where users can contribute to collectively authored content. Wikipedia is perhaps the best-known wiki on the web; WikiLeaks is the most infamous. Love it or hate it, freely sharing information through computer technology is the essence of hacker culture.

The *wikileaks.org* domain (*https://oreil.ly/RRnBw*) was registered in October 2006 (*https://oreil.ly/7cSOv*) and published its first controversial document that December: a plan to assassinate government officials, signed by a Somali political figure. Julian Assange (*https://oreil.ly/6XY89*) is generally accepted to be the founder of WikiLeaks. But as Assange, as of this writing in November 2022, is still incarcerated in the UK and fighting extradition to the US, his foundership of the site is still legally debated.

Assange has said that WikiLeaks was inspired by Daniel Ellsberg's 1971 release of the Pentagon Papers (*https://oreil.ly/uul7q*), a set of documents revealing that the US government had lied to the public about many aspects of its activities in Vietnam. Noting that two years passed between the leak and any significant media coverage about it, Assange wanted to make publicizing information more efficient. In its first decade of operation, WikiLeaks (*https://oreil.ly/x6jP6*) published at least 10 million documents. Some of the most notable include:

- Unflattering internal documents from the Church of Scientology (2008).

- Classified documents on the US military's activities in Iraq (2010), shared by former US Army soldier and network security expert Chelsea Manning. Manning was convicted of treason and spent roughly seven years in prison (*https://oreil.ly/HKy-7*), much of that in psychologically traumatizing solitary confinement.

- The US Central Intelligence Agency's "Vault7" documents (*https://oreil.ly/r6hmj*) (2017) detail multiple zero-day cybersecurity vulnerabilities.

See also "Assange, Julian" on page 18, "Manning, Chelsea" on page 168, "Zero day" on page 279

Wikipedia

Wikipedia (*https://oreil.ly/cPTJV*) is an online, collaboratively written and edited "wiki" encyclopedia, launched in 2001 by Jimmy Wales and Larry Sanger. Anyone can contribute to a Wikipedia article if other users, acting as editors, accept it. It is a massively successful ongoing project to carry out the hacker ethos of "knowledge should be free," with millions of articles in more than 300 languages. (English Wikipedia published its six millionth article in 2020!)

Wikipedia was preceded by Nupedia (*https://oreil.ly/-4C-2*), founded by Wales and edited by Sanger, which debuted in March 2000 and included a lengthy peer-review process. Nupedia wasn't successful, but Wikipedia rose from its ashes. For a full rundown, check out Wikipedia's very meta History of Wikipedia (*https://oreil.ly/vjjK9*) entry.

Windows

See "Microsoft" on page 174

WIRED magazine

If *PC World* and *Vogue* had a baby, it'd be *WIRED* (*https://oreil.ly/OCfL6*) magazine, a San Francisco-based technology lifestyle magazine that debuted in 1993 and was purchased by Condé Nast in 1998. It covers many aspects of hacker culture, like digital rights, Silicon Valley business matters, open source, and computer technological innovations. Its editor-at-large, Steven Levy, is the author of the book *Hackers: Heroes of the Computer Revolution*.

I think of *2600* and *WIRED* (*https://oreil.ly/nKb7v*) as opposite ends of the spectrum of periodicals about computer technology. *2600* is printed relatively inexpensively in black and white; *WIRED* (*https://oreil.ly/Y2lOc*) is full color and glossy. *2600* reads like a hacker bulletin board; *WIRED* covers corporate strategy as well as tech, and includes plenty of retail buying guides for tech enthusiasts.

See also "Hackers: Heroes of the Computer Revolution (2010 book)" on page 123, "Silicon Valley" on page 224, "2600 (Twenty-Six Hundred): The Hacker Quarterly (magazine)" on page 250

World War II

See "Akihabara, Tokyo" on page 6, "Cryptography" on page 63, "ENIAC (Electronic Numerical Integrator and Computer)" on page 98, "Hopper, Grace" on page 137, "DARPA (Defense Advanced Research Projects Agency)" on page 72, "Lamarr, Hedy" on page 159, "Texas Instruments" on page 242, "Turing, Alan" on page 248

World Wide Web

The World Wide Web was invented (*https://oreil.ly/BN7dW*) by Tim Berners-Lee in 1989 and became the "killer app" that made the internet widely popular with ordinary people. In the 1980s, many academics, scientists, and hacker types enjoyed the internet, often through services like email and Usenet. But the web really helped to bring the internet to the mainstream.

In the late 1980s, Berners-Lee was working at the European Organization for Nuclear Research (*https://oreil.ly/6wKxf*) (known by its French initials as CERN). He wanted to devise a better way to exchange information with other researchers. He outlined his ideas in a 1989 paper (*https://oreil.ly/wJq41*) and published a formal management proposal (*https://oreil.ly/-xXi9*) in 1990. By then, Berners-Lee had created the web's foundational technologies (*https://oreil.ly/nz74O*): hypertext markup language (HTML), the Uniform Resource Identifier (URI, later URL), hypertext transfer protocol (HTTP), and the httpd web server, which he ran from his NeXT Computer. He also created the first browser, which he called World Wide Web.

Thank goodness Berners-Lee believed in the virtues of open source. He said (*https://oreil.ly/BahBG*), "Had the technology been proprietary, and in my total control, it would probably not have taken off. You can't propose that something be a universal space and at the same time keep control of it."

See also "Berners-Lee, Tim" on page 33, "Internet" on page 145, "NeXT Computer" on page 184, "Open source" on page 189, "World Wide Web Consortium (W3C)" on page 268

World Wide Web Consortium (W3C)

The World Wide Web Consortium (*https://oreil.ly/ZTJ8X*) (W3C) is an organization founded by Tim Berners-Lee, inventor of the World Wide Web, in 1994 (*https://oreil.ly/z1-p4*) with the goal of influencing web technology standards.

W3C's stated core values (*https://oreil.ly/wBkDz*) harmonize with hacker culture:

The web is for all humanity.

The web is designed for the good of its users.

The web must be safe for its users.

There is one interoperable world-wide web.

See also "Berners-Lee, Tim" on page 33, "Internet" on page 145, "World Wide Web" on page 268

Worm

A *worm* is a type of malware that self-replicates (*https://oreil.ly/vfjrR*) and spreads from computer to computer without attaching itself to computer programs. Viruses are also malware that spreads and replicates, but using different methods; it's impossible for an item of malware to be both a worm *and* a virus. But a worm can also be categorized by its malicious actions, so an item of malware can be both a worm and spyware, for instance. Worms are often spread through Trojans and email attachments. Stuxnet is a particularly notorious example of a worm.

See also "Cybersecurity" on page 68, "Dark Web/darknet" on page 71, "Exploit" on page 101, "Malware" on page 167, "Ransomware" on page 211, "SCADA (Supervisory control and data acquisition)" on page 220, "Spyware" on page 228, "Stuxnet" on page 232, "Threat actor" on page 243, "Virus" on page 258, "Worm" on page 269

Wozniak, Steve

Steve "Woz" Wozniak (1950–) is most famous for co-founding Apple with Steve Jobs and for personally designing and building the prototype for the very first Apple product, the Apple I.

The son of an engineer, he started working with electronics and computer technology at a very early age. He describes building an intercom system with friends as a child: "We just ran a ton of telephone wire down the fences, walked down the fences, stapling them into place, hooking our rooms up so we had a little intercom." When he was 10, he got his amateur radio license. The other kids in school didn't understand Woz or his interests.

Woz briefly attended the University of Colorado at Boulder, only to be expelled for hacking the school's computers. In 1971, he enrolled at the University of California, Berkeley. While there, Woz built his first computer as a side project with his high school classmate Bill Fernandez. Although Steve Jobs attended the same high school, he and Woz didn't properly connect until university, when Fernandez introduced them.

Woz took a year off from Berkeley to earn tuition money and got a job at Hewlett-Packard designing pocket calculators, then a marvelous new technology.

Later in 1971, Woz read an article about the notorious phone phreaker John "Captain Crunch" Draper, who used "blue boxes" to hack the phone system for free long-distance calls. Woz was inspired to make his own blue boxes, shared the idea with Jobs, and the legendary two Steves of Apple got together for their very first business venture. They made thousands of dollars, selling their blue boxes for $150 each.

In 1973, Jobs was working for Atari. He was assigned the task of designing a circuit board for an arcade machine game, *Breakout*. He asked Woz for help making the board use as few chips as possible. Woz designed a remarkably efficient circuit board (for which Jobs got credit). *Breakout*, released in 1976 to commercial success, would later influence two smash hits for Japanese arcade-game maker Taito: 1978's *Space Invaders* and 1986's *Arkanoid*.

Woz and Jobs were founding members of the Homebrew Computer Club, to which Gordon French introduced the groundbreaking Altair 8800. They were inspired to get serious about making their own microprocessor-based home computer. A year later, Woz showed the club his Apple I prototype. He offered his design to HP five times, but he was rejected each and every time.

In 1976, Woz and Jobs founded Apple. Woz was the brilliant computer genius; Jobs had the brains for business and marketing. They launched the Apple I that year. The Apple II followed in June 1977, establishing Apple's reputation as a PC maker and bringing Woz and Jobs plenty of money.

Woz took up a new hobby: piloting small aircraft. In 1981, a crash badly injured his head and face and caused him to develop a condition called *anterograde amnesia*: the inability to make new memories. It forced Woz to take a temporary break from Apple. He decided to return to UC Berkeley—enrolling as "Rocky Raccoon Clark" to avoid attention from his now famous name.

Woz stopped actively working for Apple in 1985, but he is still involved with the company. Since then, following his passions, he's produced the world's first programmable universal TV remote control, taught computer classes to grade school kids, founded a startup to make consumer GPS technology, and launched Silicon Valley Comic-Con. There are much worse things a rich tech guy could be doing.

See also "Apple" on page 13, "Atari" on page 22, "Berkeley, University of California" on page 32, "Captain Crunch (John Draper)" on page 41, "Comic-Con" on page 52, "Ham radio" on page 127, "Hewlett-Packard (HP)" on page 131, "Homebrew Computer Club" on page 136, "Jobs, Steve" on page 150, "Personal computers" on page 196, "Phreaking" on page 199, "Pirates of Silicon Valley (1999 film)" on page 202, "Silicon Valley" on page 224

WYSIWYG

WYSIWYG (*https://oreil.ly/EH2s6*) (pronounced "wiz-ee-wig") stands for "What You See Is What You Get." It's used to describe applications for software development and document creation that show the person working on the software or document what it'll look like to future users. Web development and printer applications are often WYSIWYG. The Bravo document preparation program, from the revolutionary, experimental Xerox Alto computer in 1974, is considered the first WYSIWYG application.

See also "Graphical user interface (GUI)" on page 117, "World Wide Web" on page 268, "Xerox" on page 273

24

X

Xbox

See "Microsoft" on page 174

Xerox

Most people think of Xerox as a company that makes photocopiers, but it has had a profound influence in the history of computing.

Xerox was founded in 1906 (*https://oreil.ly/48WC1*) as the Haloid Company, a producer of photographic paper. In 1942, its founder, Chester Carlson (*https://oreil.ly/JiGJz*), patented his electrophotography technique, which was later renamed *xerography*. It's the technological foundation of photocopier document imaging, and in 1958, the company rebranded as the Haloid Xerox Company. It introduced the first xerographic photocopier the following year.

Since that novel invention was the catalyst for Xerox's success, the company prioritized research and development, launching its Palo Alto Research Center (Xerox PARC) in 1970. PARC's mission (*https://oreil.ly/40BOZ*) was to create "the office of the future." And indeed it did, even though the company accidentally let competitors profit from its efforts.

Douglas Englebart spent much of the 1960s developing new technology for DARPA at the Stanford Research Institute, and in 1968 he presented the most groundbreaking prototype ever, known as the "Mother of All Demos." It featured ideas that seemed bizarre at the time but are now mainstays of our modern lives: graphical user interfaces (GUIs), the computer mouse, and a hypertext-based computer network (the basic functionality of what later became the web).

The Xerox Alto computer, the first completely usable computer with a GUI and mouse, was launched at Xerox PARC in 1973, but never commercially released. Bravo, the first properly WYSIWYG document application, was developed for the Alto, and its software was made with Smalltalk, the first object-oriented programming language (*https://oreil.ly/lDdTJ*).

Other revolutionary inventions (*https://oreil.ly/40BOZ*) at Xerox PARC include Ethernet (1973); natural language processing, which is the foundation for ChatGPT (1979); optical data storage, which led to CD-ROMs and DVD-ROMs (1980); and fiber-optic networking (1982).

Many of the ideas that went into the Apple Macintosh and Microsoft Windows were inspired by the Xerox Alto, according to a 1995 interview (*https://oreil.ly/s3EXy*) with Steve Jobs.

See also "Apple" on page 13, "ChatGPT" on page 47, "DARPA (Defense Advanced Research Projects Agency)" on page 72, "Graphical user interface (GUI)" on page 117, "Jobs, Steve" on page 150, "Microsoft" on page 174, "Programming" on page 204, "Stanford University" on page 230, "WYSIWYG" on page 272

Xfce

XForms Common Environment (*https://oreil.ly/jBPJS*) (Xfce, pronounced as "ex-fuss" or "X-F-C-E") is one of many popular desktop environments for Linux- and UNIX-based operating systems. Open source operating systems generally allow users to choose their own desktop environments, unlike proprietary operating systems (such as Windows and macOS). Xfce is notable for being really lightweight compared to alternatives like GNOME and KDE, which makes it a better choice for legacy low-spec PCs. But you can also install it on a cutting-edge gaming PC from 2023!

Olivier Fourdan (*https://oreil.ly/QOLYG*) started the Xfce project in 1996 as a free alternative to the Common Desktop Environment for UNIX, which was then proprietary. Fourdan would go on to work for Red Hat.

See also "GNOME" on page 113, "Linux" on page 161, "Microsoft" on page 174, "Red Hat" on page 213, "UNIX" on page 253

Xiao Tian

Xiao Tian (ca. 1987–?) is an elusive, intriguing Chinese hacker about whom little is publicly known. She was originally a part of an all-female hacker group called the Six Golden Flowers. In 2007, she launched a website and BBS for her next group, China Girl Security Team (*https://oreil.ly/r31J8*),[1] which was active and full of cybersecurity trainings, hacker debates, and even insults through 2008.

In a September 2006 Baidu post, she said she was "turning 19 soon," which means she was probably born in the latter part of 1987. She describes (*https://oreil.ly/ZmOo2*)[2] herself as "a nerdy PHP programmer with a bit of a homebody tendency."

By 2008, she was noticed by the Western media (*https://oreil.ly/xBWW7*). It's difficult to attribute specific cyberattacks to Tian as an individual, but she and her group were especially interested in SQL injection and cross-site scripting (XSS), two dangerous cyber exploitation techniques that can even be used to breach sensitive financial data.

See also "Cybersecurity" on page 68, "Bulletin board systems (BBSes)" on page 37, "Denial-of-service (DoS, DDoS) attacks" on page 81, "Hacktivism" on page 125

---

1 The website no longer exists and is in Chinese, so I must thank the Internet Archive and ChatGPT's translation ability for their help.

2 This website is in Chinese.

25

Y

Yahoo!

Yahoo! was once the brand that defined the web in many people's minds. It was founded in 1994 by Stanford University graduate students Jerry Yang and David Filo as "Jerry and David's Guide to the World Wide Web (*https://oreil.ly/xT3pK*)." It was initially a categorized web directory (really a search engine): really just a collection of links to Jerry and David's favorite web pages, back when there were fewer than 3,000 web pages in the world. Now there are billions (*https://oreil.ly/F_8Lo*)! They soon renamed it Yahoo!, an acronym for "Yet Another Hierarchical Officious Oracle." Users could request that websites be added to the directory. For many 1990s kids with internet access, exploring its different categories felt like opening our minds to a new world.

Yahoo! was often the first site people would visit on their "web surfing" journey through the "Information Superhighway." They had a four-year head start (*https://oreil.ly/Z8zjn*) on Google, which launched in 1998. Yahoo! was the first to make an all-in-one home page for users that included search, news, weather, and email. It also pioneered the click-based ad revenue model, which would later skyrocket Google to enormous profitability.

From the dawn of the new millennium onward, Yahoo! squandered its early lead. In 2012, it attempted to regain its tech-giant status by hiring Google employee number 20, (*https://oreil.ly/8_dVR*) Marissa Mayer, as its president and CEO. But Mayer failed to reverse Yahoo!'s downfall. Verizon bought the company in 2017. Yahoo! still exists, mainly as a news portal, but it's a shadow of its former self.

See also "Google" on page 114, "Stanford University" on page 230, "World Wide Web" on page 268

Y Combinator

Y Combinator (*https://oreil.ly/-Hyef*), which launched in 2005, is the most influential "startup accelerator" in Silicon Valley. Anyone with a business idea for a Silicon Valley company and at least 10% equity in their startup can apply to one of Y Combinator's biannual funding cycles (*https://oreil.ly/LfQIh*). If Y Combinator accepts your application, you'll get $500,000 in funding and three months of mentorship and guidance.

Some of the big names (*https://oreil.ly/A8SPR*) that Y Combinator has helped to "accelerate" include Reddit, Dropbox, Airbnb, Instacart, DoorDash, Twitch, GitLab, Coinbase, and Docker. Y Combinator is basically Shark Tank for nerds, with a lot of the worst aspects of Silicon Valley culture enmeshed in it.

See also "Reddit" on page 212, "Silicon Valley" on page 224

26

Z

Zero day

In cybersecurity, a *zero-day vulnerability* (*https://oreil.ly/864Ga*) is a security vulnerability in a software or hardware product that exists for some time without the knowledge of the product's vendor (such as Microsoft for Windows, or Samsung for Galaxy Android phones) or the cybersecurity community. MITRE's Common Vulnerabilities and Exposures (CVE) database (*https://oreil.ly/ruQIR*) is a good way to check whether or not a vulnerability is a zero day.

A *zero-day exploit* is a cyberattack method of which the vendor and the cybersecurity community were previously unaware.

Nothing bad has to happen for zero-day vulnerabilities and exploits to be discovered. Sometimes penetration testers and bug bounty hunters find them before an attacker does. Other times, zero-day vulnerabilities and exploits are discovered after a *zero-day attack,* (*https://oreil.ly/Hgwmm*) when a threat actor exploits a previously unknown vulnerability or uses a previously unknown exploitation technique in a successful cyberattack.

See also "Common Vulnerabilities and Exposures (CVE)" on page 56, "Cybersecurity" on page 68, "Exploit" on page 101, "Penetration testing" on page 196, "Stuxnet" on page 232, "Threat actor" on page 243, "Worm" on page 269

Zettabyte Era

A *zettabyte* is a very large amount of computer data: about a thousand exabytes, a million petabytes, or a billion terabytes. To put that in perspective, a really good solid-state drive in a laptop in 2023 might have about 1 terabyte, and a good external hard drive around 4 terabytes.

In 2012, global internet traffic hit a milestone: it went past 1 zettabyte. In 2016, the amount of digital data in the world also exceeded 1 zettabyte. This marks such a big change in the scale of data that our current age (*https://oreil.ly/ F4aNI*) is often called the "Zettabyte Era" (*https://oreil.ly/XBflM*).

Zork

See "DOS (Disk Operating System)" on page 86

Zuckerberg, Mark

Mark Zuckerberg (1984–), founder of Facebook and Meta, had a privileged childhood in White Plains, New York. He launched what's believed to be his first website (*https://oreil.ly/4sCIR*) in 1999, when he was 15, on the Web 1.0 provider Angelfire (*https://oreil.ly/4sCIR*). It included a Java applet linking various people on "The Web," with the text (*https://oreil.ly/R6fwX*):

> If you see someone who you know and would like to be linked with but your name is not already on The Web, then you can contact me and I will link that person to you and put you on The Web. In order for this applet to work, you must email me your name.

A harbinger of things to come!

The story of how Zuckerberg started Facebook was dramatized in the 2010 blockbuster Hollywood film *The Social Network*. I think that movie is OK, but it's two hours long. I'll summarize the interesting details here without using the movie as a source. Besides, "based on a true story" movies often embellish stuff.

Zuckerberg enrolled (*https://oreil.ly/ndP5E*) in Harvard University in 2002, when the site *Hot or Not?* was peaking in popularity. That site's users rated photos of people, usually young women, according to whether they were "hot." Zuckerberg created a similar site in 2003, which he called *Facemash*—and which got him in trouble with the university. The *Harvard Crimson* (*https://oreil.ly/GqsR2*) reported at the time:

> The creator of the short-lived but popular Harvard version of the Am I Hot or Not? website said he will not have to leave school after being called before the Administrative Board yesterday afternoon. Mark E. Zuckerberg '06 said he was accused of breaching security, violating copyrights and violating individual privacy by creating the website, www.facemash.com (https://oreil.ly/OHwHN), about two weeks ago....
>
> Comments on the e-mail lists of both Fuerza Latina and the Association of Harvard Black Women blasted the site. "I heard from a friend

and I was kind of outraged. I thought people should be aware," said Fuerza Latina President Leyla R. Bravo '05, who forwarded the link over her group's list-serve.

Zuckerberg launched Facebook (originally called The Facebook), in 2004. It largely copied Friendster (*https://oreil.ly/6vuLl*), a social network popular in 2002 and 2003. "The Facebook" was originally only available to Harvard students. Then it opened to people with *.edu* email addresses, and in 2006 it opened to anyone over age 13. In the years that followed, hundreds of millions of people joined—and then billions.

Zuckerberg learned how profitable it could be to violate people's privacy. The list of Facebook's privacy violation and mass-monitoring scandals (*https://oreil.ly/3kZMa*) is long; the notorious 2014 Cambridge Analytica scandal (*https://oreil.ly/vSrOr*) is merely the tip of the iceberg. Zuckerberg became a famous billionaire, and much of his life story was dramatized in the 2010 film *The Social Network* (*https://oreil.ly/w_l4y*).

In 2021, Facebook renamed itself (*https://oreil.ly/OTGxL*) Meta, though the original social network still operates as Facebook. The shift reflects Zuckerberg's obsession with what he calls the "Metaverse"—sort of an inferior version of the 3D virtual-world game *Second Life*.

Zuckerberg had trouble generating interest in the "Metaverse," and less than a year after rebranding, Meta announced that it had lost $15 billion and would lay off 11,000 workers (*https://oreil.ly/-ObtP*).

In July 2023, Meta launched a new social network called Threads (*https://oreil.ly/54HF1*). Threads functions similarly to Twitter. But even compared to Twitter, Threads is a privacy nightmare (*https://oreil.ly/ZvmP2*) that appears to gather as much data as technologically possible on users, even including sensitive data about their health. Due to the European Union's privacy laws (especially the General Data Protection Regulation (*https://oreil.ly/NFwz2*)), as of July 2023, Meta has been unable to launch Threads in European Union countries (*https://oreil.ly/T8Kxm*). That should be a warning sign to everyone.

Meta Platforms' headquarters is at 1 Hacker Way. Zuckerberg clearly identifies as a hacker. Is he one? Perhaps—but not one that I respect.

See also "Meta" on page 171, "Silicon Valley" on page 224

About the Author

Kim Crawley is a prolific writer and researcher who specializes in cybersecurity. She has spent many years writing blogs and whitepapers for tech companies, some of the most notable include AT&T, BlackBerry, NGINX, Synack, and Hack The Box. While writing two books simultaneously in 2023 (including this one), she took the ISC2 CISSP exam and passed on her first try.

Her previous appearances on bookshelves include being interviewed in *Tribe of Hackers*, coauthoring *The Pentester Blueprint*, and authoring *8 Steps to Better Security: A Simple Cyber Resilience Guide for Business*. In addition to writing books, Kim divides her time between writing blogs and whitepapers for cybersecurity firms, playing video games, and reading books about fashion designers, rock musicians, and Japanese culture. Visit her Linktree at *https://linktr.ee/kimcrawley*.

Colophon

The cover image is by Susan Thompson. The cover fonts are Guardian Sans and Gilroy. The text font is Scala Pro and the heading font is Benton Sans.

Printed in the USA
CPSIA information can be obtained
at www.ICGtesting.com
JSHW011406290124
56244JS00016B/316